Markets and Dealers:
The Economics of the London Financial Markets

Markets and Dealers: The Economics of the London Financial Markets

edited by David Cobham

Longman
London and New York

Longman Group Limited,
Longman House, Burnt Mill,
Harlow, Essex CM20 2JE, England
and Associated Companies throughout the world

*Published in the United States of America
by Longman Publishing, New York*

First published 1992
Second impression 1995

British Library Cataloguing-in-Publication Data

A catalogue record for this book is available
from the British Library

Library of Congress Cataloging in Publication Data
Markets and dealers: the economics of the London Financial Markets /
[edited by] David Cobham.
     p.   cm.
  Includes bibliographical references and index.
  ISBN 0-582-07581-2
  1, Securities industry--England--London. I. Cobham, David P.
HG5443.L66M37 1992
332.63'2'094212--dc 20

92-20208
CIP

Produced through Longman Malaysia, CLP

Contents

Preface

The aim of this book is to explore the various organised financial markets that make up the City of London. It provides a mix of analytical and descriptive material, with a distinctive emphasis on microstructural issues, that is on the mechanisms by which trading is organised and on the roles which different market participants perform.

Students in higher education who are aiming for a career in the City will find it of obvious interest. However, they and other students may also find that the operation of financial markets constitutes a fascinating subject in its own right. Economists are too often interested only in the outcomes of market processes, but in focusing on financial markets it is necessary to investigate the processes and mechanisms of the markets themselves.

New practitioners in the City, from economic or other backgrounds, will also find the book of interest, precisely because it describes large parts of the mechanisms within which practitioners operate and with which they must be familiar.

The first chapter sets the scene: it introduces some analytical material on the nature of market making, provides a historical background and examines two markets which are not discussed more fully elsewhere. The following five chapters look in turn at the principal organised financial markets in London: those for equities, sterling bonds, futures and options, eurobonds, and money. The final chapter considers the issues involved in the regulation of financial markets. The emphases of different chapters vary with the nature of the material covered and the range of previous research in the area. Together they provide a comprehensive analysis of the financial activities conducted in the City of London.

David Cobham
January 1992
St. Andrews

Notes on contributors

Shane Bonetti

Shane Bonetti is Lecturer in Economics at the University of St. Andrews. His research interests include macroeconomic theory, game theory, countertrade, economic sanctions and international finance. He was previously Senior Research Officer in the Capital Markets Division of the Australian Treasury, and has also worked at the University of Melbourne and the Australian National University.

David Cobham

David Cobham is Senior Lecturer in Economics at the University of St. Andrews. He has published articles on UK monetary policy and control, European monetary integration and the French financial and monetary system, and is co-editor with Michael Artis of *Labour's Economic Policies 1974–79* (Manchester University Press, 1991). He was Houblon-Norman Research Fellow at the Bank of England in 1987.

E.P. Davis

Phil Davis is Adviser, Financial Structure and Regulation, at the Bank of England. He has previously worked at the Bank in the areas of monetary policy and international financial markets, and on secondment to the Bank for International Settlements in Basle. His publications include papers on financial instability, the euromarkets, institutional investors and the economics of financial centres.

Richard Harrington

Richard Harrington is Senior Lecturer in Economics at the University of Manchester. He has written and published widely on financial institutions and financial markets, and has acted as consultant to a number of national and international organisations including the Building Societies Association and the OECD. He previously worked in insurance in the City of London.

James Leslie

James Leslie is Senior Lecturer in Banking and Finance at Heriot-Watt University in Edinburgh and is a member of the Chartered Institute of Bankers in Scotland. He is the author of *International Finance and Developing Countries* (Longman, 1987) and co-author with Geoffrey Wyatt and Richard Dale of *Futures and Options: Winners and Losers* (Financial Times Business Information, 1988).

David Miles

David Miles is Lecturer in Economics at Birkbeck College, University of London. Before that he worked for several years in the Economics Division and the Money Markets Division of the Bank of England. He has published several articles on the operation of monetary policy, on the regulation of financial markets, on the economics of the housing market and on asset pricing.

Paul Temperton

Paul Temperton is Director of European Economic and Fixed Income Research at Merrill Lynch in London. He previously worked in the Economics Division of the Bank of England. He is the author of a number of articles on monetary economics, of *A Guide to UK Monetary Policy* (Macmillan, 1986), and of *UK Monetary Policy: the Challenge for the 1990s* (Macmillan, 1991).

Geoffrey Wyatt

Geoffrey Wyatt is Senior Lecturer and currently Head of the Department of Economics at Heriot-Watt University in Edinburgh. He has worked previously as a staff economist at the OECD. He is the author of *The Economics of Invention* (Wheatsheaf, 1986), and co-author with James Leslie and Richard Dale of *Futures and Options: Winners and Losers* (Financial Times Business Information, 1988).

Acknowledgements

The publishers are grateful to the following for permission to reproduce copyright material.

The Bank of England for tables 1.4, 1.5, 2.2, 3.4, 3.5, 6.1, 6.5; The Stock Exchange for tables 3.1, 3.3, 3.7.

Whilst every effort has been made to trace the owners of copyright material, in a few cases this has proved to be impossible, and we take this opportunity to offer our apologies to any copyright holders whose rights we may have unwittingly infringed.

1 Financial markets and the City of London

by Shane Bonetti and David Cobham

This chapter is designed to present some basic ideas about the role and operation of organised financial markets in an economy and to give an overview of the City of London and the markets that exist there.

Section 1.1 distinguishes between direct and indirect financial flows, and between the roles of organised financial markets and financial intermediaries. Section 1.2 provides a simple introduction to the theory of market making. Section 1.3 gives a brief historical overview of the development of the City of London. Section 1.4 gives a preview of the main financial markets in London and compares London's position with that of other financial centres. Sections 1.5 and 1.6 look in more detail at two markets not covered elsewhere in the book which underpin much of the activity in, and the relationships between, the other markets, namely the foreign exchange and swap markets. Finally, section 1.7 analyses the reasons for the emergence of financial centres in general and applies the conclusions reached to consider London's present and future.[1]

1.1 Direct versus indirect finance

A financial system can be thought of as a number of more or less roundabout channels by which flows of finance are lent by one group of economic agents, the ultimate lenders, to another group, the ultimate borrowers. Ultimate lenders are those who save out of their incomes; essentially those parts of the personal sector which are in surplus but also on occasion industrial and commercial companies and even the government (when it has a budget surplus), and to a small extent financial institutions themselves (out of their own reserves). Ultimate borrowers are those who invest in the economic sense, that is by buying productive physical assets; essentially firms, but also the government (when it has a deficit) and deficit units in the personal sector (for purchases of property, for example).

Between these two lies the financial system, a variety of financial institutions and markets whose connections to the various ultimate agents may be strong or tenuous. A useful fundamental distinction is between *direct finance* and *indirect finance.* The former refers to financial flows that take the form of lenders directly buying claims issued by borrowers, while the latter refers to flows that involve financial intermediaries who issue one sort of claim to lenders and themselves purchase a different sort of claim on borrowers. Indirect finance thus typically involves banks taking deposits from lenders and making loans to borrowers, thereby *transforming* the claims concerned. Direct finance, on the other hand, typically involves borrowers issuing equity or other debt which is purchased directly by lenders; differences between the asset preferences of lenders and the liability preferences of borrowers are then handled through the existence of secondary

1

markets which allow lenders to liquidate their own assets without the borrower being directly affected.

In this book we are concerned primarily with direct finance, and with the *organised financial markets* through which it passes in London. The latter is the financial centre of the UK, and an important international financial centre. We therefore need to add to the lists of ultimate lenders and ultimate borrowers above another, most important, source and user of finance: the overseas sector. For the City of London is to an important extent an entrepôt for financial flows between the economic agents of other countries.

1.2   An introduction to the theory of market making[2]

In most of the financial markets which are covered in this book a key role is played by agents known as market makers. In some markets this status emerged gradually over time in response to market opportunities and constraints, and in some – notably the equity market – it is regulated and institutionalised. But market makers (dealers) of some kind operate in a wide range of other markets as well.

Market makers fulfil a variety of functions. First, they act as auctioneers in the broad sense that they organise transactions, handle orders, and participate in trading more generally. Secondly, they act as price stabilisers, either in a mechanical or passive way – in so far as they tend to buy at low prices and sell at high prices so that their actions tend to reduce price fluctuations, or in a more active way – as in the New York Stock Exchange where the specialists have an 'affirmative obligation' to stabilise prices and are subject to rules that forbid them to sell stock when prices are falling or to buy when prices are rising.

Thirdly, market makers act as processors of information and contribute to price discovery, that is the process by which the market arrives at the closest possible approximation to the true price of a security. Thus market makers' price quotations reflect all the information known to them, and disseminate it to the market; their quotes therefore affect the flow of public orders and so indirectly affect prices; and in some markets they may perform a more positive role, for example in New York the specialists are expected to search actively for the market clearing price prior to the opening session.

Fourthly, and perhaps most importantly, market makers supply 'immediacy', as first explained by Demsetz (1968). In securities markets a public trader who wishes to buy or sell could simply wait for a matching sell or buy order from another public trader, but such waiting involves 'execution risk', that is the risk that an order may be executed only after some delay and/or at a different price from that at which the order was originally made. Alternatively, a public trader may buy from, or sell to, a market maker who is willing to trade immediately out of his own inventory, but only at prices which allow him to cover the costs of his operations. The role of market makers in supplying immediacy is depicted in Fig. 1.1, where the horizontal axis shows the quantity of securities traded per period and the vertical axis the price. The DD and SS curves represent the public demand and supply; their intersection determines an equilibrium price of P^e, but this price would be attainable only if buy and sell orders happened to be present in the market at the same time. D'D' and S'S' represent the market maker's demand and supply curves; they show that the market maker is willing to buy (sell) at a price slightly lower (higher) than those at which public traders are willing to deal. The intersection between the DD

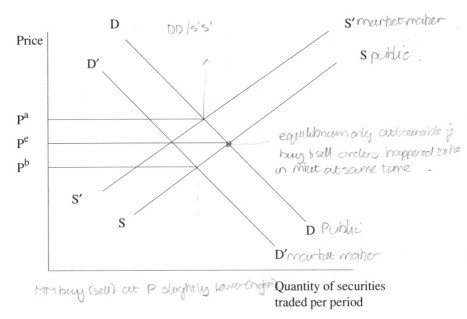

The figure shows axes with "Price" on the vertical axis and "Quantity of securities traded per period" on the horizontal axis. Curves labelled D, D', DD/s's', S' market maker, S public, S', S, D Public, D' market maker. Price levels P^a, P^e, P^b marked.

Handwritten annotations:
- DD/s's'
- S' market maker
- S public.
- equilibrium only achievable if buy & sell orders happened to be in mkt at same time.
- D Public
- D' market maker
- MM buy (sell) at P slightly lower/higher

Figure 1.1

and S'S' curves determines the price at which the market maker is (always and immediately) willing to sell to the public, that is the market maker's equilibrium ask-price, P^a. The intersection between SS and D'D' similarly determines the market maker's equilibrium bid-price, P^b. The difference between P^a and P^b is defined as the (quoted) spread; it can be regarded in the first instance as the price of immediacy (the extra payable on a round trip transaction), or as the remuneration to the market maker for the provision of this service.

To understand how market makers operate and how the spread is determined, we need to introduce the two main theories of market maker behaviour to be found in the literature: that of the market maker as risk bearer, and that of the market maker as victim of information traders. The former, which has been developed primarily by Ho and Stoll (e.g., 1981), sees the market maker as an agent with a preferred portfolio like any other agent, but who is obliged to accept a portfolio different from what she would have chosen. The market maker therefore has to be induced to take on the unwanted inventory (in securities or cash) via more favourable prices: the market maker's bid-price is therefore below her estimate of the true price of the security, and her ask-price is above it. How large this inducement needs to be depends on the riskiness of the inventory fluctuations involved, which will vary positively with the variance of the return on a security, positively with the size of the transactions concerned, positively with the risk aversion of the market maker, and negatively with the magnitude of the market maker's own capital.

The second main theory of market making, developed mainly by Glosten and Milgrom (1985) and Copeland and Galai (1983), is based on the distinction between information traders and liquidity traders. The former are traders who trade on the basis of specific information about the securities concerned, while the latter are traders who are buying and selling securities for reasons connected with their own

info traders : trade on basis of specific info about securities
liquidity traders : buying / selling to do with prof on own portfolios

3

portfolios. The key point about this distinction is that market makers stand to lose from transactions with information traders, because these traders buy only when they believe that the true price of a security is above the market maker's ask-price, and sell only when they believe that the true price is below the bid-price. On the other hand, market makers gain from trades with liquidity traders insofar as they receive the spread between bid- and ask-prices. Now if market makers widen their spreads, they will lose less from trades with information traders (since the latter will find fewer transactions now profitable); on the other hand, while they will gain more from a given transaction with a liquidity trader since the spread is now wider, liquidity traders will also be discouraged from undertaking transactions so that the volume of trades will decline. Thus profit maximising market makers will continue to operate in a market only if they can set their spreads so that their profits from transactions with liquidity traders outweigh their losses from dealings with information traders; but their ability to widen their spreads is constrained by the fact that the demand for their services is downward sloping.

The above theories are not necessarily mutually exclusive, although they focus on different aspects of the market maker's behaviour. They also have a number of common implications, of which the most important concerns the relationship between the *quoted spread* – that is the difference between a given market maker's bid- and ask- prices at a particular moment – and the *realised spread* – that is the difference between the prices at which the market maker actually deals in successive offsetting transactions. Both theories predict that market makers will tend to respond to the purchase of a security by a customer by raising their prices, and to respond to customer sales by lowering their prices.

In the case of the market maker as risk bearer, a customer purchase means that the market maker now holds less of the security than she would otherwise have preferred. She therefore tries to correct this by offering to buy at a higher price and offering to sell again only at a higher price. In the case of the market maker as victim of information traders, a customer purchase implies that the true price of a security is greater than the market maker's ask-price. She therefore raises her ask-price in order to avoid further losses of the same kind, and raises her bid-price in order to obtain more of the underpriced security. Similarly, we would expect customer sales to be followed by a lowering of bid- and ask-prices.

Hence the realised spread must be less than the quoted spread. For a customer purchase (dealer sale) at time t followed by a dealer purchase at time t+1 we find

$$P_t^a - P_{t+1}^b < P_t^a - P_t^b$$

that is, the realised spread is less than the quoted spread. For a customer sale (dealer purchase) followed by a dealer sale, we find

$$P_{t+1}^a - P_t^b < P_t^a - P_t^b$$

that is, again, the realised spread is less than the quoted spread.

It is now possible to examine directly the determinants of the spread. Four different elements can be distinguished. First, the spread will be affected by the costs of processing orders: these costs, part fixed and part variable (some varying with the number of transactions and some with their size), include the costs of office space and communications equipment, membership fees for specialised exchanges, labour costs, and so on. Second, the spread will be affected by the costs of risk bearing, that is the factors identified above in the discussion of the market maker as risk bearer: the variance of the return on a security, the size of transactions, the capitalisation of the market maker, and the latter's degree of risk aversion. Third, the spread will be affected by the cost of ignorance, which is determined by the proportion of information trades to liquidity trades, and possibly by the extent and nature of the information systematically available only to information traders. Finally, the spread will reflect the degree of competition to which market makers are subject: monopolistic market makers will widen their spreads as far as is consistent with the downward sloping demand for their services, but market makers facing competition from other market makers, from other trading mechanisms (other exchanges or other mechanisms within the same exchange), or from public limit orders[3] will be obliged to accept narrower margins which restrict their equilibrium profit rate to the economy wide normal rate of profit.

These broad predictions seem to be supported by empirical evidence, the bulk of which refers to North American stock markets. Research has found that spreads depend significantly on an activity variable of some kind (e.g. trading volume), a risk variable (e.g. the variance of the return on a security),[4] and a measure of competition (e.g. the number of market makers). Evidence also confirms the prediction that realised spreads are less than quoted spreads.

Finally, it is useful to look briefly at the economies of scale in market making, an issue which also goes back to Demsetz (1968). The latter found that spreads on individual stocks on the New York Stock Exchange were negatively related to the trading volume in the stocks, and he interpreted this as evidence of economies of scale in market making which he took to explain the concentration of dealing in individual securities on one exchange only. Demsetz's basic empirical finding has been widely confirmed, though the correct interpretation of it is less clear. It seems that there are some internal economies of scale for individual market makers over some range of output, that is, over that range their average costs are lower for higher volumes. However, there are numerous cases where multiple market makers continue to coexist, which suggests that these economies are limited and that market making is certainly not a natural monopoly.[5]

At the same time, there seem to be some external economies of scale for market makers arising from the size of the market for a security. Larger markets are typically characterised by a faster and wider flow of information (which enables and induces market makers to set quotes which are continuously nearer to the true price of a security), by greater facilities for interdealer trading (which facilitates the laying off of risk for individual market makers) and by a higher proportion of liquidity traders. Thus, in larger markets both bid-ask spreads and the 'inside spread' (that is the spread between the highest bid-price and the lowest ask-price from any market maker, also referred to as the *touch*) tend to be narrower.

These external economies of scale suggest that there may be a tendency towards natural monopoly at the level of the exchange, and this concept is revisited in section 1.7 below. But at the level of the individual market maker no such tendency seems to exist; the markets for individual securities typically involve some ongoing competition, and they are often highly contestable (that is, outside firms can easily and cheaply enter – and leave – the market because the inputs required are the same as those which they are already using for markets in other securities).

In summary, market makers in organised financial markets are economic agents who choose to specialise in buying and selling the security concerned because they

5

find it profitable to do so. The prices paid by outside traders must (in equilibrium) compensate them for the costs they incur in making markets. And the outcomes of the market processes, that is the prices and volumes traded, are determined by the interaction of the behaviour of market makers and public traders within the particular arrangements by which the market is organised.[6]

1.3 The development of the City of London[7]

The origins of London's position as a leading financial centre can be traced back many centuries. By the end of the fifteenth century the use of bills of exchange for short term finance of trade was widespread in England, and London with its ports was a major centre for internal and external trade.

Financial development accelerated in the late seventeenth century: the Bank of England was established (in 1694, as the first joint stock bank in England), forerunners of both the stock exchange and the Lloyds insurance market came into being, and the system of government finance (both taxes and loans) was reorganised, in part by drawing on Dutch practices familiar to the new king, William III, and his advisers.

During the eighteenth and early nineteenth centuries the English government fought a series of commercial wars which contributed – via the government's need for finance – to the development of the City and enabled London to challenge and then to take over Amsterdam's position as the leading financial centre in Europe. In some ways London was already a more important centre by the second half of the eighteenth century, but by the end of the Napoleonic Wars its supremacy was secure. From 1815 to 1914 both internal and external developments served to consolidate this position. The English banking system became pervasive, well organised and centred on London, while those of Scotland and Ireland also came more firmly under the sway of London and the Bank of England. At the same time Britain became a major exporter of capital (to countries outside as well as inside the Empire), with its organised financial markets (in bills, bonds and equity) heavily involved in overseas business. In addition, the pound sterling became the key reserve currency, and the Bank of England the dominant central bank in the international monetary arrangements known as the gold standard which reached their peak in the four decades up to 1914.

Paris attempted to challenge London's position, particularly through capital exports in the second half of the nineteenth century, but Paris was in a different category. As Kindleberger (1984) puts it,

London was a world financial center; Paris was a European financial center. London was an efficient financial market, handling an enormous body of transactions on a small monetary base. Paris was a rich money and capital market, efficient in the sense that it could mobilize savings and pour them in a given direction, such as the Thiers *rente* or Czarist bonds, but inefficient in its much higher ratio of gold reserves to total financial transactions as compared with London. (p. 268)

The First World War, with the demise of the gold standard and the unequivocal shift in world power away from Britain and towards the United States, caused London to lose its status as the leading international financial centre. Britain's short lived return to the gold standard in 1925 did little to restore the pre-war position, and the use of exchange controls from the 1930s made restoration impossible. The Second World War shifted the international balance of power further away from Britain. The US was now by far the most important economy in the world, and New York became for a while in the 1950s the leading international financial centre.

After the war the continuation of exchange controls and the relatively slow economic growth of the UK meant that the City of London's international role remained a shadow of its pre-1914 self, while the domestic financial system was now heavily protected. However, from the late 1950s London began to find a new role for itself through the emergence of a series of interconnected international money and capital markets centred on the City.

The main impulses to this development were the large scale arrival of US companies in western Europe, the controls on banking in the US in the form of reserve requirements and Regulation Q (which limited the deposit rates banks could offer), and US exchange controls including the Interest Equalisation Tax of 1963–74 (which made it unattractive for foreigners to borrow dollars in New York). US banks thus had an incentive to open branches in Europe, where they could more easily service their American customers now operating in Europe and where they could borrow and lend dollars outside the jurisdiction of US interest rate and exchange controls. A further initial impulse to the development of the eurodollar market was the desire of East European governments to hold their dollar reserves somewhere outside the US where they were not susceptible to confiscation. Easier access to the UK in terms of language, law and business culture, together with the relatively light regulation provided by the Bank of England for international financial activity, made London the natural home for the developing eurocurrency markets. At this stage the euromarkets were mainly money markets; they included wholesale interbank deposits and (from 1966) certificates of deposit, but also a small capital market in the form of eurobonds.

A new impetus to financial developments in London was provided by the breakdown of the Bretton Woods international monetary arrangements in 1971–73, and the first and second oil price shocks of 1973–74 and 1979–80. These created the opportunity for an enormous growth of eurocurrency activity in the form of the recycling of oil exporters' surpluses as syndicated credits to many third world and some industrialised countries. London, with its existing eurocurrency activities and its reputation for political neutrality (as compared to the US, for example, where Arab countries were initially unwilling to deposit their petrodollar surpluses), was again the natural base.

Thus it was that during the 1960s and the 1970s the phenomenon dramatised by Plender and Wallace (1985, pp. 15–16) as the 'two Cities' developed: the domestic City, based on the Stock Exchange and the domestic banks and institutional investors, organised largely in self regulating and often cartellised 'clubs', and sharing in many of the long standing inefficiencies of the UK economy; and the international City, dominated by foreign banks and securities houses involved in the euromarkets, lightly regulated, dynamic and competitive. The dividing line between these two Cities was the system of exchange controls. There were some cross influences: for example, UK banks were active in the eurocurrency markets while US banks became involved in lending to UK industry (on rather different terms from those used by the UK banks, who were then obliged to introduce variable rate medium term loans themselves); and the brokers and jobbers of the London Stock Exchange became involved in the trading of eurobonds, which was organised more informally and with dual rather than single capacity.

However, for the most part the two Cities remained divided until the abolition of exchange controls by the new Conservative government in 1979. This was undertaken for ideological but also for conjunctural reasons (to restrain the appreciation of sterling and offset the current account surpluses associated with North Sea oil). It had a major impact on the City of London by opening up the domestic financial system to international competition and thereby setting in train something of a financial revolution. The 1986 Big Bang on the Stock Exchange is the best known element of this revolution, but major changes were also introduced in the 1980s in a variety of other domestic markets.

In the international markets themselves, the boom in international bank lending in the wake of the oil price shocks led in its turn to the debt crisis of 1982, in which debtor countries suddenly appeared likely to default. The associated loss of confidence in banks and the decline in their credit ratings precipitated a switch from indirect to direct finance and the take off of the market in eurobonds (which had existed since the 1960s), another worldwide unregulated market centred on London.

The City of London developed, then, both as the financial centre of England and the UK and as a leading international financial centre. It lost much of its international role in the years after 1914, but found a new one in the 1960s. While the earlier position was based largely on British economic and political power and capital exports, the new role was more that of an entrepôt financial centre, borrowing from the residents of one country to lend to those of another. In this London benefited from a number of 'first mover' advantages: the UK was the first host to eurocurrency business, one of the first major countries to abolish exchange controls and the first European country to undergo radical stock market reform. By the end of the 1980s, however, a number of other centres, notably Paris and Frankfurt in Europe, were seeking to challenge London's position. We defer consideration of this competition until section 7.

1.4 The London financial markets

London exercises a role in international financial markets which is much larger than the UK's share in international trade and investment, and which contrasts sharply with the UK's relatively poor economic performance in many other areas. This

Table 1.1 Asset positions of banks in major financial centres
(As at end-1990, $US billion)

	External Domestic Currency	External Foreign Currency	Internal Foreign Currency	Total	%
Financial Centre					
London	98	971	315	1384	19
Tokyo	418	533	498	1449	20
United States	512	66	0	578	8
Other	476	2833	496	3805	53
Total	1504	4403	1309	7216	

Source: Bank for International Settlements, 1986, pp. 127–8.

dominance is evidenced by the size and diversity of the financial markets and institutions based in London.

London is the second most important source of international bank lending, but remains the largest centre in terms of foreign currency lending to non-residents. Table 1.1 presents the international asset position of the major international financial centres. Japan's position of overall dominance as the largest international supplier of bank funds is associated with its persistent positive trade balance. However, London's share of foreign currency lending to non-residents, a measure of pure entrepôt financing, is 22% and that of Tokyo is only 12%.

Table 1.2 Banking Institutions in London: number, size and activities

Type	Number	Total Deposits (£'000m)	of which % Sterling	% of Assets in market loans
Retail banks	21	376	81	24
British merchant banks	31	49	65	54
Other British banks	167	46	46	36
American banks	44	125	14	55
Japanese banks	29	230	15	72
Other overseas banks	288	362	25	59
Total	580	1188		

Notes: The number of banks is as at 12 January 1990. There is some double counting where banking institutions have created multiple corporate identities for taxation or organisational purposes. Total deposit figures are as at September 1991. Percentage of assets in market loans is as at December 1990.
Sources:
Bank of England Quarterly Bulletin, Volume 30, Number 1.
Bank of England Quarterly Bulletin, Volume 31, Number 4, Tables 3.2–3.7.
Bank of England Quarterly Bulletin, Volume 30, Number 1, Tables 3.2–3.7.

London is host to a large and diverse array of foreign banks. However, while the number of banks represented in London has grown considerably in the past decade, most international business is booked by a small number of large banks.[8] Table 1.2 indicates the range of banking institutions in London and gives some salient features of their balance sheets. It shows clear differences in the sources and uses of funds for different classes of banks in London. The majority of foreign bank liabilities are denominated in currencies other than sterling. The majority of British bank liabilities are sterling denominated. Foreign bank asset structures, particularly those of Japanese banks, are much more heavily based on the wholesale money markets than those of British banks. London is also host to 120 foreign non-bank securities houses from a wide range of countries (Table 1.3).

In addition to traditional banking activities, London serves as the base for a diverse array of additional financial markets and institutions. It has the fourth largest stock exchange when measured by market turnover, and the third largest when measured by total market capitalisation, and the London market is far more internationalised than other exchanges.[9] It has one of the world's largest markets in domestic government bonds, and a significant turnover in US, German and other foreign government bonds. It also has a major share of syndications and of secondary market trading of eurobond issues: London accounts for 65% of

Table 1.3 Foreign securities houses in London

Country	Number	Total Staff
Australia	12	548
Austria	1	112
Bahrain	1	29
Canada	11	679
France	2	557
Germany	2	272
Hong Kong	1	25
Italy	2	51
Japan	37	3414
South Korea	3	10
Netherlands Antilles	2	120
Singapore	1	5
Sweden	3	99
Switzerland	5	407
United Arab Emirates	1	10
United States	36	8056
TOTAL	120	14394

Source: The Banker, Nov. 1989.

eurobond issues, 62% of eurobond bookrunners, and 76% of eurobond secondary market dealers.[10]

London is the base for a large number of financial and commodity futures and options markets,[11] which accounted for around 6% of the global market in derivative financial instruments in 1989.[12] It contains one of the largest markets for risk insurance and reinsurance. It is a major centre for corporate finance and (together with Edinburgh) for international fund management.

Finally, London is one of the principal hubs of swap market dealing (see section 1.6), and has the dominant international foreign exchange market, accounting for more than 30% of average global daily turnover.

1.5 The foreign exchange market[13]

1.5.1 The operations of the foreign exchange market

The foreign exchange (forex) market provides a means of buying and selling the currencies which are required for transactions in international goods and assets markets. The majority (64%) of forex contracts negotiated on the London forex markets are spot contracts. The remainder are mostly forward contracts. Options and futures contracts make up only one percent of London forex market turnover. While there are 365 forex market dealing institutions, the ten largest institutions account for 35% of London market turnover.[14]

The majority of forex trades involve buying or selling $US. Trades between other pairs of currencies, 'cross currency' deals, though not impossible are far less frequent. Thus an institution wishing to sell Uruguayan pesos and buy Greek drachmae will usually enter a pair of matched transactions. It sells Uruguayan pesos and buys $US, and simultaneously sells $US and buys Greek drachmae. The reasons for choosing this apparently inefficient circuitous route from pesos to drachmae are twofold. First, there are economies of scope in forex markets. The larger the daily volume of transactions in any particular market, the smaller the probability of failing to find another party prepared to buy or sell the required amount of the desired currency. Thus forex markets naturally tend to make some particular currency the key currency. This increases the liquidity of the market and decreases the probability that deals will be frustrated, as can occur in a 'thin' market. Second, forex market trading is information intensive. It therefore makes sense for forex dealers as a group to minimise the costs of information processing by focussing on one or a few currencies as key currencies, and for historical and other reasons the chosen currency is the $US.

In contrast to many equities and securities markets, there are no officially designated market makers in forex markets. But there are many dealers who stand ready to buy or sell particular currencies at bid- and ask-prices which they quote continuously. Trading in global forex markets occurs virtually 24 hours a day. Market makers typically operate dealing rooms in each of the three major time zones. Their aim is to achieve risk cover. Thus, if a market maker sells spot sterling for $US (for delivery in 48 hours), then she will seek a matching or offsetting transaction in which she sells the same amount of $US for sterling. Until such a matching transaction can be found, the market maker faces the risk that variations in the £/$US exchange rate will eliminate profitability.

Foreign exchange deals are frequently arranged by brokers who perform the service of matching deals and passing information for a fee. Such brokers are particularly important in the London market, although there has been a recent slight decline in the proportion of forex deals arranged by them to 38% by value of London forex turnover.[15]

1.5.2 London's foreign exchange market

London's historical dominance of the forex market derived from the role of the pound as the key international reserve currency. Though that mantle long ago shifted to the $US, London remains the dominant international centre for forex trading. This can be illustrated by three distinct pieces of evidence.

Table 1.4 Average daily foreign exchange market turnover

Financial centre	Average daily turnover (US$ bn)	
	1989	1986
London	**187**	**90**
New York	129	58
Tokyo	115	48
Switzerland	57	n.a.
Singapore	55	n.a.
Hong Kong	49	n.a.

Source: Bank of England, 1989b.

First, the estimated average daily turnover of the London forex markets substantially exceeds that of any other financial centre. Estimates for the average daily turnover in the six largest forex centres, taken from the April 1989 Central Bankers' survey of forex activity, are presented in Table 1.4.[16] They show that, although London had the largest forex turnover, the turnover of the Tokyo and New York markets grew more rapidly between 1986 and 1989.

Second, while a majority of London forex contracts are written in $US/£ or $US/DM, the currency composition of London forex turnover is significantly more diverse than the currency composition of turnover in the other major exchanges (Table 1.5).[17]

Table 1.5 Currency composition of foreign exchange market turnover

Currency	Financial Centre		
Exchange	London	Tokyo	New York
$US/£	27	4	15
$US/DM	22	10	33
$US/¥	15	72	25
$US/SwFr	10	4	12
Other	26	10	15
	100	100	100

Notes: SwFr is Swiss Francs. Figures are in percentage terms.
Source: Bank of England, 1989b.

Finally, Goodhart and Demos (1990) have invented a technique for indirectly measuring forex market activity, and the relative importance of different trading centres. Their technique exploits the fact that forex markets use screen based systems to communicate indicative prices. While a range of screen based systems are available, the Reuters system is the clear market leader. Forex market makers regularly update bid- and ask-prices displayed on Reuters for the currencies in which they deal. Goodhart and Demos suggest that the frequency with which dealers in a particular centre enter new prices on the Reuters system might provide some proxy evidence regarding the centre's relative importance in the forex market. Greater relative frequency of price changes indicates greater relative importance of that centre. Table 1.6 provides the relevant data for London, Tokyo and New York as a source of Reuters price quotations for three of the major $US exchange rates. While there is some danger that these figures give a biased representation of the geographic distribution of forex turnover,[18] the figures in Table 1.6 would appear to accord fairly well with the direct survey evidence presented in Table 1.4 above, at least as far as London is concerned, although they give greater weight to Hong Kong and Singapore. This indirect price quotation evidence therefore reinforces our conclusion that London is the dominant financial centre in the forex markets.

Table 1.6 Reuters foreign exchange quotations by currency and financial centre

	% of Dm/$US	% of £/$US	% of ¥/$US	% of Total
Financial centre				
London	19.1	36.9	17.3	23.1
Singapore	16.5	18.4	12.2	15.6
Hong Kong	20.3	7.5	13.8	14.9
New York	13.7	13.4	14.3	13.8
Tokyo	4.0	8.6	18.0	9.8
Zurich	9.0	2.1	8.9	7.2
Sydney	7.0	2.6	6.8	5.8
Toronto	2.8	4.8	3.1	3.4
Other	7.6	5.7	5.6	6.4

Notes: The category 'other' covers 11 smaller trading centres accounting together for 6.4% of quotations. The fourth column is calculated by taking a weighted average of the first three columns. The weights are the proportions of each exchange rate in total price quotations. These proportions were: Dm/US$ 41%, £/$US 26% and ¥/$US 33%.
Based on 491,251 price announcements from early- to mid-1989.
Source: Goodhart and Demos, 1990, p. 10.

1.6   Swap markets[19]

The swap is a relatively recent financial innovation. The swap market enables the parties to a swap agreement to alter their interest rate or currency exposure. Although isolated examples of swap like instruments are known to have existed in the mid-1970s, a developed international swap market did not appear until the early 1980s.

The swap is a natural extension of back-to-back or parallel loans. A back-to-back loan involved two firms or institutions, say from the US and the UK, each borrowing at home and passing on their loans to each other. Back-to-back loans developed when exchange controls were in force in the United Kingdom in the 1970s, as a way of enabling companies operating abroad to obtain cheaper finance by exploiting their comparative advantages in their own national credit markets. Swaps achieve broadly the same results as back-to-back loans in a single transaction.

1.6.1   Types of swap

There exist two main species of swap: the interest rate swap and the currency swap. An interest rate swap is an agreement to exchange interest payment streams. In effect, each party agrees to fulfil the other's interest payment obligations. An interest rate swap does not affect the obligation of the debtor to repay the principal on the loan. Interest rate swaps simply enable each counterparty to alter the characteristics of their interest payments. The most common type of interest rate swap involves an exchange of fixed for floating interest rate payments, or vice versa.

A typical interest rate swap works as follows. Consider a firm which has debt outstanding at a fixed interest rate of 10% per annum. Assume that, perhaps as part of a larger risk diversification portfolio management strategy, the firm wishes to switch from fixed to floating interest rate debt. It strikes a contract with a counterparty under which the counterparty pays the firm 10% per annum, while the firm pays the counterparty some flexible interest rate plus or minus a premium. This premium takes account of the expected direction and magnitude of changes in interest rates over the duration of the swap contract, and includes some fee payable to the market maker arranging the swap. The flexible interest rate is usually LIBOR, the London Interbank Offered Rate, which is the key money market rate in the London eurodollar market. The firm continues to pay its creditors the 10% interest obligation, but is in turn paid the same amount by the counterparty. In effect, the counterparty pays the 10% interest payment. The firm pays the counterparty LIBOR plus or minus the agreed premium.

The interest rate swap market experienced spectacular growth in the early to mid-1980s, but the rate of growth diminished towards the end of the decade. The size and distribution of the interest rate swap market is indicated in Table 1.7. While the $US interest rate swap market accounts for a majority of outstanding interest rate swaps, interest rate swaps in other currencies have recently grown in importance.[20]

Table 1.7 Composition of the interest rate swap market

Market	1989 stock $US bn	%	1990 flow $US bn	%
$US	1288.3	62	294.6	52
¥	195.5	10	67.5	12
£	160.0	8	59.6	11
DM	133.0	6	48.4	9
Other	287.3	14	91.4	16
Total	2064.1		561.5	

Notes: Stock figures are as at end 1989. 1990 flow figures are annualised estimates based on data for the first half of 1990. Figures are for the nominal principal on which the swap agreement is based.
Source: Bank for International Settlements, 1986, p. 142.

These figures do not give an entirely accurate picture of the size of the financial flows generated by the swap market. This is so for two reasons. First, although it is conventional to measure the size of the market by the principal of the debt involved, the principal is 'notional' in that an interest rate swap involves an exchange of interest payment streams but no exchange of principal payments. Second, in order to minimise transaction and administration costs, standardised swap contracts usually include a 'netting' clause under which a single net payment will be made each period by the party owing the greater sum at the payment date.

A currency swap is an agreement to exchange payments in one currency for payments in another currency. Unlike interest rate swaps, currency swaps involve an exchange of both principal and interest payments. At the end of 1989, the outstanding notional principal value of currency swaps was $US 450 billion.[21] Thus the currency swap market is about one fifth the size of the interest rate swap market. Table 1.8 indicates the composition of new currency swaps in the first half of 1990.

Table 1.8 Composition of new currency swaps

Currency	1990 flow $USbn	%	Against $US %
¥	42.3	33	49
$A	16.4	13	30
SwFr	15.4	12	48
DM	12.2	10	50
Ecu	8.4	7	51
£	8.1	6	37
$C	7.2	6	85
Other	16.9	13	56
TOTAL	126.9	100	49

Notes: Figures are for the nominal principal on which the swap agreement is based. $A and $C are the Australian and Canadian dollars respectively. SwFr is Swiss Francs. The figure in the third column is the proportion of currency swaps from that currency which were swaps against $US. Figures are annualised estimates from data for the first half of 1990. Recent stock data for currency swaps is not readily available.
Source: Bank for International Settlements, 1986, p. 143.

The sustained growth of the swap markets can be attributed to two particular factors, in addition to the inherent attractiveness of the swap as a financial instrument. The first factor is the introduction by the International Swap Dealers Association (ISDA) of standardised dealing terms, contracts and documentation for swap agreements in 1985. This has substantially reduced the transaction costs of swap agreements. Second, sustained growth has been fostered by a series of product innovations in swap markets.

While interest rate and currency swaps are the two major simple forms of swap instrument, various 'synthetic' or 'derivative' swap instruments have appeared in the past decade which combine elements of both types of swaps with a number of other features. A 'zero coupon swap' is an interest rate swap in which the fixed rate payments are compounded over the life of the swap, and are payable only on the maturity of the swap. A 'circus swap' is a swap from fixed interest rate obligations in one currency to floating interest rate obligations in another currency, or vice versa. Nearly half of all new currency swaps in 1990 were circus swaps. 'Swaptions' are swap contracts in which the counterparties have the option to cancel or to invoke the swap contract obligations. The parties will make their choice on the basis of movements in the relevant interest and exchange rate variables up to the time at which the option may be exercised. Swaps with 'caps' and 'collars' limit the extent of permissible variations of payments to be made by one of the counterparties. Swaps with caps limit the extent to which a counterparty's payments under the agreement can increase. Of course, the beneficiary of this limitation must pay a premium in order to enjoy the benefit. Swaps with a collar limit the permissible extent of variation in payments under the swap contract in both directions, up and down. The combined size of the market for swaptions and swaps with caps and collars is about the same as the market for simple currency swaps, but the market for simple currency swaps is growing significantly less rapidly than the market for derivative currency swaps.

A 'commodity swap' is a form of derivative swap in which the payments the counterparties agree to make to each other are determined by forward commodity prices, rather than forward interest and exchange rates. In particular, one party agrees to make payments at a fixed rate, the other makes payments pegged to the market price of some commodity. The recent growth of the commodity swaps market has been stimulated by commodity price instability following the Iraqi invasion of Kuwait. However, the commodity swap market is only 3% of the size of the interest rate swap market.

1.6.2 The motivation for swaps

The motivations for entering swap contracts vary. Four primary motivations can be identified. First, swap markets provide a means of exploiting comparative advantage to obtain low cost financing. For instance, consider a firm wishing to obtain finance in yen for a Japanese project. Assume that the firm is unknown in Japanese finance markets but well known in German finance markets. Its relatively strong reputation will allow it to issue bonds in German markets with a substantially smaller interest rate attached. The firm will therefore choose to issue deutschemark denominated bonds, then to conduct a currency swap from deutschemark to yen. Swap markets therefore permit easy arbitraging between national credit markets. A large proportion of currency swaps are swaps out of funds acquired in new eurobond issues.[22] Note that this kind of swap market activity gives rise to 'transparency risk', the risk that the financial position of the firm is not accurately indicated by its balance sheet. This arises because swaps are 'off-balance sheet'. A swap does not eliminate a firm's legal liability to pay its creditors, so swaps do not alter the currency and interest rate composition of liabilities represented in the balance sheet.[23]

Second, swap markets provide a means of hedging currency or interest rate exposure. For instance, imagine that a Swiss firm has a debt portfolio primarily denominated in US dollars, but that its revenues are primarily in Swiss francs. It faces a risk that the US dollar will appreciate against the Swiss franc, so that its net profit after debt servicing will be substantially smaller when measured in Swiss francs. To eliminate this risk, it can enter a currency swap, changing the nature of its debt portfolio from US dollars to Swiss francs. This creates a natural hedge, such that variations in the Swiss franc/$US exchange rate no longer affect the firm's profitability measured in Swiss francs.

Third, swaps provide a relatively easy method of implementing debt management strategies. For example, assume that a French public sector body has a debt portfolio consisting solely of floating rate US dollar debt. Assume that its view is that in the medium term US interest rates will rise and French interest rates will fall. Without the mechanism of swap markets, the organisation would need to engage in the issue of new floating rate securities on French markets, and in the repurchase of existing $US debt on US markets. Swap markets provide a means of achieving the same result as these two transactions, by entering a single swap transaction. The swap contract would involve a shift from floating rate $US to floating rate French franc liabilities. More generally, swap markets provide a relatively cheap means of diversifying the currency or interest rate composition of a debt portfolio.

Finally, like all financial markets, swap markets provide an opportunity for speculation. For example, assume that the general market view is that the $US is likely to appreciate against the yen in the medium term. This will mean that there will be a risk premium payable by a counterparty wishing to switch from yen to $US, and a risk premium payable to a counterparty wishing to switch in the opposite direction. A firm which believes that, contrary to the market consensus, the $US is likely to depreciate against the yen, can engage in a swap from $US to yen. If the firm's speculation regarding the $US/yen exchange rate is correct, it will profit by the amount of the risk premium payable to it under the swap contract.

1.6.3 The operation of the swap market

Commercial or governmental institutions rarely engage directly in swaps with each other. Swaps are usually conducted via a market maker, a commercial or investment bank. The market maker maintains a 'swap book' which it attempts to keep balanced by entering into offsetting swap contracts. Thus, if it agrees to pay fixed rate $US in exchange for floating rate sterling, it attempts to find another counterparty wishing to receive floating rate sterling and pay fixed rate $US. The swaps balance each other, so that the market maker faces no interest or exchange rate risk, but earns fee income from both of the counterparties. Note that balancing the swap book in this way does not entirely eliminate risk for the market maker. The market maker always faces a default risk, the risk that a counterparty will not honour its obligations. The fee charged by the market maker will depend positively upon the credit rating and reputation of the counterparty.

This traditional practice of swap matching has been superseded since 1984 in the more liquid swap markets by the widespread adoption of 'warehousing'. The market maker enters into a swap with one counterparty while taking out a temporary hedge in the bond or futures markets. The maximum acceptable period of warehousing varies across market makers, from one day to several weeks. Swaps involving less well traded currencies continue to be managed on a matched deal basis. For the more liquid contracts, the swap market has now reached a stage of maturity similar to that in other organised financial markets, in which market makers with large swap books appear to be willing to hold open a swap during the interim period, accepting the attendant currency and interest rate risk.

Swap prices are usually negotiated by closed telephone auction. The end user invites a number of market makers to nominate the terms under which they would be prepared to agree to the proposed swap. For instance, in an interest rate swap from fixed to floating liabilities, each market maker will offer a spread over LIBOR. Some of the bidders will be eliminated immediately, because their lowest bid is significantly larger than those of their competitors. Each of the remaining bidders is then given an opportunity to revise its lowest spread over LIBOR. Usually, the lowest bidder is chosen, although the credit rating of the market maker may well influence the choice between close bids. The successful bidder then confirms the swap details by telex.

There would appear to be several dominant market makers in each swap 'sub-market'.[24] This is a consequence of the significant economies of scale which swap book balancing and market making creates. A dealer with a small swap book in a particular pair of currencies and limited contacts will naturally find it more difficult to balance its book quickly following a major transaction. Correspondingly, a dealer with a small swap book will need to inflate its bid to account for the increased interest or exchange rate exposure risk which it undertakes by entering a swap agreement. In contrast, a market maker with a large and rapidly growing swap book and a well developed customer base can anticipate fewer problems in quickly finding a series of swaps which offset a large swap transaction. In consequence, the risk premium charged by a market maker with a large swap book tends to be smaller. Therefore dealers with a large swap book tend to make more competitive bids to the end user.[25]

It is worth mentioning finally that something of a pall has been cast over swap markets, and the robustness of the London swap market in particular, by a ruling of the House of Lords in 1991. The Law Lords decided that UK local authorities are not empowered to enter swaps. All existing obligations of the local authorities under such contracts were declared null and void. The market makers involved in the swaps in some cases faced substantial losses. This decision, although it directly affected swaps valued at only £70 billion, raised more general doubts as to the legal validity of swap transactions entered into with other non-corporate counterparties, such as building societies[26] and pension funds. It is not yet clear whether this development will adversely affect the viability of the London based swap markets.

1.7   London as an international financial centre

1.7.1   The clustering of financial activity

It is not immediately obvious why financial activity should tend to gravitate towards a few places rather than be spread evenly throughout economies. The question has been addressed, at general or specific levels, by writers such as Robbins and Terleckyj (1960), Dunning and Morgan (1971), and Kindleberger (1974).[27] More recently, Grilli (1989) and Davis (1990) have focused on London's prospects in the light of the current general process of financial liberalisation; the present discussion is based on their analyses.

Davis approaches the issue through the economic analysis of the location decisions of firms. That analysis emphasises the supply of factors of production, the demand for the product and external economies, each being considered in terms of a given site relative to alternative sites. In addition, the existence of sunk costs at a given site, on the one hand, and uncertainty about conditions and costs at other sites, on the other hand, will tend to induce inertia, while 'stress' on a firm at a given site may induce relocation. Finally, for multinational enterprises factors such as tariff barriers, political stability and strategic considerations in oligopolistic markets are important.

When this analysis is applied to financial firms, the factors of importance on the supply side seem to be the following: the rights of establishment in a particular location; the supply of skilled personnel (whose cost may be affected by local tax rates); the supply of premises; the supply of equipment and machinery; and the supply of funds, whose cost may be influenced by reserve requirements and regulation, by stamp duties and other fiscal arrangements, and by the efficiency of payment and settlement systems. However, it seems unlikely that the differences between financial centres in these factors would be very large in the long run; they are certainly in principle susceptible to modification by appropriate policy measures. On the demand side, the efficiency and speed of modern communication suggests that the location of customers is unlikely to be too important, except in so far as differences in time zone are concerned.

On the other hand, sunk costs can be considerable in financial activities, in particular the sunk costs of building relationships with other financial firms and with clients. The heterogeneity of some financial activities – for example, primary issues or the secondary trading of heterogeneous equities – means that trust and confidence on the part of customers and firms involved in joint projects are crucial to sales. The contacts a financial firm develops in a particular site are therefore valuable, and militate against relocation elsewhere.[28] However, under the heading of stress, Davis suggests that shocks such as the emergence of serious excess capacity in a particular centre or the intensification of competitive pressures as the result of the 1992 process may cause financial firms to consider relocating.

External economies of scale and economies of agglomeration[29] are likely to be of great importance for financial firms. First, concentrations of financial firms in one place lead to improved flows of information,[30] higher liquidity and greater efficiency in organised markets. Second, proximity between related markets (e.g. spot and derivative markets, eurobond and swap markets, forex and euromarkets in general) will similarly improve information, liquidity and efficiency. Third, financial activities which require joint action by a range of similar or differing firms – e.g. loan syndication on the one hand, or primary issues involving underwriting on the other – can be undertaken more easily and with more confidence when close and regular contacts are feasible. In addition, the concentration of financial firms induces a similar concentration of firms supplying the requisite professional services such as accounting, legal and computer programming services, and therefore reduces the cost of these services, while there are infrastructural economies of scale in payment and settlement systems and in non-professional services such as the transportation of documents. At the level of the firm, economies of scope, arising from the simultaneous supply of related products or the simultaneous satisfaction of related demands, may also be important.

The location of financial firms may be affected by strategic behaviour (both predatory and defensive), for example, if firms move geographically as part of attempts to enter particular markets. The arrival of some Japanese banks and securities houses in London in the 1980s can be interpreted in this way. Variations in regulatory regimes as between different centres may also be important.

On the basis of this discussion Davis argues that, while a variety of factors may have been involved in the original growth of an international financial centre, once that growth has started the external economies of scale and economies of agglomeration tend to sustain it. Moreover, some of these economies are dynamic rather than static, that is they increase as the number of firms in a single location increases. For example, the benefits of contacts rise with the number of firms contacted, while 'liquidity attracts liquidity'. Moreover, a growing centre will gradually acquire a better reputation as a place for business and this will attract further business and new firms. Thus after some critical mass is reached growth may become self-perpetuating, with the marginal benefits to new entrants continuously rising. Conversely, there must be a possibility of cumulative departure from, and therefore decline of, a given financial centre.

Davis then goes on to analyse international financial centres as oligopolistic firms competing against each other to attract financial activity, in an 'industry' characterised by increasing returns to scale and economies of scope, and with large sunk costs. Established centres find their low average costs reinforced by intertemporal dependencies: low costs now lead to lower costs in the future by the transmission of expertise, while large 'sales' now attract larger 'sales' in the future through the building up of reputation. At the same time in a large centre the 'fixed costs' – notably financial infrastructure in the form of payment and settlement systems – are spread more widely over a greater number of markets and financial institutions.

Collusion between centres is unlikely and centres are unable to exercise strong market power because, with the globalisation of financial activity, customers can switch between existing centres or even move to new potential centres; and because major changes in technology or in relative regulation can severely affect a centre's competitive position. Smaller financial centres, on the other hand, may be able to establish and maintain niche positions, for example in locally based markets which require detailed local information and contacts, but they will find it hard to break through into becoming major international financial centres.

Grilli (1989) uses a more formal and rigorous model, but one which is less multi-dimensional. The essence of it is the notion of increasing returns from thick market externalities, as first discussed by Diamond (1982), that is, the idea that trade is easier when there are a larger number of potential trading partners. In Grilli's application the productivity of financial firms depends on the size of the market in which they are operating, hence firms tend to cluster together in 'hot spots'. Grilli finds empirical confirmation for this hypothesis from an examination of the location of international bank deposits; non-bank (individual) investors seem to put more emphasis on bank secrecy and withholding taxes, but interbank deposits gravitate towards markets with greater thick market externalities.[31]

1.7.2 Conclusion: the prospects for London

The analyses of Grilli and Davis should be seen as complementary rather than mutually exclusive. They concur, moreover, in arguing that the widespread financial liberalisation (partly associated with the 1992 process) is unlikely to damage London's position as an international financial centre, and may even strengthen it: financial activities repatriated to their home countries by the deregulation there may be outweighed by activities previously held in their home countries by direct controls which are now attracted to London.[32] This view needs to be tempered, however, by a recognition of the damage done to London by the perpetual delays in introducing an efficient settlement system for equities (see Chapter 2) and by the continuing uncertainties about swap transactions in London (section 1.6 above).

More generally, we may conclude that London's initial rise as an international financial centre was due to a number of factors, from the early development of internal financial instruments and markets through Britain's initial industrial supremacy and its place at the apex of the gold standard. This position was largely lost in the period after 1914, although much of the financial culture that had sustained it continued to exist. London found a new international role, of a somewhat different sort, as a home for the euromarkets that developed from the late 1950s; that role was then expanded by a number of radical internal reforms whose effects are still being felt, in the rest of Europe as well as in the UK.

However, London's new position as an international financial centre is now buttressed by a variety of economies of scale, of scope and of agglomeration. Policy makers need to continue to be vigilant in view of the possibility of predatory strategic moves from other European centres.[33] One issue of particular current concern is the attitude of the UK government to European economic and monetary union. While many of the City's activities are of an entrepôt nature there must be a serious danger that financial activities in the coming single European currency will gravitate to the countries which adopt that currency, and the UK might lose out if it chooses to remain aloof. Nevertheless, London is at the very least playing from a position of considerable strength.

Notes

1   Shane Bonetti was primarily responsible for sections 4–6, and David Cobham for sections 1–3 and 7.

2   The last decade and a half has seen a rapid growth of the academic literature on this subject. The reader who wishes to delve further is recommended to look at the introduction in Goodhart (1989, Chapter I) and the surveys by Stoll (1985) and Schwartz (1988, Chapter 12), on which this section draws.

3   That is, orders from the public for sales or purchases at prices which are not currently available in the market but may become so if prices move.

4   The risk may be related to the proportion of information to liquidity traders active in a particular security, so that it is not possible to differentiate empirically between the two main theories of market making.

5   A natural monopoly is a situation where one firm can produce the entire output of an industry more cheaply than any combination of more than one firm, i.e. where the long run average cost curve slopes continuously downwards. Typical examples are utilities such as electricity distribution, telecommunications, etc., where the concept of natural monopoly is evoked to explain the need for regulation even if competition is legally permitted.

6   The differences between different trading mechanisms are discussed below most explicitly in Chapter 2 in connection with the equity market.

7   For further discussion see in particular Kindleberger (1974, 1984), and also Dunning and Morgan (1971).

8   Bank of England (1986c, pp. 371–3).

9   Equity turnover and market valuation data are examined in greater detail in Chapter 2.

10   Bank of England (1991b, p. 527). See Chapter 4.

11   These are the International Petroleum Exchange, the Agricultural Futures Exchange, the London Gold Market, the London Silver Market, the Baltic International Freight Futures Exchange, the London Commodity Exchange (London FOX), the London International Financial Futures Exchange, the London Metal Exchange, and the London Traded Options Market.

12   Davis (1990, Appendix I).

13   This section draws on Bank of England (1986b), (1989b), Burnham (1991), and Harrington (1991).

14   Bank of England (1989b).

15   Bank of England (1989b, p. 534). It is worth noting that until their abolition in 1985 on the initiative of the Bank of England there were fixed scales for brokerage commissions in this market issued by the Bank itself. (Bank of England, 1986a.)

16   The figure of $US 187 billion daily turnover understates the size of the London market to the extent that it excludes an average of $US 12 billion per day intermediated by London brokers between principals abroad. (Bank of England, 1989b, p. 532.)

17 We can measure diversity by the index D:

$$D = \left(\frac{1}{n}\right) \sum_{i=1}^{i=n} \left[\left(\frac{100}{n}\right) - s_i\right]^2$$

where s_i is the percentage share of currency i in turnover, and n is the number of currency classes. Note that D=0 implies perfect diversification, and the larger is D the less diverse is the currency mix. From the data in Table 1.5, the diversity index is 42.8 for London, 61.6 for New York and 683.2 for Tokyo. The large figure for Tokyo is a consequence of the dominance of $/yen contracts in the turnover of the Tokyo forex market.

18 See Goodhart and Demos (1990) for the appropriate qualifications.

19 This section draws on Bank of England (1987), Bank for International Settlements (1986, pp. 37–60), and Bank for International Settlements (1991).

20 Interest rate swaps denominated in currencies other than the dollar accounted for 48% of new contracts in the first half of 1990 compared to only 24% in the first half of 1987. (Bank for International Settlements, 1986, p. 143.)

21 A currency breakdown of the stock data comparable to that in Table 1.7 is not available. (Bank for International Settlements, 1986, p. 143.)

22 Bank of England (1987, p. 71).

23 Bank for International Settlements (1986, p 59) notes that standard accounting practice is to omit swaps from financial accounts.

24 Bank of England (1987, p. 70); Gehrig (1990).

25 The foregoing discussion of swap pricing is highly simplified. In reality, the valuation and pricing of swap transactions involves a very high degree of conceptual and mathematical difficulty. The interested reader is referred to Bicksler and Chen (1986).

26 The UK Building Societies Commission claims that under the Building Societies Act (1986), societies are empowered to make swaps. (McDougall, 1991.)

27 See also Lewis and Davis (1987, Chapter 8).

28 The importance of contacts was emphasised by Robbins and Terleckyj (1960) in their study of New York and by Dunning and Morgan (1971) who conducted a sample survey of business contacts of City of London workers. Davis (1990) argues convincingly that technological improvements in communications are unlikely to eliminate the need for co-location of financial firms, particularly for non-homogeneous products. Certainly workers in the City maintain that face-to-face personal contacts are an important complement to telephone and fax communication.

29 Economies of agglomeration are reductions in cost that arise from the locational concentration of firms and industries.

30 Particular attention was drawn to information by Robbins and Terleckyj, who coined the term 'knowledge in a hurry'. They argued that the short run volatility of security prices creates a need for knowledge of current prices, and that 'clustering tends to occur whenever the high risks of an activity can be modified through the frequent swapping of information and ideas.' (Robbins and Terleckyj, 1960, p. 35.)

31 However, Grilli uses GNP as a proxy for thick market externalities, which makes sense only for financial centres whose position is based on the size of

their hinterland economies. This is not entirely correct for the UK in the recent period, and certainly not correct for centres like Hong Kong and Singapore which are not included in his analysis.

32 Grilli criticises Kindleberger's (1974) prediction that Brussels might become the financial centre of the European Community but, as Grilli would surely agree, matters were very different in 1974, before the abolition of UK exchange controls, the burgeoning of the euromarkets and the revolution in the City of London itself.

33 Previous measures of support by the Bank of England for the City's position as an international financial centre have included its early welcome for eurocurrency business, its contribution to the financial infrastructure in the creation of the Central Gilts Office, and its more general pressure for liberalisation as in the abolition of minimum commissions in forex broking and in the stock exchange.

Bibliography

Bank for International Settlements (1986) *Recent Innovations in International Banking* (the Cross Report). BIS.

Bank for International Settlements (1991) *61st Annual Report*. BIS.

Bank of England (1986a) The changing foreign exchange markets, *Bank of England Quarterly Bulletin*, **26**, 211–15.

Bank of England (1986b) The market in foreign exchange in London, *Bank of England Quarterly Bulletin*, **26**, 379–82.

Bank of England (1986c) International banking in London, 1975–85, *Bank of England Quarterly Bulletin*, **26**, 367–78.

Bank of England (1987) Recent developments in the swap market, *Bank of England Quarterly Bulletin*, **27**, 66–74.

Bank of England (1989a) London as an international financial centre, *Bank of England Quarterly Bulletin*, **29**, 516–28.

Bank of England (1989b) The market in foreign exchange in London, *Bank of England Quarterly Bulletin*, **29**, 531–35.

Bank of England (1990) The role of brokers in the London money markets, *Bank of England Quarterly Bulletin*, **30**, 221–7.

Bank of England (1991a) Developments in international banking and capital markets in 1990, *Bank of England Quarterly Bulletin*, **31**, 234–45.

Bank of England (1991b) The international bond market, *Bank of England Quarterly Bulletin*, **31**, 521–8.

Bicksler, J. and **Chen, A.H.** (1986) An economic analysis of interest rate swaps, *Journal of Finance*, **41**, 645–55.

Burnham, J.B. (1991) Current structure and recent developments in foreign exchange markets, in S.J. Khoury (ed.), *Recent Developments in International Banking and Finance*, (vols IV and V). Amsterdam.

Copeland, T.C. and **Galai, D.** (1983) Information effects on the bid-ask spread, *Journal of Finance*, **38**, 1457–69.

Davis, E.P. (1990) International financial centres – an industrial analysis, *Bank of England Discussion Paper*, **51**.

Demsetz, H. (1968) The cost of transacting, *Quarterly Journal of Economics*, **82**, 33–53.

Diamond, P. (1982) Aggregate demand management in search equilibrium, *Journal of Political Economy*, **90**, 881–94.

Dunning, J.H. and **Morgan, E.V.** (1971) *An Economic Study of the City of London*. Allen & Unwin.

Gehrig, T. (1990) Natural monopoly in intermediated markets, *LSE Financial Markets Group Discussion Paper*, **83**.

Glosten, L.R. and **Milgrom, P.R.** (1985) Bid, ask and transaction prices in a specialist market with heterogeneously informed traders, *Journal of Financial Economics*, **14**, 71–100.

Goodhart, C.A.E. (1989) *Money, Information and Uncertainty*, 2nd edn. Macmillan.

Goodhart, C.A.E. and **Demos, A.** (1990) Reuters screen images of the foreign exchange market: the yen/dollar and the £/dollar spot market, *LSE Financial Markets Group Discussion Paper*, **105**.

Grilli, V. (1989) Europe 1992: issues and prospects for the financial markets, *Economic Policy*, **4**, 388–421.

Harrington, R. (1991) The London financial markets, in C.J. Green and D.T. Llewellyn (eds.), *Surveys in Monetary Economics*, Vol 2: *Financial Markets and Institutions*. Blackwell.

Ho, T. and **Stoll, H.** (1981) Optimal dealer pricing under transactions and return uncertainty, *Journal of Financial Economics*, **9**, 47–73.

Kindleberger, C.P. (1974) The Formation of Financial Centers: A Study in Comparative Economic History, *Princeton Studies in International Finance*, **36**, Princeton University.

Kindleberger, C.P. (1984) *A Financial History of Western Europe*. Allen & Unwin.

Lewis, M.K. and **Davis, K.T.** (1987) *Domestic and International Banking*. Philip Allan.

McDougall, R. (1991) A sorry tangled tale, *The Banker*, January, 29–30.

Plender, J. and **Wallace, P.** (1985) *The Square Mile*. Hutchinson.

Robbins, S.M. and **Terleckyj, N.E.** (1960) *Money Metropolis*. Harvard University Press.

Schwartz, R.A. (1988) *Equity Markets: Structure, Trading and Performance*. Harper & Row.

Stoll, H. (1985) Alternative views of market making, in Y. Amihud, T. Ho and R. Schwartz (eds) *Market Making and the Changing Structure of the Securities Industry*. Lexington Books.

2   The equity market

by David Cobham

This chapter examines the market for equity in London. It starts by differentiating in section 2.1 between different types of trading structure used in equity markets, noting briefly the advantages and disadvantages of each. Section 2.2 provides an account of the historical development of the London stock market, concentrating on the consolidation of its particular trading structure in the early years of the twentieth century and on the post-1945 trends and pressures that culminated in the Big Bang reforms of October 1986. Section 2.3 considers the restructuring of the London Stock Exchange, examining the choice of a new dealing system for equities and the opening up of membership to outsiders. Section 2.4 looks at primary issues and the second (and third) markets, and section 2.5 considers a variety of post Big Bang adjustments to the system. Section 2.6 evaluates the new dealing system in terms of the quality of market that it has produced, and via some international comparisons. The market in London for international equities is the subject of special attention in section 2.7, which also considers the prospects for competition and or collaboration with other European stock markets. Section 2.8 provides a brief conclusion.[1]

2.1   Trading structures for equity markets[2]

The trading structure of a market means the mechanisms by which orders are aggregated and prices are determined. The most basic distinction is that between *batch* (or *call*) markets and *continuous* markets.

The former are markets in which trade takes place at discrete intervals by means of auctions: orders for a particular stock are allowed to accumulate over time and the market is then *called*, usually at pre-specified times, with the price being determined in a single auction process. This auction can be verbal and iterative, that is the auctioneer starts the process by calling a price which is then adjusted in response to traders' shouted orders, the latter themselves being modified in response to the information about demand and supply which is revealed in the course of the process. Alternatively, the auction may be written and non-iterative, that is the auctioneer assembles previously submitted orders, sets the price at the equilibrium level (or as near to it as is possible), and reports which trades have been executed.

Continuous markets are those in which trading can take place at any time, whenever buy and sell orders cross. Markets of this sort are either *matching* markets or *dealer* markets. Matching markets are ones in which trade takes place when one public order crosses another, while in dealer markets there are recognised dealers who must decide and quote publicly the price at which they are ready to buy or sell out of their own inventories, and trade takes place whenever a trader accepts that price. Thus the former are called 'order-driven', and the latter 'quote-driven'.

Batch markets used to be common in continental Europe; for example, the Paris market consists of a 'forward' market in which trading used to be conducted by means of verbal auctions (*à la criée*) and a 'cash' market in which trading used to be conducted through written auctions (*par cassiers*). However, the reforms of recent years have seen the replacement of batch markets by continuous trading in many cases (including Paris). Continuous markets have been used for rather longer in the Anglo-Saxon countries. The London Stock Exchange (both before Big Bang and since) and the NASDAQ market in the US are examples of dealer markets. New York and most of the other US exchanges are hybrids; they combine a matching system with the use of specialists who are private (but officially recognised) dealers but who operate the order book. Pure matching markets, on the other hand, can be further subdivided into those that use an order book (where an exchange official records orders and effects transactions when orders cross) such as (part of) the Tokyo stock exchange, those that involve the use of a board (on which prices are posted and transactions recorded) such as the Hong Kong exchange, and those that involve crowd trading (the stock market equivalent of pit trading) such as the Zurich stock exchange.

In most cases stock exchange trading structures evolved gradually over time, but in recent years exchanges have sought more deliberately to choose the trading structure best suited to their purposes and aspirations. The key considerations involved in such a choice are cost and efficiency. Batch markets are cheaper to operate, and within that category written auctions are cheaper than verbal auctions (where traders or their agents must be present during the process); continuous markets, on the other hand, are more expensive to operate because more personnel (and/or more electronic technology) are required, and dealer markets are generally more expensive than matching markets. On the other hand, price discovery is more efficient in continuous than in batch markets: market prices reflect more closely the fundamentals, and for given fundamental conditions prices are more stable and less volatile. Continuous markets can handle large volumes with low unit costs, and dealer markets with well capitalised dealers may be most cost effective at handling large volumes with large individual transactions.

Recent work by Pagano and Roell (1992) has suggested that ordinary traders face lower average trading costs in (continuous) auction markets because public orders can cross directly rather than passing through an intermediary. On the other hand, there may be significant execution risk in auction markets, that is transaction prices may be widely dispersed around the expected value of a security, whereas in dealer markets execution risk is zero. In addition, in both dealer markets and floor based markets dealers may be able to distinguish liquidity from information traders and therefore to offer the former better prices; such markets are better for identified ordinary (liquidity) traders, but worse for information or unidentified traders.

2.2   The development of the London Stock Exchange up to Big Bang[3]

Some sort of market in securities had existed in London since the late seventeenth century, but the London Stock Exchange was formally established only in 1773. For a long period it was in competition with outside dealers in London, although there was no other organised marketplace, and its monopoly position was consolidated only in the late nineteenth century. For much of that century it had a largely complementary relationship with the various provincial stock exchanges in Great Britain and Ireland, but the revolution in communications and the trend towards larger and less localised joint stock companies towards the end of the century led to the London Stock Exchange becoming the dominant hub of an integrated securities market,[4] although it formally merged with the other exchanges only in 1973. It also merged with the International Securities Regulatory Organisation, the representative body for international bond dealers in London, to form the International Stock Exchange of the United Kingdom and the Republic of Ireland in December 1986, but reverted to calling itself the London Stock Exchange in 1991.

From its early years the London exchange had close connections with the British government; in particular a very large part of its turnover was in government bonds, e.g. during and after the Napoleonic Wars of the late eighteenth and early nineteenth centuries. At the same time it had a strong overseas orientation. In the 1820s, for example, there was a high turnover in foreign bonds, and from the 1840s issues of, and turnover in, foreign railway equities were of primary importance to the market. On the other hand, the London Stock Exchange had a relatively weak relationship with British industrial and commercial companies, many of which at this stage were relatively small and localised and therefore either raised funds through their nearest provincial stock exchange or relied on internal finance (for example, very little of the early finance for the British rail system was provided through the London Stock Exchange). Thus in 1914 only 40% of all securities listed on the London exchange (equity and bonds) were domestic, while 60% were foreign.

Over the next three decades, however, the London stock market was gradually converted for the first time into an essentially domestic market. During the First World War, and again during the Second, there were large sales of British holdings of overseas securities, while the inter-war period saw a general decline after 1929 in the importance of international trade and capital flows and from 1931 the introduction of exchange controls. After the Second World War exchange controls continued, if anything in a more severe form, and the London Stock Exchange became somewhat inward looking and undynamic, organised along the lines of a 'club' with self regulation and restrictive practices, but protected by exchange controls from overseas competition.

The organisation and trading structure of the exchange had evolved in a long, and sometimes uneven, process from its origin in Jonathan's Coffee-house, but was consolidated in the early part of the twentieth century in two main features. First, the intermediaries of the market were separated into two distinct groups with distinct functions: brokers acted as the agents of outside customers, seeking to buy or sell on their behalf at the best possible terms, while jobbers acted as principals, buying and selling on their own account from and to the brokers. This *single capacity* was incorporated in the rules of the exchange in 1909. Secondly, brokers charged fees to their customers on the basis of a scale of *minimum commissions* first established in 1912.

The original development of single capacity in the eighteenth and early nineteenth centuries seems to have been both the result of a natural tendency towards specialisation and a response to the demand from customers for a guarantee of the integrity of those acting on their behalf; single capacity meant that brokers had no interest themselves in the terms on which their customers traded. However, the jobber/broker distinction was becoming blurred in the later part of the nineteenth century when improved communications enabled jobbers to establish direct contacts with brokers on other provincial and overseas exchanges, and brokers began to quote prices themselves in order to compete for such business with the jobbers. The reassertion of single capacity in 1909 was designed in part to oblige business between London dealers and provincial brokers to be conducted via London brokers.

The introduction of minimum commissions had been mooted long before by brokers who wanted to protect their incomes from too much competition, but what made the difference in 1912 was the argument that single capacity required minimum commissions. Without the latter, jobbers could circumvent the single capacity rule by having their outside business passed through the books of an obliging broker for a nominal fee. Brokers would then be tempted to protect themselves by matching deals between their own clients or even acting as principals (fulfilling customers' orders out of their own inventories), thus removing business from the jobbers, who would then be under even more pressure to deal directly with outsiders in order to protect their own turnover and income. Thus minimum commissions were needed, it was argued, to preserve single capacity.[5]

In the period after the Second World War a number of disparate pressures and forces gradually developed and finally combined to force radical change upon the London Stock Exchange in the 1980s. The first of these trends was the growth of the importance of institutional investors. Investment trusts had existed from the second half of the nineteenth century, and unit trusts since the 1930s, but their share in overall holdings of securities had been relatively unimportant. It was only after the war with the growth of pension funds and the associated rise in the life business of insurance companies that institutional investors came to hold a large and increasing proportion of UK securities. The Wilson Committee reported that institutional investors' holdings of ordinary shares had risen from 19% of the total in 1957 to 47% in 1978 (and their holdings of gilt-edged from 17% to 46% over the same period), while later figures suggest a further rise in the proportion of equities held to 57.6% in 1981 and 57.9% in 1989.[6] Meanwhile, personal sector direct holdings of equities fell from 66% in 1957 to 28% in 1981 and 21% in 1989.[7] These trends are significant for two reasons: first, institutional investors tend to deal in much larger amounts and more actively, and secondly, they tend to share the same views (as the result of their dependence on similar sources of information and advice) and therefore to trade in the same direction at the same time. Thus the liquidity of the market was adversely affected.

The second major trend was the growing pressure upon the capital resources of the jobbers, and to a lesser extent those of the brokers, as the result of both the rise of institutional investors and the generally slow growth of stock market activity (real turnover actually declined over much of the 1950s and 1960s). This pressure led to a significant reduction in the number of jobbing firms, mainly through mergers which increased both the capital and the personnel resources of firms (see Table 2.1); and at the same time to an increase in anti-competitive practices such as the operation by two or more jobbing firms of a joint book on a particular security and agreements between jobbers on minimum price spreads (which could be reduced by negotiation for large deals with institutional investors). The reduction in the number of broking firms over the same period was rather smaller; for them the main effect of the rise of the institutions was to encourage competition in non-price forms (since price competition was excluded by minimum commissions) such as hospitality and the provision of research.

Table 2.1 Membership of the Stock Exchange

	Brokers		Jobbers	
	Firms	Principals	Firms	Principals
1920	475	1513	411	1465
1930	461	1646	358	1248
1940	426	1630	278	n.a.
1950	364	1743	187	791
1955	329	1791	135	632
1960	305	1886	100	545
1965	270	1893	60	417
1970	192	1810	31	273
1975	284	2129	21	231
1980	240	2104	19	203
1984	209	2034	17	183
1986	207	2189	18	247

	Firms	Individual members
1987	357	5433
1989	389	5114
1991	413	5192

Notes: Figures before 1973 cover London firms only, from 1974 regional firms as well.
1984 (figures relate to January) is the low point before the Big Bang-induced rise.
From 1987 firms trade as dual capacity.
Source: Quality of Markets Quarterly Review, Jan.–April 1991.

A third important trend in this period was the London Stock Exchange's growing exposure to competition. The first sign of the coming trend was an attempt to set up an electronic security trading system outside, and in competition with, the Stock Exchange in 1972. The Automated Realtime Investments Exchange Ltd (ARIEL) was set up by a group of merchant banks and institutional investors to provide a cheaper dealing service. It was opposed by the Bank of England (which meant that it never became a serious market for gilt-edged) and it suffered from some fiscal disadvantages vis-à-vis the Stock Exchange. It never captured a significant share of transactions but it may be said to have exerted substantial pressure on the Stock Exchange all the same, because the latter responded by halving the fixed commissions on large deals in order to avoid a loss of business.

However, the event that really opened the market to the winds of competition was the UK government's decision to abolish exchange controls in the autumn of 1979. The immediate consequence was a major outflow of capital over the next few years as the institutions sought to diversify their portfolios into the previously forbidden territory of overseas securities. This should have represented a good business opportunity for UK brokers, but the latter lacked the connections and expertise to handle the transactions.[8] More importantly still, it had now become much easier to trade UK securities outside the UK, notably in New York in the form of American Depository Receipts (ADRs),[9] and a significant share of domestic security business began to migrate abroad. In 1984 it is said that more ICI shares

29

were traded in this way in New York than in London.[10] International competition between stock exchanges was being opened up by deregulation, notably in the US, and by cost reductions associated with improved communications and computer technology. Such competition highlighted the undynamic, inefficient and undercapitalised nature of London Stock Exchange member firms. On the other hand, the abolition of exchange controls in the UK, at a time when many other industrialised countries (but not the US or West Germany) retained important restrictions, suggested that the London Stock Exchange might find a new role for itself as a dynamic international entrepôt market.

A further source of pressure for change in the late 1970s and early 1980s was the growth of near breaches of the single capacity rule. Brokers were doing an increasing number of 'put-throughs', that is deals between their clients which they matched and then had confirmed by a jobber, who received a small fee for his service, less than he would have obtained from the normal handling of such business.[11] Both jobbing and broking firms were by now active in the eurobond market which was relatively unregulated at this time and where both of them acted as principals. Finally, from 1980 jobbers as well as brokers were allowed by the Stock Exchange to deal with foreign principals, who operated on a dual capacity basis.

Thus, in the late 1970s and early 1980s a number of forces and pressures were coming together to push the Stock Exchange towards radical reform. One further factor, which appeared initially as a stimulus to change but later became a drag upon it, was the reference of the Stock Exchange rule book to the Restrictive Practices Court in February 1979, following the extension of the 1956 Restrictive Practices Act in 1976 to cover services as well as goods. *Prima facie*, the Exchange appeared to be operating a number of restrictive practices, notably on minimum commissions and on barriers to entry into membership and to broking and jobbing. However, the Exchange prepared to defend itself, largely on the basis of the 'link argument' that single capacity required minimum commissions to protect its existence – essentially the same argument that had been instrumental in the introduction of minimum commissions in 1912. The Exchange's case, a statement of some 250 pages, was put to the Court in 1981, and the case was expected to be heard early in 1984. It was, however, precisely in these early years of the 1980s that the pressures for change grew noticeably more intense, following the abolition of exchange controls and the possibility this opened up that the London stock market could lose a very large part of its position to overseas markets. Yet the Stock Exchange found it could not introduce changes at this point, for fear of implicitly admitting guilt with respect to restrictive practices. Eventually, after the general election which returned the Conservative government to power in June 1983, pressure from the Bank of England (which was keen to find a new role for itself in the aftermath of the problems associated with monetary targeting) led to the problem being handled in a different way. In July 1983 the government (represented by Cecil Parkinson, the new Secretary of State for Trade and Industry) and the London Stock Exchange (led by Nicholas Goodison) reached an Accord. Under its terms the Exchange agreed to abolish minimum commissions and open up its membership by the end of 1986, while the government agreed to lift the reference to the Restrictive Practices Court (which later turned out to require a special Act of Parliament).

The government's behaviour in all this was heavily criticised at the time, for it seemed obvious it was favouring its friends and abrogating the due course of the law in a way that was at the very least a snub to the Office of Fair Trading which had been responsible for preparing the case against the Stock Exchange. However, in retrospect it seems clear that the government's actions resulted in as big a shake up of the Stock Exchange as could have been wished for; and, while the timing of the Accord was bound to provoke suspicions, the government's aim was straightforward reform (for example, it had not yet become as enthusiastic as it did later about either privatisation or the spread of share ownership).

Initially it was thought that single capacity would survive, and the government had not expressed hostility towards it. However, before long the 'link argument' was put into reverse. If minimum commissions had to go, then single capacity would not be able to survive; in which case the Stock Exchange had to start looking for a new trading structure to replace the previous system since that had depended on the separation of brokers and jobbers. Among the members of the Exchange there was considerable apprehension at first about the likely changes, but in time this apprehension was overridden, for it became clear that members could make enormous potential gains out of the purchases of the existing partnerships by outside firms which had now become possible.

2.3 The restructuring of the London Stock Exchange[12]

2.3.1 The choice of a new dealing system

The Stock Exchange sought a new trading structure which would provide continuous dealing at low transactions costs and with high liquidity, and one that would be suitable for international security business, where it hoped for a strong development, as well as domestic security business. It examined two existing models, that of the New York Stock Exchange (NYSE) and that of the National Association of Securities Dealers Automated Quotation (NASDAQ) system; other existing models such as those of the continental European bourses at this time did not satisfy the basic criteria specified above.

The NYSE, which was identified in section 2.1 as a hybrid matching dealer market, is often referred to as a broker-to-broker auction market with specialist participation.[13] It operates on a central trading floor with trading 'posts' for different securities where the specialist operates the order book and trading takes place through the 'crowd' of brokers and specialists. The market is order driven, that is to say it is changes in the flow of orders brought to the market by brokers on behalf of their clients which is the proximate cause of changes in price. The role of the specialist was originally to take limit orders (that is, orders in the form 'buy (sell) so many of security X at or below (above) price Y') and execute them whenever possible, but later the specialists acquired a more important role as dealers, and with it an 'affirmative obligation' to maintain orderly markets and minimise price fluctuations. At the same time, however, the extent of competition between specialists declined markedly, so that by the 1970s there were no posts with more than one specialist operating. In 1976 the NYSE introduced a new category of registered competitive market makers who were required to make bids and offers that would narrow the quoted spread or increase the size of an existing quote if asked to do so by a floor official or a broker, but the impact of the RCMMs has been limited. The NYSE also encompasses in effect three other trading mechanisms: it opens each day with a clearing transaction, while small deals can be transacted via an automated execution service, and large 'block' trades are generally negotiated 'upstairs' at member firms' offices and then brought to the trading post on the floor for execution.

The Stock Exchange rejected the NYSE model as inappropriate for London, on a variety of grounds. Such an auction market, it was argued, was suitable only for trading in securities with large volumes of transactions in both directions, whereas many of the securities listed in London were not traded intensively enough. The specialist's price smoothing role and concepts such as limit orders, open outcry dealing, and trading halts (which could be called by specialists in order to assist in the smoothing of prices) were alien to London. It was difficult to see who in London might assume the role of specialist. A floor based market would not enable London easily to exploit its time zone advantages by allowing extended dealing hours. Moreover the efficiency of the NYSE auction system was in any case under pressure since block trading handled upstairs now accounted for over 40% of all business.

Since that time the shortcomings of the NYSE have been shown up more strongly in the crash of October 1987, when it became clear that the New York specialists were undercapitalised in much the same way as the London jobbers before Big Bang. More generally, however, it is worth emphasising that the New York and London traditions are very different, in that the NYSE system puts a premium on price stability, even at the expense of trading halts, whereas London has always opted for continuity of trading over price stability.

The second model considered by the Stock Exchange, that of NASDAQ,[14] is a system of competing market makers operating through a computerised network set up in 1970 to unify the previously fragmented 'over-the-counter' (OTC) market in which the availability of information about alternative quotations for a given security had been very imperfect. Since its inception the NASDAQ market has grown rapidly and established itself as the second largest exchange in the USA after the NYSE in terms of market capitalisation and turnover. Essentially, the quotations of geographically dispersed market makers are assembled and disseminated through electronic screens, enabling brokers to find the best prices; trades are then conducted by telephone. NASDAQ members operate in dual capacity, and may choose to become market makers in particular securities, in which case they are able to show their quotations (bid and offer prices) on the NASDAQ screens. More recently an automatic small order execution service has been introduced for deals of up to 1000 shares. The electronic technology involved facilitates inspection, investor protection and regulation.

The Stock Exchange judged the NASDAQ system to represent a good model for the new London market. It was a 'quote-driven' system with private negotiations of bargains, in line with London's own traditions. It could accommodate more members, including those from the UK regions and from outside the UK, and would enable the Exchange to operate for longer hours if it wished. It would allow members to choose to operate in single or dual capacity. And, unlike the NYSE system, it would allow bargains between members to be settled through the existing TALISMAN electronic system (set up in 1979).

As from October 1986, therefore, all members of the Stock Exchange would become 'broker/dealers' and could choose whether to operate in single or dual capacity, and whether or not to become market makers in particular securities. Market makers would compete with each other in making a market (offering the best prices) rather than just in matching orders. Members who chose to become market makers would be committed to dealing, that is they would be obliged to buy or sell at the prices they were quoting, but in return they would receive certain privileges: the ability to post their quotes on the screens, access to stock borrowing facilities, trading accounts in the TALISMAN electronic system for jobbers and market makers, and exemption from the stamp duty levied on security transactions. The market makers' quotations would be displayed on SEAQ (Stock Exchange Automated Quotations system), which would have three levels: Level 1, the Investor Service, would show the best quotes currently available for each alpha and beta security, plus some other information for alpha stocks; Level 2, the Dealing Service, would show all the quotes for each security posted by each market maker; and Level 3, the market makers' input facility, would enable the market makers to enter their quotes on to the screens.

Stocks were divided into four categories – alpha, beta, gamma and delta – on the basis of market capitalisation, turnover, number of market makers, and number of shareholders. For alpha stocks market makers had to quote prices that were firm up to a specified number of shares (e.g. 100,000), and to report the basic information on all transactions for publication by the Exchange directly in the trade reports on the screens: these would show the time of the last deal, the prices of the last four deals and the total amount of shares traded so far during the day. For beta stocks market makers had to quote firm prices, but trades were to be reported only the next day in the Stock Exchange Daily Official List. For gamma stocks only indicative prices were to be quoted, and for delta stocks only an interest had to be expressed; in both cases trades were reported next day in the Daily Official List. All price and trade information is stored on computer, so that the Stock Exchange Surveillance Division can reconstruct the position of the market at any particular time.

This trading structure, explicitly modelled on NASDAQ, differs from it in four main respects. First, there are greater penalties in London for market makers who cease to make markets at any time. Second, SEAQ market makers compete on the number of shares for which their quotes are firm as well as on the price, whereas NASDAQ market makers quote for a standard 100 shares only. Third, market making is somewhat more concentrated in London, both overall (in terms of the number of market makers and the share in overall activity of the few largest) and in terms of the average number of market makers in individual securities. Finally, SEAQ market makers, unlike their NASDAQ counterparts, only rarely operate by matching trades instead of taking them directly onto their own inventories.[15]

2.3.2 The opening up of the Stock Exchange

Traditionally stock exchange firms had to be partnerships with unlimited liability, but from 1970 they could become limited companies with outside shareholders provided that no single shareholder had a stake of more than 10% and provided the individual members retained unlimited liability. However, the pressure on firms' capital resources and the growing internationalisation of financial activity (which required UK firms to have links with firms from other countries that were differently organised) combined to induce the Exchange to allow an increase in the maximum stake for an outsider from 10% to 29.9% (that is, just below the limit at which, under the Takeover Panel rules, a purchaser would normally be obliged to bid for the whole of a firm) in 1982. In July 1984, when the Big Bang changes were clearly in sight and outside financial institutions were buying up existing member firms at a rapid rate, the Stock Exchange declared a moratorium on the creation of

10% ~ 29.9% ~ 100%

new member firms, until March 1986. Finally, on the basis of a vote in June 1985 whose result had been widely anticipated, 100% ownership of member firms by a single non-member together with limited liability corporate membership of the Exchange were to be permitted as from March 1986.

There had been one or two large outside stakes in stock exchange firms purchased before the Accord, notably the 1982 purchase by Security Pacific (a US firm) of a share in broker Hoare Govett. However, the Accord unleashed a frenzied wave of purchases and takeovers, mostly during the first half of 1984, in which nearly all the London brokers (except Cazenove) and nearly all the London jobbers (except Smith New Court, which floated itself directly on the exchange instead), and then many of the provincial firms, were bought up. After that attention turned to the 'marzipan layer', that is the senior personnel in broking and jobbing firms who were not partners and could be lured away by high salaries and 'golden hellos' (themselves largely a response to earlier 'golden handcuffs' offered by purchasers) into other firms. Reid (1988, pp. 44, 66–8) estimated that over £1.5bn was spent in buying up the existing firms, money which went into the pockets of former partners and was therefore 'withdrawn', and another £1.5bn was then invested in the new securities firms that were created. These figures have to be set against an estimate of £150–200m for the total capital of UK stock exchange firms at the start of 1983.[16]

2.4   Primary market arrangements

2.4.1   Primary issues

While the bulk of activity on the equity market relates to the purchase and sale of existing securities, the market also provides for the issue of new securities; indeed the *raison d'être* of the secondary market is its role as support for the primary market.

Primary issues are of two broad kinds: initial public offerings involved in the flotation of new companies on the Stock Exchange, and those providing additional funds for already listed companies. Within the former category, one of the main mechanisms is the offer for sale (at fixed prices), in which an issuing house (merchant bank or securities house) offers shares to the public on behalf of a company. Typically the issuing house underwrites the issue as well as handling all the administrative arrangements, and then passes most of the risk on to sub-underwriters, normally major institutional investors. The second main mechanism is the placing, in which the issuing house uses its contacts to place the shares with investors. In October 1986 the upper limit on a placing which had been £3 million was raised to £15 million on the Official List and £5 million on the Unlisted Securities Market (USM). A third, but less popular mechanism is the tender in which the shares are auctioned. A fourth mechanism which has been of great importance in recent years is the privatisation, in which shares are partly offered for sale and partly placed.

Table 2.2 shows the number of IPOs on the main market in each category over the years 1985–89, the sums raised and the costs involved. The latter include both the direct costs and the discounts, that is the extent to which shares are sold at prices below the market prices that are established shortly after. Such discounts can best be regarded as reflecting the need for an incentive to persuade investors to purchase securities whose trading price is unknown at the time of purchase. There appear to

34

be economies of scale in terms of direct costs, but not discounts. Within a given size category (but not overall because placings predominate in the lower sizes and offers for sale in the largest size), placings appear to involve lower direct costs but much larger discounts. Privatisations (which have been for much larger amounts of money) have incurred significantly larger discounts. Later work has found that discounts on the USM were around 1% larger than those on the main market.[17]

Table 2.2 Initial public offerings, Official List, 1985–89

	Offers for sale	Tenders[1]	Placings	Privatisations[2]
Number	94	11	120	15
Sums raised (£m)	5855	361	725	16661
Costs (%) by amounts raised:				
Up to £5m raised:				
Direct costs	13.8		11.4	
Discount	8.7		14.1	
£5–10m raised:				
Direct costs	10.1		7.7	
Discounts	7.8		14.9	
More than £10m raised:				
Direct costs	6.9		5.9	
Discounts	8.8		13.4	19.6
Total by Issue Method				
Direct costs	8.8		9.3	
Discounts	8.5		14.3	19.6

Notes: [1]Figures for costs included with offers for sale because size of sample small.
[2]No figures for direct costs given as these were mostly not borne by company and therefore not comparable.
Source: Bank of England (1990).

Historically the most important mechanism by which already listed companies obtained additional equity funds was the rights issue, in which a company offers additional shares to its existing shareholders, usually at a discount; those who do not wish to take up the offer can sell their 'rights' instead. Shareholders' right to first choice on such additional issues is referred to as the 'pre-emption right'. However, in recent years companies have sought to make use of other mechanisms for raising funds, notably *placings*, in which additional shares are placed as in an IPO; *vendor placings* in which one company buys out another with a fresh issue of its own shares for which it arranges a placing; and *bought deals* in which a new issue of shares is sold en bloc to a securities house, which then sells the shares on to its own clients. Institutional investors wanted to retain their privileges in the form of pre-emption rights, while companies felt they could raise funds more cheaply and broaden their shareholder base, notably by issuing abroad. A compromise reached in 1987 requires companies to obtain shareholders' agreement to the 'disapplication' of pre-emption rights at regular intervals and to limit their non-rights issues to 5% of the issued capital per year.[18]

Table 2.3 gives figures for the last decade for selected items: money raised by new companies, rights issues by existing companies and overall equity funds raised. While there is substantial year-to-year fluctuation, it is clear that overall money raised and rights issues were relatively high in the mid-1980s, but fell off towards the end of the decade. This was mainly in response to the 1987 crash which lowered equity prices and therefore increased the cost in terms of future dividend payments of raising funds in this way, and rights issues in particular have revived more recently.

Table 2.3 Money raised by companies (£m)

	Money raised by new companies			Rights issues (UK and Irish)	Total funds raised by equity sales (Listed, UK and Irish)
	UK and Irish		Overseas		
	Listed	USM + TM			
1980	241	13	–	1061	1098
1981	631	75	94	1981	2493
1982	1169	74	89	914	1776
1983	1592	165	935	2088	2569
1984	5950	182	1106	1741	6899
1985	1462	202	182	4182	4775
1986	8874	290	10180	5728	14019
1987	5002	214	131	8861	18648
1988	3790	323	842	6039	9935
1989	7578	188	1271	4961	12626
1990	7095	48	707	5224	12035

Source: Stock Exchange Quarterly with Quality of Markets Review, April–June 1991.

2.4.2 The second and third markets

Apart from the main market, called the Official List, the London Stock Exchange also contains a second stock market, the Unlisted Securities Market (USM), and – until it was closed at the end of 1990 – the Third Market (TM).

The USM was set up in 1980 primarily to make access to the capital market easier for companies not eligible for, or not desiring, a full listing. Thus the requirements for admission to the market are less strict, and therefore less expensive, than those for the Official List, as can be seen in Table 2.4. By mid-1991

844 companies had been admitted to the USM, and £5201m had been raised. Of the 844 companies, 178 had graduated to the Official List, 176 had been taken over by other companies, and 98 had left the market because of reorganisation or the cancellation of their quotation, leaving 392 firms continuing to trade. The trading structure for USM stocks is essentially the same as for the less liquid stocks on the Official List: typically a rather small number of market makers, with large bid-ask spreads and low turnover (see section 2.5.3 below).

In its early years the USM was widely regarded as successful.[19] Since the 1987 crash, however, it has stagnated somewhat, with both turnover and prices falling relative to those on the Official List. In February 1990 the minimum trading record required for entry to both the USM and the Official List was changed in response to the EC Directive on the Mutual Recognition of Listing Particulars; these changes brought the London markets more into line with practice in other European exchanges, and reduced the difference between the two sets of entry criteria.

The Third Market was set up in June 1987 to provide a home for companies which did not meet the conditions for admission to the USM, and whose shares were at that time trading in the unregulated over-the-counter market, which had grown rapidly in the 1980s. Conditions for admission were less strict, but companies had to be 'sponsored' by a broker or bank, and potential sponsors turned out to be very cautious. By its peak at the end of the first quarter of 1990, 92 companies had been admitted and £195m had been raised. However, this was well below expectations and, in the light of the implications of the EC Directive referred to above, it was decided to close the market at the end of 1990. By that time, of the original 92 companies 2 had been transferred to the Official List, 4 had been taken over, 48 had been reorganised or had their quotations cancelled, and 38 had been transferred to the USM.

2.5 Adjustments to the system

2.5.1 The introduction of inter-dealer brokers

At the time of Big Bang the gilt-edged market was designed to include a category of market participant called inter-dealer brokers (IDBs), and these were also introduced into the equity market shortly after Big Bang. The equity market had always involved transactions between market makers, or between market makers and broker dealers acting as principals; but the introduction of IDBs made such transactions easier and confidential. The IDBs operate electronic screens, made available only to market makers, on which offers or bids by market makers can be posted anonymously. Although they merely match orders rather than buying and selling out of their own inventories the IDBs act as principals to the market makers on each side of a transaction in order to preserve confidentiality. Thus individual market makers can unwind long or short positions in particular stocks by transactions with other market makers, without revealing their own identities. The existence of the IDBs therefore increases the immediate resources of the individual market maker and the liquidity of the market as a whole. Intra-market turnover typically amounts to 50–60% of customer business in terms of value, with average bargains being roughly five times the size of customer bargains.

Table 2.4 The ISE's three markets

	Official list	USM	Third Market
Minimum market capitalisation	£700,000 for equities (but normally sponsors look for companies over £10 million for market liquidity and cost reasons)	No minimum	No minimum
Minimum trading record	3 years (previously 5)	2 years (previously 3)	Usually 1 year
Annual turnover of company	No minimum but sponsors normally look for over £10 million	No minimum	No minimum
Annual profit before taxation	No minimum but sponsors normally look for over £1 million	No minimum but normally over £500,000	No minimum
Minimum percentage of shares which must be held publicly	25%	10%	No minimum
Latest audited results in prospectus	Within six months	Within nine months	Usually within nine months unless a greenfield company
Threshold percentage for circulars to shareholders on acquisitions and disposals after flotation	15% of the assets or profit before taxation or equity being issued	25% of the assets or profit before taxation or equity being issued	No threshold, but recommended at 25%

Publicity requirements:

	Official list	USM	Third Market
Introductions and Placings	One formal notice in a national daily newspaper and circulation of listing particulars in the Extel Statistical Services.	One formal notice in a daily newspaper and circulation of prospectus in the Extel Statistical Services.	One formal notice in a daily newspaper and circulation of prospectus in the Extel Statistical Services.
Offers for Sale	Listing particulars to be published in two national daily newspapers and circulated in the Extel Statistical Services	One formal notice in a daily newspaper	One formal notice in a daily newspaper

Market capitalisation end-1989 (£m)	514,854	9139	582
Number of companies end-1989	2015	448	69
Turnover 1989 (£m)			
customer business	241,312	4482	434
intra–market business	148,699	511	39
Velocity(%)	46.9	49.0	74.6

Sources: Quality of Markets Review, Winter 1988–89, p. 20, July–Sept. 1990, p. 17, and various issues for statistics.

Information & spreads

2.5.2 Excess capacity and the rule changes of February 1989

The Big Bang changes were accompanied by a massive entry of new firms and new capital into the London equity market, which has led to a continuing excess capacity. While there had been 13 jobbers under the old system, at the moment of Big Bang there were 33 and in May 1991 – despite some 20 withdrawals – there were still 25 market makers in equities.

The reasons for such 'excess entry' into financial markets are not well understood, but they seem to be related on the one hand to the contestability of such markets, and on the other to factors such as 'the generally "one-off" or "non-repeatable" nature of entry, the difficulty of forecasting demand in financial markets and the desire to maintain "relationships" even though short to medium-term losses may be made in the relevant sector', combined with the weakness of the takeover sanction in the finance industry (Davis, 1988, p.36). Whatever the reasons, the results have been predictable: the financial performance of London Stock Exchange member firms (excluding gilt-edged market makers) has been consistently disappointing. Profits of only £24m for calendar year 1987 (dominated by fourth quarter losses of £375m) were followed by losses for 1988 of £195m, and the improvement in 1989 when profits amounted to £504m was followed by losses of £353m in 1990; in the first half of 1991 there were profits of £179m. Within these totals, dealing profits are much more volatile than either other income elements such as commission revenues and corporate fees or expenditure items such as establishment and staff costs.[20]

One early reaction to these problems was the price war between market makers which broke out in the summer of 1988 when some of the leading market makers first reduced sharply their quoted spreads, and then reduced the size in which they were quoting. They claimed that this would enable them to avoid being 'hit' by other market makers for large deals while at the same time allowing them to continue to offer large deals by negotiation to institutional investors. The reduction in the transparency of the market which these moves implied led to the setting up of a Special Committee on Market Development (the Elwes Committee), whose interim report of January 1989 led to the implementation of two controversial rule changes in February of that year.

1. The first of these was the removal of market makers' obligation to deal with one another at their quoted prices. The argument for it was that this would prevent so called 'fair-weather' market makers from unwinding their positions on the big market makers. However, the fact that the former were for the most part US and other overseas securities houses, while the latter were the large UK firms (whose placing power was much greater so that they had less need to unwind their positions in this way), led inevitably to accusations that the rule change favoured the old boys of the London Stock Exchange club. More analytically, the issue depends on the importance attached to the quick dissemination of information in the market. It could be argued that the rule change would force market makers to unload their positions by changing their quotes which would disseminate more efficiently the news that a major one-way deal had been done. By contrast, without the rule market makers would tend to protect themselves by widening their spreads or reducing their quote sizes, both of which impair the quality of the market (Kyle and Roell, 1989).

2. The second rule change was that details of alpha transactions for more than £100,000 would now be published only the next day, although cumulative volumes would still be published. Here it was argued that this would prevent other traders, notably other market makers, from being able to work out the size of a market maker's book and profiting from this information; market makers would therefore be able to offer better quotes. However, it can also be argued that, when last trade publication is absent, market makers will widen their spreads to protect themselves against the possibility of losing out to a market maker who has just made a large one way deal and then repositioned his quotes. There are therefore two effects in opposite directions on the width of spreads, and which dominates is not obvious (Kyle and Roell, 1989).

A more extensive discussion of this issue by Franks and Schaefer (1990, 1991)[21] has also cast doubt on the case for universal immediate trade publication. They consider a variety of evidence to the effect that information based trades may be less frequent and important than sometimes thought (so that investors may suffer less from ignorance of the terms of recent trades). They argue that simple comparisons between NASDAQ and SEAQ are inappropriate because large trades tend to be matched on NASDAQ but inventoried on SEAQ. In addition, NASDAQ market makers have a certain flexibility with respect to the prices they report for transactions, and because of the lower level of concentration their books are less likely to become visible to other market professionals. Moreover, the weight that investors themselves put on immediate publication is not clear, since in a number of securities traded on both markets SEAQ International (where no trade publication at all occurs) does larger volumes of business than NASDAQ.

Franks and Schaefer thus argue that immediate publication would reduce the capacity to handle large transactions on SEAQ; that it could be circumvented easily enough in ways that would have adverse side effects; and that any reduction in the profitability of market making induced by immediate publication could have undesirable consequences for the degree of concentration in market making on SEAQ. More generally, they argue that there is a trade off between transparency, immediacy and liquidity, that no market has complete transparency and that SEAQ transparency is not obviously less than that on NASDAQ; and they suggest that transparency on SEAQ might be better improved by refining the NMS system introduced in January 1991 so as to allow a significantly higher proportion of trades to be published immediately, and by action to bring the screen quotes closer to the prices at which trades are dealt (given the evidence[22] that nearly half of trades by value take place inside the touch).

2.5.3 The problem of less liquid stocks

A rather different problem with the new trading structure, which remained submerged in the period immediately after Big Bang but became more visible following the 1987 crash and the 1989 mini-crash, concerned those stocks – the majority of those listed in London – in which the turnover was low. These stocks were typically those of small companies where ownership was concentrated (particularly in the hands of directors and a small number of specialised institutional investors); in some stocks there was less than one transaction on average per day.

As time went on, these stocks tended to have few market makers dealing in them, wide spreads and in some cases limited immediacy as well as limited liquidity. For example, in late 1990, some 200 stocks had only one market maker. Similarly, while average bid-ask spreads (in percentage terms) in alpha stocks fluctuated between October 1987 and December 1990 around 2, with a low of 1.22 pre-crash and a high of 3.28 at end-October 1987, average spreads for beta stocks widened from 2.38 pre-crash to around 7 in late 1990, and those on gamma stocks widened from 3.77 to 12 at the end of 1990.

The nature of the problem was clear – the competing market maker system is not efficient for stocks with low turnover. Indeed, according to a later report by the Exchange a significant proportion of trades in these stocks, especially larger trades, were now either being dealt at prices outside the touch or being 'brokered', that is actively matched by a broker (or market maker) seeking a counterparty instead of being inventoried by the market maker.[23] However, the appropriate solution was not obvious.

2.5.4 The rule changes of January 1991

In July 1990 the Stock Exchange Council approved a number of related rule changes, based on the final report of the Elwes Committee. The centrepiece of these was the abandonment of the alpha/beta/gamma/delta classification in favour of a classification based on the Normal Market Size (NMS) of each stock.[24]

The NMS of a stock can be thought of as 2.5% of its average daily turnover over the preceding 12 months. More precisely, it is derived by calculating the stock's 'NMS Shares' as

$$\frac{\text{value of customer turnover in previous 12 months}}{\text{closing mid-price on last day of quarter}} \times 10{,}000$$

and then finding the appropriate NMS 'band' according to Table 2.5 (which also gives the number of SEAQ securities in each band).[25]

This identification of an NMS band for each security made possible a more flexible trade publication regime. For all shares with an NMS equal to or greater than 2000 (about 900 stocks including more or less all the old alphas, two thirds of the old betas and a sixth of the old gammas), price and volume, details of transactions of up to three times the NMS would be published immediately and those of transactions greater than three times NMS with a 90 minute delay. Details of transactions in shares with an NMS of 1000 or less would be published in the

Table 2.5 NMS bands

NMS band	Share equivalent	Number of SEAQ securities
500	0–667	919
1000	668–1333	367
2000	1334–2400	217
3000	2401–3750	151
5000	3751–6667	168
10,000	6668–12,000	144
15,000	12,001–18,000	63
25,000	18,001–33,000	83
50,000	33,001–60,000	53
75,000	60,001–93,000	18
100,000	93,001–160,000	8
200,000	>160,000	0
	Total	2191

Source: Stock Exchange Quarterly with Quality of Markets Review, July–Sept. 1991, p. 86.

Daily Official List the next day. The Stock Exchange calculated that these changes implied an improvement in transparency for some 610 stocks (accounting for some 20% of turnover), a deterioration for two stocks (0.4% of turnover) and a mixed effect (improved publication for prices but a new 90 minute delay for volume) for 169 stocks (most of the former alphas, which accounted for 74% of turnover).[26]

The NMS was also used in new rules regarding the minimum quote size for market makers (1 × NMS except for special exemptions); regarding the London Stock Exchange's automatic execution service (see section 2.5.7 below); and regarding market makers' obligation to trade with each other (which was reinstated for trades up to the NMS size).

At the same time, the Stock Exchange introduced a requirement for all agency crosses (matched trades) arranged at or outside the touch to be exposed to the most competitive market maker, in order to consolidate the order flow and make all trades contribute to price formation. And it reached an agreement with the larger market makers designed to ensure that there would be at least two market makers for every stock listed.

While it is obviously too soon to assess the effect of these rule changes, the Stock Exchange itself claimed in its review of some six months later that quote quality had improved, with touches narrowing (mainly, however, due to the increase in volumes) and a higher proportion of trades being dealt at, rather than inside, the touch, but there had been a decline in the relative number of large trades in stocks where visibility had increased.[27]

2.5.5 Settlement

The existing system of settlement and registration of securities in London is paper based rather than computerised, and hence time consuming and expensive. Moreover, since the early nineteenth century settlement has been organised around a fixed period called the Account, usually of two weeks in length, with each stage in the settlement process occurring on a particular day after the end of the Account in which the transaction took place.[28] Since at least 1981 there has been talk of introducing a new computerised settlement system in London, but the idea was initially set aside under the pressure of the Big Bang reforms and was later held up by disagreements between the various parties concerned (which include the companies whose shares would be registered, the institutional investors, brokers and market makers, and the existing company registrars, most of them owned by banks).

More recently the London Stock Exchange has come under intense pressure, both from the improvements made elsewhere (notably in Germany and France) and from bodies of experts such as the Group of Thirty and authorities such as the Bank of England. After repeated delays it now looks as though a new system – the latest version of TAURUS (Transfer and Automated Registration of Uncertificated Stocks) – will come on stream sometime in 1993, with a shift to three day rolling settlement sometime thereafter, and the demise of the Account system. The Exchange projected some very large savings in costs as the result of the change. However, the delays have been expensive, not least in the continuation of the 0.5% stamp duty, which the government had announced in the 1990 Budget would be phased out when TAURUS was finally introduced.

2.5.6 Stock lending[29]

One of the privileges which market makers enjoy is their access to stock borrowing facilities, arrangements by which market makers can borrow stock (or cash) of which they are short. Such facilities date from the second half of the nineteenth century in the gilt-edged market, and from the 1960s in the case of the equity market. In the former, the amount of stock lending outstanding has averaged between £5 and £6 billion in recent years, while in the equity market it fluctuates between £1 and £2 billion.

Stock lending fulfils two main functions. First, it ensures that delays in settlement of bargains at one stage are not passed on into delays at subsequent stages: market makers borrow to cover themselves against (anticipated) delays in receipts of stock so that they can themselves deliver on time. Second, stock lending improves the resources available to market makers, making it easier for them to sell short and therefore enabling them to make better quotes in larger sizes: it thus improves the liquidity of the market as a whole. In addition, stock lending enables the institutional investors who provide the loans to obtain a lending fee on top of the standard return from holding securities.

Stock lending is organised through stock exchange money brokers (of whom there are ten, most of them operating in the gilts market as well as the equity market). Under current arrangements market makers *must* use money brokers as the source of stock loans, and *only* market makers may so use them. The money brokers act as principal to both the market makers and the institutional lenders, in order to preserve confidentiality. All loans are secured against collateral (in cash or other securities), and the fee involved is calculated as so many days' interest on the value of the stock involved, with the interest typically split 3:1 between institutional lender and money broker. Any dividends continue to accrue to the lender and are treated as so doing for tax purposes.

Complexities in the tax arrangements for stock lending have provided one focus for the work of the recently established Stock Borrowing and Lending Committee, a consultative body of practitioners including the regulatory and tax authorities which is chaired by a Bank of England official. The Committee has also been concerned to set up appropriate arrangements for the lending of overseas securities, both by UK lenders (where the tax issues are simpler) and by overseas lenders, as part of London's efforts to preserve its competitive advantages vis-à-vis other financial centres (see Bank of England, 1991b).

The introduction of the TAURUS electronic settlement system will facilitate stock lending, while the eventual move to three day rolling settlement is expected to increase the amounts but reduce the periods for which market makers need to borrow. In the meantime there is some continuing debate about access to these facilities and about the role of money brokers. Both the Stock Exchange and the Bank of England have felt obliged to argue publicly that market makers' restricted access to money brokers is a necessary *quid pro quo* for market makers' commitment to make continuous markets in all conditions. In the overseas equity market, on the other hand, market makers are not required to borrow through money brokers, but the latter retain an important role in bringing interested counterparties together.

2.5.7 Retail investors

Small transactions by private clients account for a large proportion of the business of stock exchange firms. More precisely (from Table 2.10 in section 2.6.1 below), bargains of up to £2000 made up 45% of the total number of bargains in 1991 (down from a post-Big Bang peak in 1987 of over 50%), while bargains between £2000 and £10,000 made up another 32% (as in 1987). By value, of course, these transactions were much less significant, with bargains up to £10,000 accounting for only 5% of the total value of transactions in 1991 (down from a peak of nearly 8% in 1987). However, these transactions are relatively expensive to handle, due to the diseconomies of small scale operations, and commission rates are much higher than those for large transactions. Thus transactions of up to £10,000 contributed some 30% of total commission revenue in 1991 (against a peak of 39% in 1987). The London Stock Exchange therefore faces a problem, that its members are heavily dependent on small investors whose holdings of shares and propensity to deal in them seem to be on a long term downward trend despite privatisation.

The Exchange tried to solve this by introducing its Stock Exchange Automatic Execution Facility (SAEF) after considerable delays in 1989. This initially allowed brokers to make deals for their clients in up to 1000 alpha or beta shares via computer terminals rather than phones. The orders are automatically routed to the market maker showing the best quotes, confirmed, reported and entered into the settlement mechanism. Since the rule changes of January 1991, bargains in up to 10% of each stock's NMS can be handled in this way, which means that far more shares can be traded via SAEF and some can be traded via SAEF in much larger amounts than before. Brokers can also 'preference' orders to particular market makers even though the latter may not be making the best price, if the latter display a '+' sign on the screen to indicate that they will provide execution of small orders at whatever the best price is at the time.

Small investors have also been able to use the automatic execution facilities available from Kleinwort Benson (the Best system set up in 1987) and BZW (Trade, set up in 1988) and others. These firms (which like other market makers are also obliged to provide small scale execution services through SAEF) operate such services as part of their normal market making function and/or in direct and active competition with SAEF. In some respects they are clearly superior to SAEF. For example, it may be possible to trade a wider range of stocks and in larger sizes, and the services are normally provided free (unlike SAEF, which levies a small charge per transaction). Market estimates suggest that around 10% of the number of bargains (but a much smaller percentage of the value) goes through these systems, and that most of the volume goes through Trade and BEST, while SAEF has been unsuccessful in attracting business.

The functioning of these systems reduces the chance of congested telephone lines, but it has done little to reduce the commission rates charged to small investors by brokers (Table 2.10). Some alleviation of the charges may be brought about by the eventual introduction of the TAURUS electronic settlement system. But for the moment at least the London Stock Exchange is caught between the real diseconomies of small scale operations and the government's repeatedly proclaimed desire to see wider share ownership.

2.6 The efficiency of the new dealing system

2.6.1 Market quality since Big Bang

London Stock Exchange publications regularly refer to the 'quality of the market' which the Exchange provides, which is then assessed with respect to a number of criteria: liquidity, depth, visibility and transactions costs.[30]

Table 2.6 Turnover on the London Stock Exchange (£bn)

	Domestic equity*	Overseas equity	British government securities*	Fixed interest securities
1980	30.8	..	151.7	..
1981	32.4	..	146.0	..
1982	37.4	..	203.4	..
1983	56.1	..	210.8	..
1984	73.1	..	268.7	..
1985	105.6	..	261.5	..
1986	181.2	..	424.4	..
1987	283.1	109.6	574.5	..
1988	191.7	79.6	547.3	49.3
1989	264.2	169.1	531.5	62.7
1990	205.2	294.0	450.9	59.7
1991	234.1	283.4	489.3	41.0

Notes: * customer business only.
.. not available.

Source: Quality of Markets Quarterly, various issues.

Table 2.7 Velocity of domestic equity

		Velocity
1986	Q1	64.0
	Q2	55.6
	Q3	50.9
	Q4	56.5
1987	Q1	77.3
	Q2	66.8
	Q3	63.5
	Q4	59.3
1988	Q1	52.4
	Q2	49.7
	Q3	43.2
	Q4	49.2
1989	Q1	60.1
	Q2	53.3
	Q3	53.5
	Q4	43.4
1990	Q1	41.3
	Q2	41.8
	Q3	44.7
	Q4	46.3
1991	Q1	49.4
	Q2	43.0
	Q3	44.6
	Q4	40.9

Note: velocity equals (annualised) turnover as percentage of the market value at the beginning and end of the period.
Source: calculated from *Quality of Markets Quarterly*, various issues.

The liquidity of a market in this context can be measured in terms of *turnover* – the value of transactions – and *velocity* – the value as a proportion of the market value of the underlying securities. Table 2.6 shows the turnover in domestic equity, overseas equity (from 1987 when figures are first available) and, for comparison, in gilt-edged securities and (other, private and public sector) fixed interest securities. Table 2.7 shows the velocity for domestic equity (the comparable measure for overseas equity would not be helpful because a high proportion of the securities may be traded elsewhere). It is clear that in domestic equity turnover increased significantly in the mid-1980s, before and particularly after Big Bang, with velocity reaching a high in the first quarter of 1987. However, turnover fell back after the October 1987 crash, with velocity returning to the levels of 1984–85 (not shown in the table). Both picked up again in 1989 but dipped again after the mini-crash of

Good comparisons

October 1989. These figures suggest that the Big Bang changes provided a strong temporary boost to activity in the Exchange, but how much of this boost remains as a longer term phenomenon is unclear. In overseas equity, on the other hand, although the figures overstate the recent rise (because in earlier years not all such transactions were recorded), it is clear that London has been able to attract a very large amount of business, which is now greater than its domestic business (see section 2.7.1 for further discussion). It should also be noted that turnover in gilt-edged securities is much higher than that in domestic equity, while turnover in fixed interest securities is much lower.

The depth of the market refers to two things: the degree of competition between market makers, and the ability of investors to deal in large quantities without a deterioration in prices. At the overall level, while before Big Bang there were 13 jobbers in London, the new trading structure started with 33 market makers in domestic equity and retains around 25 (as the result of 12 arrivals and 20

Table 2.8 Market makers per share

(a)	Average number of market makers per share			
	alphas	betas	gammas	deltas
October 1986	14.8	11.4	3.3	0.5
September 1987	13.7	6.6	3.5	1.0
September 1988	15.0	7.2	3.6	1.1
September 1989	13.7	6.1	3.2	1.1
September 1990	11.9	5.3	2.3	n/a

Source: Quality of Markets Quarterly Review, various issues.

(b)	Shares by number of market makers, September 1991	
Number of market makers	alphas	betas
16–17	19	
14–15	72	
12–13	30	1
10–11	30	1
8–9	76	1
6–7	177	26
4–5	322	238
2–3	165	938
0–1	–	8
Total shares	891	1213

Note: alphas and betas refer here to stocks with NMS of 2000 (or above) on the one hand and 1000 (or below) on the other.
Source: Stock Exchange Quarterly with Quality of Markets Review, July–Sept. 1991.

withdrawals, up to September 1991). Within these totals, while before Big Bang 5 jobbers handled some 80% of transactions, in December 1988 the largest 8 market makers handled 80% of business and in early 1990 7 market makers accounted for a little over 80% of transactions in alpha stocks.[31] In terms of individual securities, Table 2.8(a) shows the average number of market makers per share in the main categories used up to the end of 1990, while 2.8(b) shows the position in September 1991 in terms of the new categories. Given that transactions are concentrated on a relatively small number of shares,[32] these figures show that for most transactions there is a high level of competition between market makers even though it has declined slightly since Big Bang. More importantly, perhaps, the marginal cost for a market making firm of extending the range of shares in which it makes markets is low, so that market making for any individual share is highly contestable.

Table 2.9 Spreads and touches for alpha shares (%)

	Average spread	Touch at yellow strip	Touch at largest quote size
Old alpha stocks			
October 1987 (pre-crash)	1.22	0.83	0.88
End-October 1987	3.28	2.00	2.21
End-December 1987	2.18	1.52	1.59
June 1988	1.71	1.15	1.19
December 1988	1.44	0.85	1.02
June 1989	1.37	0.87	0.98
December 1989	1.92	1.19	1.28
June 1990	1.89	1.20	1.29
December 1990	2.51	1.61	1.67
June 1991	2.31	1.49	1.53
September 1991	2.22	1.35	1.39
FT–SE 100 stocks:			
June 1991	1.68	1.08	1.12
September 1991	1.70	0.93	1.00

Source: Stock Exchange Quarterly with Quality of Markets Review, July–Sept. 1991, p.86.

The ability to deal in large quantities without adverse price effects can be examined by considering the difference between the touch for alpha shares at yellow strip and at largest quote size, as in Table 2.9. The touch is the difference between the lowest ask-price and the highest bid-price, in percentage terms and averaged over the shares concerned. The yellow strip is the section of the SEAQ screens which is highlighted for each stock, showing the best quotes available and the size to which they refer. Typically this is well above the minimum quote size, but less than the largest quote size. Thus the difference between the two touches represents the widening of the spread which investors have to pay if they wish to deal in larger amounts. The figures concerned in Table 2.9 show that the 'size premium', as this difference is sometimes called, has usually been small as a proportion of the touch, although it has widened sharply in periods of increased uncertainty such as the 1987 stockmarket crash. At the same time, the average largest quote size per share has fluctuated over time, but (although no precise measures of the pre-Big Bang position exist) there is general agreement that it has been consistently much higher since than before Big Bang.

'Visibility' refers to the amount of information which is available to traders and the speed with which it is published. It is clear that the new trading structure involves in general a much higher degree of visibility, in so far as all market makers' quotes are assembled together on screen instead of jobbers' mid-prices being shown on the floor. Moreover, trade publication was significantly better in the October 1986 – February 1989 period and has been so again since January 1991, although it was less good in the intervening months. In addition, Big Bang was followed by a process of reclassification of securities which increased the number in the more visible (especially the alpha) categories, and the January 1991 changes have led to a much larger number of securities being in the top category for visibility.

There are three elements to transactions costs in equity markets: the commissions charged by brokers, the stamp duty payable to the government, and the difference between bid- and ask-prices. With respect to the first of these, the pre-Big Bang expectations of significant falls in commissions faced by institutional investors carrying out large transactions but smaller falls or even increases in those for small transactions, have been generally borne out. As Table 2.10(a) shows overall average commission rates fell from 0.43% in 1986 (pre-Big Bang) to 0.33% in 1987 and then stabilised at 0.26. Within the total, commissions on the smallest deals fell between 1986 and 1989 but returned most of the way to their original level in 1990, while those on the next two categories rose in each year up to 1990. However, for deals between £50,000 and £1,000,000 there were major reductions. The second part of Table 2.10 shows one aspect of this. Since 1986 a proportion of transactions have been done 'net', i.e. without commission being charged, either because large clients are dealing directly with market makers or because their brokers act towards them as principals, and this proportion is much higher for larger transactions.[33] These changes obviously reflect the economies of scale involved in broking operations, on the one hand, and the superior bargaining power of large investors, on the other.

The second element of transactions costs is the stamp duty (identified by Jackson and O'Donnell, 1985, as a major contributor to the uncompetitiveness of the pre-1986 London market). From the mid-1970s this was 2%, until it was restored in 1984 to its previous level of 1%. It was then halved again from the date of Big Bang in October 1986, and is due to be eliminated altogether when the Stock Exchange's new settlement system, TAURUS, is finally introduced.

The third element of transactions costs is the touch, that is the difference between the highest bid-price and the lowest ask-price. Figures for the touches and spreads on alpha stocks are given in Table 2.9; while they have fluctuated quite widely in response to the 1987 and 1989 crashes in particular, the overall trend since October 1987 has clearly been one of increase (and enough to outweigh the minor falls thought to have occurred around the time of Big Bang[34]). However, care needs to be

Table 2.10 Commissions on equity transactions

(a)			Average commission rate			
Bargain size	1986	1987	1988	1989	1990	1991
0–600	6.81	6.15	5.41	5.31	6.26	6.11
601–2,000	1.53	1.81	1.89	1.84	2.03	2.02
2,001–10,000	1.26	1.27	1.30	1.37	1.44	1.42
10,001–20,000	0.72	0.70	0.75	0.79	0.94	0.81
20,001–50,000	0.58	0.41	0.39	0.37	0.43	0.38
50,001–100,000	0.41	0.28	0.24	0.24	0.25	0.23
100,001–250,000	0.32	0.20	0.19	0.18	0.20	0.19
250,001–1,000,000	0.31	0.17	0.16	0.16	0.15	0.16
>1,000,000	0.14	0.12	0.16	0.11	0.11	0.15
All bargains	0.43	0.33	0.28	0.26	0.26	0.26

(b)		Size distribution 1991			
Bargain size	% of bargains	% of value with comm.	% of value without comm.	total	share of commission revenue
0–600	23.1	0.2	0.0	0.2	4.2
601–2,000	22.3	0.7	0.0	0.7	5.4
2,001–10,000	31.7	3.5	0.3	3.8	20.7
10,001–20,000	6.0	1.8	0.4	2.2	6.6
20,001–50,000	5.1	3.2	1.0	4.2	6.0
50,001–100,000	3.7	5.2	1.7	6.9	6.0
100,001–250,000	4.1	13.3	4.1	17.4	12.3
250,001–1,000,000	3.5	30.6	11.2	41.8	25.6
>1,000,000	0.5	17.3	5.5	22.8	13.2
Total	100.0	75.8	24.2	100.0	100.0

Source: Quality of Markets Quarterly, various issues; *Stock Exchange Quarterly with Quality of Markets Review*, July–Sept. 1991.

taken with the comparisons here, first because some of the widening of touches and spreads reflects the increase in the number of stocks designated as alphas (from 62 at the time of Big Bang to 168 in December 1990). The FT–SE 100 stocks, for which the June 1991 touches are not so much larger than those for alphas in October 1987 (pre-crash) probably give a more correct picture. Moreover, these touches do not take account of trades executed inside the best quotes, which have been important for institutional investors in recent years.

Overall then, it seems that transactions costs have probably gone down for larger trades but less so for smaller ones since Big Bang. But within the total it has been the cut in stamp duty that has made the biggest contribution.

Table 2.11 International Equity Market Comparisons (£bn)

	Market value of domestic equities				Turnover (equities)					
	1974	1983	1988	1990	1974	1983	1988	1990 domestic	1990 foreign	1990 total
New York	205.4	1048.0	1307.6	1389.1	41.5	526.9	749.2	..	..	748.5
Tokyo	51.3	369.9	2121.7	1482.8	17.6	160.4	1273.9	730.3	7.3	738.2
NASDAQ		158.1	196.3	165.5		129.7	194.8	243.2	15.9	259.1
London*	31.1	155.7	393.2	445.0	6.3	28.1	202.6	157.1	147.8	304.9
Federation of German Stock Exchanges* of which	19.4	57.3	139.3	194.4	2.4	25.2	102.0	286.6	6.7	293.3
Frankfurt*	..	..	126.9	176.5	..	..	58.2	172.8	4.3	177.1
Paris	..	26.3	123.7	159.3	..	7.9	37.8	64.9	2.5	67.4

Note: .. Not Available
   * Turnover figures halved for comparison purposes

Sources   1974   *Stock Exchange Fact Book,* 1975
         1983   *Stock Exchange Official Yearbook,* 1984–85
         1988   *Quality of Markets Quarterly,* Jan.–March 1989
         1990   Market value from *Stock Exchange Quarterly,* April–June 1991
              Turnover from *Bank of England Quarterly Bulletin,* May 1991

2.6.2   International comparisons

In assessing the success of the Big Bang reforms and the state of the London Stock Exchange more generally, it is also useful to look at the 'international league position' of the London market and its relative performance during the 1987 crash and the 1989 mini-crash.

Table 2.12   International velocity comparisons

| | | Turnover as % of end-year domestic market value | | | |
| | 1974 | 1983 | 1988 | 1990 | |
				domestic	total
New York	20.2	50.3	57.3	..	53.9
Tokyo	34.3	43.4	60.0	49.3	49.8
NASDAQ	..	82.0	99.2	146.9	156.6
London	20.3	18.0	51.5	35.3	68.5
			41.4 *		
Federation of German					
Exchanges	12.2	44.0	73.2	147.4	150.9
of which,					
Frankfurt	..	..	45.9	97.9	100.3
Paris	..	30.0	30.6	40.7	42.3

Notes: * domestic turnover only.
     .. not available.
Source: calculated from Table 2.7.

   One of the objectives of the reforms was clearly to improve the international competitive position of the London market. Tables 2.11 and 2.12 provide some data on the relative positions of major world stock markets, starting with the data for 1974 (before the May Day reforms of the NYSE) and 1983 which were highlighted in Jackson and O'Donnell (1985). In these years the London market was well behind the New York and Tokyo markets in terms of the market value of the stocks listed and in turnover; in 1983 NASDAQ was slightly ahead on market value and many times so on turnover. Data of this sort are subject to a number of qualifications, mainly relating to the specificities of different exchanges,[35] and should in any case be considered in relation to the size of the 'hinterland' economies of the various exchanges, so that the trends for a particular exchange are more significant than the relativities between them. Thus perhaps the most telling point is that made by Table 2.12: between 1974 and 1983 the rate of activity, in the sense of the velocity, rose significantly in both New York (where the May Day reforms intervened) and Tokyo, but declined in London.
   The 1988 figures, however, which cover a slightly quieter period after the October 1987 crash (and London's Big Bang) show a considerable improvement in London's relative position, with both market value and turnover above those for NASDAQ and a much larger increase than in the other main markets in velocity, even if only domestic turnover is considered (the amount of foreign equity turnover

for the other exchanges in 1988 was negligible). By 1990 (when Tokyo's short lived pre-eminence had subsided with the Nikkei index and property prices, falls that were followed by the unfolding of a series of financial scandals) London was clearly in third place, but this was heavily dependent on the rise in foreign equity dealing in London, which accounted for nearly half of its turnover but much lower proportions of turnover for the other major exchanges. On the Frankfurt exchange, where activity was boosted in 1990 by the expectations surrounding German reunification, turnover in domestic equities briefly exceeded that for London but turnover in foreign equities remained small. It seems, therefore, that London's relative position has improved since the early 1980s, and most of this improvement can be attributed to the Big Bang reforms (including the establishment of SEAQ International in 1986), London is at least no longer losing out, but it remains a much smaller stock market than those of New York or Tokyo.

The October 1987 crash (and its smaller successor in 1989) are interesting for what they show about the ability of trading systems to survive under unusual pressure. During the 1987 crash all major stock markets (with the partial exception of Tokyo) experienced falls in share prices of around 30%. The New York market experienced serious problems with specialists unable to fulfil their price smoothing obligations and with trading halts whose effectiveness was undermined by the ability of investors to continue trading on the indices through the futures and options markets in Chicago. The NASDAQ market all but collapsed as market makers withdrew their services. The Tokyo market underwent repeated and prolonged trading halts, with a consequent sharp reduction in activity. In London, however, there was continuous trading despite the enormous rise in volume; and there were no defaults or bankruptcies of market makers or brokers, although it later became known that some market participants had made substantial losses over the days concerned.

On the other hand, the quality of the market provided in London undoubtedly deteriorated, although mostly in the way that would be expected in such a situation: there were major increases in spreads and touches and in the size premium (see Table 2.8 above) and a halving of 'market size', that is the total of the quotation sizes of market makers for each share. In addition, 'fast markets' had to be declared by the Stock Exchange on seven occasions over the period Monday–Thursday 19–22 October, for a total of six hours. 'Fast markets' are declared when prices are changing so fast that market makers and/or the SEAQ system itself cannot keep the quotations up to date, and the declaration means that market makers' quotes are no longer firm but merely indicative. There were also widespread claims in the City that market makers were slower to answer their telephones than was justified by the rise in volume; these claims were always denied by the Exchange itself, but it introduced shortly afterwards a system enabling it to monitor telephone delays of this sort in any future episode.

The new trading system seems therefore to have held up relatively well during the crash, and the Stock Exchange itself expressed public satisfaction with its performance. It explicitly rejected the American practice of trading halts and argued that there was a need for more index arbitrage in the UK to keep the cash and derivatives (futures and options) markets more closely in line, thus taking the opposite view to that put forward by the Brady Report in the US.[36] More significantly, while all the main markets experienced increases in share price volatility, the evidence suggests that the rise in London was if anything smaller than that in New York.[37]

2.7   The international equity market in London

2.7.1   SEAQ International

The London Stock Exchange's market for the trading of international equities was set up in early 1986. SEAQ International is a screen based price display system on which market makers quote in much the same way as on the SEAQ domestic market; transactions are then arranged by telephone. The market is relatively lightly regulated, with trade details published only the next day, but most investors active in the market are professionals and average bargain sizes are large.[38]

As shown in Table 2.6 above, turnover of foreign equity in London has grown rapidly. Only about half of this turnover is actually on SEAQ I (the rest being traded in a less formal, 'over the counter' market), and some of the increase represents an improvement in reporting (due to the introduction of the SEQUAL trade reporting and confirmation system in February 1990) rather than a rise in the underlying volume. Nevertheless, it is clear from the figures in Table 2.11 above that London has established itself as much the most important market in the world for foreign equity trading, with its nearest competitor, the NYSE, probably doing only a quarter of London's turnover.[39]

As of the end of September 1991 there were 55 registered market makers on SEAQ I, including most of the 25 market makers from the domestic equity market and a range of other mainly non-UK firms. SEAQ I carried firm quotes for 409 different stocks, and indicative quotes for another 185. Of the companies quoted the largest number is from the US (187 at the end of 1990) followed by Japan and South Africa (114 and 96 respectively), and then by Canada (36) and a range of West European countries (for example France 43, Holland 35, Germany 22 and Sweden 21). In terms of absolute turnover, however, Japan (26.5% of foreign equity turnover in London in 1990), Germany (23.2%), France (11.8%) and Holland (8.3%) are the most important, while the ratio of the turnover in a country's shares in London to the turnover in the domestic market is particularly high for Holland (52.9% in the first quarter of 1991), Sweden (45.0%), Switzerland (35.5%) and France (29.5%).[40]

The reasons for London's position, and the contrasts between London and other European equity markets, have been studied in a series of path breaking papers by Pagano and Roell (1990a, 1990b, 1991).[41] Briefly, London is not particularly competitive for small retail transactions but it is highly competitive for large transactions and it is here that the demand for immediacy, which London with its well organised dealership market can satisfy better than any of the continental exchanges, is most important. This preeminence is a reflection both of London's more general specialisation in financial activities, as discussed in Chapter 1, and of the 'first mover' advantage it achieved by initiating major reforms in the mid-1980s before the continental bourses had begun to think in global terms.

2.7.2   European cooperation and competition

The stock markets of the European Community countries, grouped together in the Federation of Stock Exchanges in the EC, spent two years discussing plans for the cooperative promotion of cross-border share trading. These plans focused on the creation of Euroquote, a joint network which would start by disseminating stock prices and company news and was expected to develop into a comprehensive trading mechanism, eventually linked to cross-border settlement arrangements. However, cooperation was hindered by different perceptions and different interests and was ultimately sabotaged by rivalries centred on the leading position of London; in May 1991 the venture was abandoned.

There are, of course, some difficult issues involved in the design of an appropriate trading system to span the European stock exchanges and carry all the main European stocks. Amihud and Mendelson (1991), which is the outstanding paper in this area, have argued from analytical work and US empirical evidence that the optimal design should enable the benefits of consolidation of the order flow – greater liquidity, depth and pricing efficiency – to be obtained without losing the benefits of competition. This will occur if trading is centred on one particular market but traders have access to alternative markets or trading mechanisms if they wish, that is if the main market is clearly contestable. They therefore propose that efforts at integrating the European stock markets should aim to provide interfaces between trading mechanisms and between portfolio management, order execution and settlement systems, so that traders can choose on which market and in what way to transact an order. In addition, they propose the construction of an EC-wide clearing transaction to operate at discrete pre-specified times. The underlying idea is to facilitate competition between markets and trading mechanisms so that they remain highly contestable even though the order flow tends to concentrate on particular markets and mechanisms. Pagano (1991) has suggested, however, that in the European context there may be significant and persistent fragmentation rather than concentration of the order flow.

In the event, the failure of the Euroquote joint venture has given a further stimulus to national stock market reforms. Almost all the continental European stock exchanges have been changing their trading systems in the last few years, partly in attempts to prevent the leakage of transactions from national markets to London. Reform has typically taken the form of the introduction of continuous trading, the ending of brokers' and dealers' monopoly positions and the abolition of minimum commissions. Paris has introduced continuous computerised order matching (Cotation Assistée en Continu, CAC), for example, and is considering relaxing restrictions on block trading. The German Federation has been wrestling with Frankfurt's repeated attempts to computerise trading and the other regional exchanges' desire to preserve their own positions, while the Federal government is now taking the lead in pressing for reforms. On the whole, settlement systems have proved easier to modernise successfully than dealing systems (except in London), while turnover taxes have been eliminated in Germany and are under review elsewhere.

At the time of writing (early 1992) there was little sign of the continental exchanges winning back transactions on a substantial scale from London.[42] However, the intense competition[43] now taking place means that something akin to the Amihud-Mendelson proposals (but without the EC-wide clearing transaction) is likely to emerge by default.

2.8   Conclusions and prospects

The equity market in London has been transformed in the last decade from what was a rather inward looking club into a more open and dynamic exchange with a strong international profile. One symptom of this change was the July 1991 vote to replace the Stock Exchange Council with a smaller Board, on which listed companies and institutional investors will be represented for the first time.

The market is now relatively efficient for large (wholesale) transactions in both the top domestic stocks and many overseas equities, providing a level of immediacy that cannot be found elsewhere in Europe and compares well with the American exchanges, at a reasonable cost. However, it is much less efficient for stocks with lower levels of turnover and for small scale (retail) transactions; for very illiquid stocks the trading mechanism provides immediacy only with difficulty and at a high cost, while for very small transactions the costs are substantial by comparison with the likely returns. At the same time, the market suffers from a lack of transparency, at least for non-professional investors, and the settlement process continues to be cumbersome and expensive. Finally, there remains a significant excess of market making capacity.

By early 1992 the London Stock Exchange was known to be considering a number of proposals designed to remedy the defects in the trading mechanism. The main idea underlying the proposals was that different sorts of customers (including both companies and investors) could be served better if the market were segmented explicitly by type of investor. Thus a market for large wholesale transactions in both domestic and overseas stocks could exist alongside, connected to but separate from, a market for smaller scale transactions particularly in the smaller domestic stocks. While the former, as a market for professionals, could be more lightly regulated, for example in terms of trade publication requirements, the latter would be more closely regulated in order to protect less informed investors. Appropriate linkages between the two markets would be required to ensure that all trades contributed to price discovery and that small investors as well as large obtained the best possible prices.

The Exchange was also considering a system of authorised 'sole traders' in illiquid stocks in order to consolidate the order flow and thereby improve liquidity. These firms would both make markets and match orders in the securities for which they were responsible, committing themselves to continuous operations in return for the privilege of sole access to all business in the securities concerned. They would then be closely supervised to prevent them exploiting their monopoly positions to make excess profits. In the meantime, however, the Stock Exchange has introduced a Company Bulletin Board Service which allows traders to post electronically firm or indicative orders in illiquid securities.

On the other hand, the eventual introduction of the TAURUS electronic settlement system can be expected to bring about a significant reduction in the cost of trading equities in London, a reduction which will be magnified by the simultaneous abolition of stamp duty. The latter will of course eliminate one of the privileges of market makers, and it remains to be seen whether any compensation can or will be offered. The related move to three day rolling settlement will remove a proportion of the short term 'trade credit' that exists at present, but any consequent reduction in transactions is likely to be relatively small.

Thus while the London equity market still suffers from serious excess capacity, and therefore provides rather modest returns to its market makers, the changes of the last decade have established it clearly as one of the world's major stock exchanges, with a particularly strong position in international equity trading; future changes are certainly intended to strengthen that position.

Notes

1   I am grateful to Richard Harrington and Michael Tahir for comments on an earlier version.
2   A more detailed discussion can be found in Chapter 2 of Cohen *et al.*, 1986; however it should be noted that the pace of change, particularly in the continental European stock markets, has been such that some of their empirical material is now out of date.
3   See Morgan and Thomas (1962) and Michie (1987) on the earlier period, and Thomas (1986) on the post-war years.
4   See Michie (1987, Chapter 1).
5   The role of rivalry between the London and provincial stock exchanges in these developments has been emphasised particularly by Michie (1987, pp. 20–3, 270–1), who also argues that these rule changes weakened the efficiency of the national securities market and the international competitive position of London.
6   See Wilson Committee (1980, Appendices, pp. 500–1), and Doggett (1991).
7   The reason for the disparate trends in personal sector and institutional holdings over the 1980s is that there was a marked increase in overseas holdings of UK equities and a similar rise in UK institutions' holdings of overseas equities.
8   Plender and Wallace (1985, p. 48) quote an estimate that 95% of the overseas investments made by the top 20 pension funds were handled by foreign firms.
9   ADRs are receipts issued by American securities houses or banks against their own holdings of overseas shares; ADRs are traded in dollars and holders receive dividend payments in dollars, so that they represent a convenient way for US residents to deal in overseas securities.
10 Plender and Wallace (1985, p. 23).
11 The Wilson Committee (1980, p. 104) reported that put-throughs were 'generally believed to account for about 10 per cent of turnover, and rather more in certain specialised sectors of the market'.
12 Useful contemporary accounts of Big Bang can be found in Bank of England (1985a, 1987a), Thomas (1986) and Goodhart (1987).
13 The NYSE is discussed in some detail in the *Stock Exchange Quarterly*, Sept. 1984; a more recent account can be found in *Quality of Markets Quarterly Review*, Jan.–March 1991. A more detailed analysis can be found in, for example, Schwartz (1988).
14 See, for example, *Stock Exchange Quarterly*, Sept. 1984 and April–June 1991.
15 These differences are explored by Franks and Schaefer (1990).
16 Graphic accounts of these events, together with some discussion of the success or failure of the different strategies pursued, can be found in Plender and Wallace (1985) and Reid (1988); see also Thomas (1986, 1989).
17 Jenkinson and Espenlaub (1991). See also Bank of England (1990) for a discussion of the trends in the use of the different mechanisms and the costs involved over the period considered.
18 See Bank of England (1987b) and Thomas (1989, Chapter 8) for further details.
19 See Bank of England (1985b); Buckland and Davis (1984).
20 *Stock Exchange Quarterly with Quality of Markets Review*, Jan.–March 1991, pp. 13–18; July–Sept. 1991, pp. 25–6.
21 Franks and Schaefer (1991) is a summary of the authors' (1990) report which was commissioned by the Department of Trade and Industry.

22 Cited from Clemons and Weber (1989, p. 7), which found that 80% of bargains accounting for nearly half of turnover by value were dealt at the touch, but 18% of bargains accounting for 45% of value were dealt inside the touch (while 1.4% of bargains accounting for 6.7% of value – the largest trades – were dealt outside the touch).

23 *Stock Exchange Quarterly with Quality of Markets Review*, July–Sept. 1991, pp. 27–32.

24 See *Quality of Markets Quarterly Review*, Jan.--March 1990, pp. 15–21, which refers to a report by Elroy Dimson and Paul Marsh of the London Business School discussing alternative measures of the liquidity of a stock.

25 The 10,000 in the denominator is described as 'a national average shares per institutional trade across all stocks' (*Quality of Markets Review*, Oct.–Dec. 1990, p. 8), but it can also be thought of as the result of dividing by 250, the rough number of business days in a year, and then taking 2.5% of the quotient.

26 *Stock Exchange Quarterly with Quality of Markets Review*, April–June 1991, p. 35.

27 *Stock Exchange Quarterly with Quality of Markets Review*, April–June 1991, pp. 35–7.

28 The original reason for this system was to allow time to overcome the problems of communication and transport, but later its advantages – the facilitation of short term speculation which increases activity and liquidity – were perceived and the system was continued (Michie, 1987, p. 264).

29 This section draws on Bank of England (1991a, 1991b) and on *Quality of Markets Quarterly Review*, Jan.–March 1991, pp. 21–24.

30 Tonks and Webb (1989) provide an assessment covering much of the same ground in terms of the traditional industrial economics categories of structure, conduct and performance, whereas the Stock Exchange's own focus, and that followed here, is on the output of this exchange as one exchange competing with others.

31 The first figure is from *Quality of Markets Quarterly Review*, Winter 1988–89, p. 13, and the second is estimated from a diagram in *Quality of Markets Quarterly Review*, Jan.–March 1990, p. 18.

32 In 1990, for example, 58% of customer turnover was in the 100 shares that make up the FT–SE 100 index.

33 It fell, however, for the largest category of transactions in 1991, and this accounts for the increase in the average commission rate from 0.11% to 0.15% on such transactions.

34 *Quality of Markets Quarterly*, Autumn 1987.

35 Some of them are discussed in Bank of England (1991c).

36 See *Quality of Markets Quarterly*, Winter 1987/88, e.g. p. 8, for the London Stock Exchange's views, and Dale (1988) on the US post-crash debate.

37 See Bank of England (1988), Mullins (1989) and Thomas (1989: pp. 217–19) for further discussion of the crash.

38 Howell and Makepeace (1991) give $275,000 as the average bargain size on SEAQ I, compared to $50,000 for Frankfurt and less than $25,000 for Paris. Figures from the *Stock Exchange Quarterly with Quality of Markets Review*, July–Sept. 1991, give the average bargain sizes in 1990 as £33,400 for SEAQ and £155,635 for SEAQ I.

39 Bank of England (1991c, p. 247).

40 Data in this paragraph are taken from Bank of England (1991c, p. 248), and from *Stock Exchange Quarterly with Quality of Markets Review*, July–Sept. 1991, pp. 84–5.
41 See also Walgenbach (1990) which includes data on costs of securities transactions in different markets.
42 *Bank of England Quarterly Bulletin*, November 1991, p. 492.
43 The European markets, and London in particular, also face competition from the NASDAQ International system which was finally approved by the US Securities and Exchange Commission in October 1991.

Bibliography

Amihud, Y. and **Mendelson, H.** (1991) How (not) to integrate the European capital markets, in A. Giovannini and C. Mayer (eds.) *European Financial Integration*, Cambridge University Press.
Bank of England (1985a) Change in the Stock Exchange and regulation of the City, *Bank of England Quarterly Bulletin*, **25**, 544–50.
Bank of England (1985b) The unlisted securities market, *Bank of England Quarterly Bulletin*, **25**, 537–43.
Bank of England (1987a) Change in the Stock Exchange and regulation of the City, *Bank of England Quarterly Bulletin*, **27**, 54–65.
Bank of England (1987b) Pre-emption rights, *Bank of England Quarterly Bulletin*, **27**, 545–9.
Bank of England (1988) The equity market crash, *Bank of England Quarterly Bulletin*, **28**, 51–8.
Bank of England (1990) New equity issues in the United Kingdom, *Bank of England Quarterly Bulletin*, **30**, 243–52.
Bank of England (1991a) The gilt-edged stock lending market since Big Bang, *Bank of England Quarterly Bulletin*, **31**, 220–4.
Bank of England (1991b) Current issues in securities lending, *Bank of England Quarterly Bulletin*, **31**, 225–7.
Bank of England (1991c) Global equity turnover: market comparisons, *Bank of England Quarterly Bulletin*, **31**, 246–9.
Buckland, R. and **Davis, E.W.** (1984) The Unlisted Securities Market, *Lloyds Bank Review*, October, 32–43.
Clemons, E.K. and **Weber, B.W.** (1989) International Stock Exchange: assessment and recommendations, quoted in Franks and Schaefer (1990).
Cohen, K.J., Maier, S.F., Schwartz, R.A. and **Whitcomb, D.K.** (1986) *The Microstructure of Securities Markets*. Prentice-Hall.
Dale, R. (1988) Financial regulation after the crash, *Royal Bank of Scotland Review*, June, 3–17.
Davis, E.P. (1988) Industrial structure and dynamics of financial markets; the primary eurobond market, *Bank of England Discussion Paper*, **35**.
Doggett, T. (1991) The 1989 Share Register Survey, *Economic Trends*, January, 116–21.
Franks, J.R. and **Schaefer, S.M.** (1990) Large trade publication on the International Stock Exchange, mimeo, London Business School, November 1990.
Franks, J.R. and **Schaefer, S.M.** (1991) Equity market transparency, *Stock Exchange Quarterly with Quality of Markets Review*, April–June 1991, 7–11.
Goodhart, C.A.E. (1987) The economics of 'Big Bang', *Midland Bank Review*, Summer, 6–15.
Howell, M. and **Makepeace, M.** (1991) London's SEAQ seeks to raise its profile in global equity market, *Financial Times*, 2.5.91.
Jackson, P.D. and **O'Donnell, A.T.** (1985) The effects of stamp duty on equity transactions and prices in the UK Stock Exchange, *Bank of England Discussion Paper*, **25**.

Jenkinson, T. and **Espenlaub, S.** (1991) Costs of raising capital on the USM, *Stock Exchange Quarterly with Quality of Markets Review*, July–Sept. 1991, 7–11.

Kyle, A.S. and **Roell, A.A.** (1989) Comments on recent developments and proposals concerning dealing practices in the UK equity market, *LSE Financial Markets Group Special Paper*, **17**.

Michie, R.C. (1987) *The London and New York Stock Exchanges 1850–1914*. Allen & Unwin.

Morgan, E.V. and **Thomas, W.A.** (1962) *The Stock Exchange: Its History and Functions*. Elek Books.

Mullins, M. (1989) Meltdown Monday or Meltdown Money? Causes of the Stock Market Crash, in R. O'Brien and T. Datta (eds.), *International Economics and Financial Markets*. Oxford University Press.

Pagano, M. (1991) Discussion (of Amihud and Mendelson 1991), in A. Giovannini and C. Mayer (eds.) *European Financial Integration*, Cambridge University Press.

Pagano, M. and **Roell, A.** (1990a) Trading systems in European stock exchanges: current performance and policy options, *Economic Policy*, **10**, April, 65–115.

Pagano, M. and **Roell, A.** (1990b) Shifting gears: an economic evaluation of the reform of the Paris Bourse, *LSE Financial Markets Group Discussion Paper*, **103**.

Pagano, M. and **Roell, A.** (1991) Dually-traded Italian equities: London vs. Milan, *LSE Financial Markets Group Discussion Paper*, **116**.

Pagano, M. and **Roell, A.** (1992) Auction and dealership markets: what is the difference?, *European Economic Review*, forthcoming.

Plender, J. and **Wallace, P.** (1985) *The Square Mile*. Hutchinson.

Reid, M. (1988) *All-Change in the City*. Macmillan.

Schwartz, R.A. (1988) *Equity Markets: Structure, Trading and Performance*, Harper and Row.

Thomas, W.A. (1986) *The Big Bang*. Philip Allan.

Thomas, W.A. (1989) *The Securities Market*. Philip Allan.

Tonks, I. and **Webb, D.** (1989) The reorganisation of the London stock market: causes and consequences of 'Big Bang', *LSE Financial Markets Group Special Paper*, **20**.

Walgenbach, B. (1990) International competition between stock exchanges, *Intereconomics*, 307–12.

Wilson Committee (1980) – Committee to Review the Functioning of Financial Institutions, *Report with Appendices*, Cmnd 7937, HMSO.

3   The sterling bond market

by Richard Harrington

Sterling bonds have been traded in London for centuries; they have been issued by commercial undertakings, by foreign governments and their agencies and above all by the British government. The origins of an organised market in the debt of the government can be traced to the end of the seventeenth century and during the following hundred years the growth of the Stock Exchange itself was closely bound up with the growth of government debt.

The market in UK government bonds was a very large one by international standards up until recent times. This was due both to periods of heavy issues of stock, usually in connection with war finance, and to the fact that the UK, unlike many other countries, experienced neither political revolutions accompanied by debt repudiation nor bouts of hyper-inflation which destroyed the real value of fixed-interest securities. The Napoleonic Wars brought about a large increase in the government debt and, in the twentieth century, so did the First World War and the Second World War. By 1946, the total of marketable government stock comfortably exceeded annual national income while the total national debt (including non-marketable debt and short-term instruments) was well in excess of twice annual national income.[1]

But in more recent times, the real value of outstanding government stock has been declining. Creeping inflation during the 1950s and 1960s and periods of rapid inflation in the 1970s and 1980s reduced real values while the Conservative administration of the 1980s at first reduced the government's borrowing requirement and then, during three years, ran a fiscal surplus and repaid debt. Meanwhile a number of governments abroad were running large and sustained budget deficits, the financing of which was steadily expanding the size of other markets in government debt. In the USA, the financing of unusually high federal government deficits (averaging over $150 billion throughout the 1980s) has produced a government bond market of a size equivalent to more than £1,000 billion or more than eight times the size of the UK government bond market. And in Japan, Italy, Germany and France large regular government deficits were leading to a steadily growing volume of outstanding government securities.

In 1991, British government finances again moved into deficit and the projections are that the deficit will grow but notwithstanding this the market in UK government bonds will remain, by international standards, a medium-sized one for the foreseeable future.

But if in recent years the market in British government bonds has declined in size, the market for other sterling bonds has grown. The exchange controls which had been strictly enforced for over forty years were removed in 1979 and this enabled both sovereign and corporate borrowers from abroad to issue sterling-denominated bonds in London. And as nominal rates of interest declined from the high levels of the 1970s and early 1980s, there was also an increasing number of British companies seeking bond finance.

Sterling bonds, other than those of the UK government, may be issued in one of two distinct ways. The traditional way involves a public offer for sale with a published prospectus and listing on the London Stock Exchange; distribution tends to be mainly to investors resident in the United Kingdom. The alternative way is by means of an issue of sterling eurobonds where no prospectus is issued and where the bonds are distributed through banks and security dealers to an international investor clientele; sterling eurobonds may be listed on the London Stock Exchange but need not be. Issuing bonds in the form of eurobonds has a number of advantages (discussed below) and this method of issue has now become the dominant one.

In what follows, we look first at the market in British government securities and then consider the market for other sterling bonds.

3.1 UK government securities

3.1.1 The size of the market

Table 3.1 shows the number and value of UK government bonds (gilt-edged) outstanding at end September 1991.[2] Over 100 stocks were listed with a total nominal value of just under £125 billion and a market value slightly in excess of this. At the same date, the market value of all company securities listed on the International Stock Exchange of the United Kingdom and the Republic of Ireland[3] was almost £1,970 billion. At end December 1990, the size of the international bond market was estimated by the Bank for International Settlements to be $1,472.5 billion (£763.15 billion).[4]

Table 3.1 UK government bonds outstanding 30 September, 1991[*]

	No. of securities	Nominal value (£m)	Market value (£m)
Short term (0–7 years)	39	53,950.7	55,524.4
Medium term (7–15 years)	29	38,437.3	40,612.0
Long term (over 15 years)	13	16,346.5	16,301.9
Undated	9	3,213.4	1,148.3
Index linked	13	12,851.7	16,555.5
Total	103	124,799.6	130,142.1

*Sterling government bonds, i.e. excluding one ECU- denominated bond issued in February, 1991.
Source: Stock Exchange Quarterly, Autumn 1991, Table A.1.

The nominal value of government stock outstanding changes continually due to a number of factors of which the most important are redemptions and conversions of existing stocks, the issue of new stock, and the annual inflation-adjustment to the nominal value of index-linked stock. Over time, the dominant influence on the nominal size of the government bond market will be the public authorities' need to borrow and the means by which this need is met. In Britain, borrowing needs of all public authorities are largely centralised and expressed as a public-sector borrowing requirement (PSBR). Apart from the years 1988-90 when the PSBR was negative (i.e. a public-sector financial surplus), this borrowing requirement has been met by sales of marketable debt (principally bonds) and of non-marketable debt (principally savings certificates and deposits with the national savings bank).

Although, in the early 1980s, the government made a successful attempt to make non-marketable debt more attractive, it is sales of marketable debt which remain the dominant means of funding the PSBR. This is reflected in the fact that at end-March 1991, government bonds outstanding constituted nearly 70 per cent of the total national debt in market holdings.[5] Table 3.2 shows the amounts of net sales of UK government bonds in the years 1981–1991. The three years in which the public sector was in surplus and repaying outstanding debt may be seen as exceptional; the normal pattern is for the government to be a net seller of debt.

Table 3.2 Net official sales of UK government bonds 1981–1991

	Conventional	Index-linked	Total
1981	6,318	1,817	8,135
1982	4,195	2,262	6,457
1983	7,049	2,441	9,490
1984	7,305	1,271	8,576
1985	7,912	1,643	9,555
1986	5,465	1,411	6,876
1987	3,222	1,387	4,609
1988	−5,450	418	−5,032
1989	−18,507	180	−18,327
1990	−6,778	−556	−7,334
1991*	6,462	536	6,998

Notes:
The sums show the total cash value as opposed to nominal value of stocks bought and sold. Only sterling bonds are included which means that the proceeds of the one ECU bond issued by the UK government (in February, 1991) have not been included.
* Quarters I-III only
Source: Bank of England Quarterly Bulletin, Table 8, May 1990, November 1991.

As can be seen from Table 3.1, just over one-tenth of the nominal value of outstanding government bonds is now in the form of index-linked stocks. The value of these stocks is uprated each year in line with changes in the retail price index. For other stocks (conventional stocks), the nominal value is fixed in terms of pounds sterling and hence all such stocks decline in real value due to price inflation. During the 1980s, inflation in Britain measured by the retail price index averaged around 6 per cent per annum; a rate sufficient to halve the real value of a fixed sum of money in twelve years. Conventional stocks and index-linked stocks are discussed further in sections 3.1.2 and 3.1.3 below.

Table 3.3 provides figures for turnover in British government securities for the years 1985–1991. Prior to the reform of the market in October 1986 (see below) all transactions were on behalf of customers but subsequently there has been much trading between market makers as well as transactions with customers as the table shows.

Table 3.3 Turnover in British government securities 1985–1991

	Customer business		Intra-market business		Total		No. of
	Total value (£m)	No. of bargains	Total value (£m)	No. of bargains	Total value (£m)	No. of bargains	business days
1985	261,529	757,364			261,529	757,364	253
1986	424,415	797,092			424,415	797,092	253
1987	574,478	720,944	601,374	396,731	1,175,851	1,117,675	253
1988	547,301	611,668	581,810	299,036	1,129,111	910,704	253
1989	531,529	501,241	456,112	187,326	987,640	688,567	252
1990	450,879	501,090	522,305	152,872	973,184	653,962	253
1991	489,290	482,897	623,423	134,850	1,112,714	617,747	253

Note: Prior to late 1986, the market operated on the basis of single capacity, hence figures for 1985 and 1986 are for customer business only.
Source: Stock Exchange Quarterly, Oct.–Dec. 1991, Table C.1.

Since the reform, the number of bargains per day has averaged nearly 3,300 with the average size of bargain reaching nearly £1½m in 1990. From a longer-term perspective, it can be said that the number of transactions per day has shown no tendency to increase since the mid-1970s; there was a surge in total number of transactions during 1987 and 1988 due to a large number of deals between the newly established market makers but both transactions on behalf of customers and intra-market business has fallen back since then. On the other hand, the average value per transaction has risen steeply since the early 1980s; this reflects both the increasing size of transactions with customers and the fact that modern intra-market business is typically conducted through deals of high value (over £4m on average in 1991).

3.1.2 Conventional bonds

The majority of government bonds, those described in Table 3.2 as 'conventional', are of fixed nominal value and pay a fixed amount (the *coupon*) each year, usually in two instalments. Most have a fixed maturity date and are redeemable at par, i.e. £100 is payable for each £100 nominal value of stock. For example, Treasury 9¾ per cent stock 2002, issued in January 1992, pays annual interest at the rate of £9.75 per £100 nominal value of stock in equal instalments on 27 February and 27 August each year until the redemption date of 27 August 2002.

Government bonds will not usually be issued at par; each £100 nominal value of stock will usually be sold for less than £100. Table 3.4 gives details of government bond issues during the last three months of 1991 and shows that, of the five issues, three were made at prices below par and two at prices above par. Once issued, bonds will, of course, be subject to continual price fluctuations as a result of changing market demand and only by chance will market price be equal to par value.

This means that the effective return or *yield* will differ from the coupon. Two yields can be defined. The *running yield* is given by dividing the *coupon* by current market price and then multiplying the result by 100 in order to express it as a percentage. For example, the Treasury 9¾ per cent stock 2002 instanced above

Table 3.4 Issues of government stock 1st October, 1991 – 31st December, 1991

Stock	Amount (£m)	Date issued	Method of issue	Price at issue	Details of payment	Yield at issue[1]	Yield when fully sold[2]	Date when fully sold
9% Conversion 2011 'B'	1,500	28 November	Auction	93.5	Part paid[2]	9.75	9.75	28 Nov. '91
10% Conversion 1996	200	29 November	To Bank	100.2813	In full	9.92	9.86	5 Dec. '91
10% Treasury 2001	200	29 November	To Bank	100.5625	In full	9.89	9.86	4 Dec. '91
9½% Conversion 2005	100	29 November	To Bank	97.6875	In full	9.81	9.81	2 Dec. '91
8½% Treasury 2007 'A'	1,000	13 December	To Bank	93.25	Part paid[3]	9.33	9.28	9 Jan. '92

[1] Gross redemption yield per cent.
[2] With 33.5 payable at issue and the remainder on 18 December, 1991.
[3] With 20 payable at issue, 40 on 13 January, 1992 and the remainder on 14 February, 1992.
Source: Bank of England Quarterly Bulletin, February, 1992.

stood at a price of £103 ³⁄₃₂ (£103.09375)[6] at the close of business on Friday 28 February, 1992 when the running yield could be derived as follows:

$$\frac{£9.75 \times 100}{£103.09375} = 9.46\%$$

But holders of Treasury 9¾ per cent stock 2002, if they held the stock until redemption in August 2002, would only receive back £100 for each £100 nominal amount of stock; i.e. they would lose capital value of £3.09375 on each £100 nominal amount of stock. When this loss is allowed for and expressed in terms of an annual (negative) return over the holding period, it is possible to derive a *redemption yield* comprised of both *running yield* minus annualised capital loss. In the case of Treasury 9¾ per cent stock 2002 the redemption yield, at end-February 1992, was 9.27%.

For most purposes comparison of bonds is in terms of *gross redemption yields* as these best reflect the expected return on an investment in terms both of *coupon* payments and capital gain or loss. But the composition of the total expected return is important for tax purposes: *coupon* payments are taxed as income; capital gains are not subject to taxation, capital losses cannot be offset against other taxable income. For many of the larger investors in gilt-edged stock, their investments are tax-free (approved pension funds, life assurance companies in respect of their pension business, registered friendly societies) so this distinction is irrelevant; but for others subject to tax (banks, building societies, many personal investors) it is obviously of importance. Tax-paying investors will, other things being equal, prefer bonds which have a low coupon but which are expected to show a capital appreciation.

To cater for different demands, the Bank of England issues bonds with widely differing coupons. In general, low-coupon bonds will have a lower *gross redemption yield* because they will be attractive to tax-paying investors concerned to maximize their *net redemption* yield after payment of taxes.

During the late 1970s, the Bank of England issued three variable-rate stocks with interest payable half-yearly at an annual average ½% above the daily average rate of discount on 91-day Treasury bills over a previous six-month period. These stocks were attractive to banks and discount houses but did not meet with strong demand elsewhere and no more were issued subsequently. None are presently outstanding.

As with coupons, there are different preferences among investors regarding term to maturity. Pension funds and life assurance companies tend to prefer medium-term and long-term bonds while banks and building societies tend to prefer short-term bonds. The Bank of England is happy to respond to market demand and issues stocks across a wide range of maturities.

As can be seen from Table 3.1, there are nine government stocks outstanding which have no final maturity; they are irredeemable bonds. These are a historical survival and no new irredeemable stocks have been issued for many years. The oldest in existence – 2½% consols – dates from 1750. Having been issued in another era, all of these stocks have low *coupon* rates (from 2½% to 4%) and hence their market value in a time of high nominal interest rates tends to be low. In total they accounted for less than 1% of the market value of government bonds outstanding at end-September, 1991.

3.1.3 Index-linked bonds

Since 1981, the Bank of England has issued a number of index-linked bonds where both capital sum and interest payments are increased in line with changes in the retail price index (RPI). The principle is straightforward. Suppose a bond issued on 1 January, 1990 paying £2 per annum; if during the year 1990 inflation as measured by the RPI were 5%, then on 1 January, 1991 each nominal £100 of the bond as issued would be worth £105 and the interest to be paid thereon in 1991 would be £2.10. If inflation continued at the rate of 5% per annum, then by 1 January, 1992 each £100 original nominal value of the bond would be worth £110.25 and the interest due thereon in that year would be £2.205.

In practice things are a little more complicated. The indexing is done with respect to a lagged value of the RPI and both the increase in capital value (the uplift) and the increase in interest payments depend on the rate of change of the price index to a period eight months earlier. Thus for a bond issued on 1 January, 1990, the base for indexing would be given by the level of the RPI in April, 1989; the uplift for capital value in January of each subsequent year would depend on the change in the RPI to April of the preceding year and all sums paid in interest would depend on the level of the RPI eight months before the payment date. This lagged indexing means that throughout the trading during any six-month period, the precise money value of the next interest payment is known. It also means that the real value of the redemption payment will vary according to the rate of inflation during the last eight months' life of a bond and so calculations of real yields to redemption can only be made on the basis of assumed rates of inflation. For this purpose it is now common to assume an inflation rate of 5%.

The retail price index was rebased in January 1987. The old index (January 1974 = 0) then stood at 394.5 and the new index was launched as usual with base 100. For all index-linked stocks issued prior to January, 1987, it is necessary therefore to adjust downward their base for indexing by the multiplicative factor of 100/394.5.

All index-linked stock issued to date have carried low coupons (2% or 2½%). Maturities vary but they tend to be longer than those for conventional stocks; only three of the 13 stocks outstanding at end-September, 1991 had maturity dates before the end of the century and several still had terms to maturity in excess of 20 years.

The money price of index-linked bonds varies due to the influence of two separate forces. Firstly there is the regular uplift in line with the (eight months prior) changes in the RPI. But then, in addition, prices move up and down due to changes in demand. Calculated *gross redemption yields* (real) on index-linked bonds vary just as do *yields* (in nominal terms) on conventional bonds.

As an example, consider 2% index-linked Treasury 2013 first issued on 21 February 1985. The base for indexing is derived from the RPI of June 1984 and is (after adjustment to allow for the rebased RPI) 89.2. In September 1991, the Bank of England issued the latest of a number of additional amounts (*tranchettes*) of this stock. Had the issue been at par (i.e. had the real return on outstanding amounts of this stock been exactly 2½%), it would have been issued at a price determined by the RPI eight months earlier in January 1991. Then the index stood at 130.2 so the uplifted value of a nominal £100 of 2% index-linked Treasury 1996 would have been equal to:

$$£100 \times \frac{130.2}{89.2} = £145.96$$

But in September 1991 interest rates on index-linked stock were well above 2½%, so the Bank of England issued the new tranchette at a price of £110.625 to give an estimated real gross yield to maturity of 4.22%.

3.1.4 The organization of the market since October 1986

The market in government securities was drastically reformed in October 1986 at the same time as the general – Big Bang – reforms of security trading in Britain discussed in Chapter 2 above. Prior to the reform, dealing in government securities had taken place on the floor of the London Stock Exchange[7] between brokers (acting on behalf of clients in an agency capacity) and jobbers (acting on their own behalf as principals). Trading was organised on the same lines as for other securities;[8] but, after a number of preparatory changes introduced during the preceding months, the trading system was completely restructured on Monday, 27 October 1986.

The most significant of the changes was the ending of single capacity with its sharp demarcation between the function of broker and that of jobber and the creation of a number of gilt-edged market makers (GEMMs) able to act in the dual capacity of broker and dealer. The GEMMs hold stocks of government securities and deal on their own account both among themselves and with final customers or their agents. There were other important changes. A new type of intermediary, the inter-dealer broker (IDB), was created to facilitate intra-market dealings in conditions of anonymity. A new settlement system came into being with the creation jointly by the Bank of England and the London Stock Exchange of the Central Gilts Office. The Bank of England extended formal and explicit supervision to all traders and brokers in the government bond market. Dealing in government bonds, along with dealing in other securities, moved off the floor of the London Stock Market sooner than anticipated and became a wholly screen-based activity.

In principle, any security dealer that is a member of the Stock Exchange can trade in government securities; but the market is subject to the powerful influence of the Bank of England and the latter has chosen to offer a package of rights and responsibilities to those whom it recognises as market makers in government securities, i.e. the GEMMs. In practice, they are the only important regular market makers and as such collectively constitute the trading core of the market.

The basic obligation of GEMMs is 'to make on demand and in any trading conditions, continuous and effective two-way prices at which they stand committed to deal in appropriate size ... thereby providing continuous liquidity for the investing public'.[9] That is to say, GEMMs provide a quote-driven market[10] at all times and regardless of market conditions. They are required by the Bank of England to deal in all outstanding gilt-edged stocks including index-linked stocks and may, if they so choose, deal in other sterling fixed-interest securities; in certain sterling money-market instruments; and in derivatives of these securities and instruments, e.g. futures and options on gilts. They may not deal in equity shares nor in securities convertible into equity shares. Recently, the Bank has agreed to GEMMs being allowed to deal in ECU-denominated liabilities of the British government.

GEMMs are required by the Bank of England to be separately established as companies or partnerships in the United Kingdom with their own dedicated sterling capital. Substantial shareholders are required to give assurances that they accept ultimate responsibility for the liabilities of the GEMM in question. The Bank discusses regularly with each GEMM about the size of transactions in which it is committed to deal and about the risk exposure that it can accept. There is no single requirement for capital but permissible risk exposure is governed for each GEMM by the amount of capital that it has. At the inception of the new market arrangements in October 1986, there were 27 GEMMs with an aggregate capital of £595 million. By end-December 1991, the combined effect of a small number of new entrants and a larger number of withdrawals had reduced the total number of firms to 18 and aggregate capital was down to £432 million.[11] Although new firms continue to enter the market, most commentators expect the total number of GEMMs to decline further.

However there does not appear to be large over-capacity in the government bond market to the extent believed to exist in the equity market. Although GEMMs in the aggregate made substantial losses during the years 1987–89, the market as a whole became profitable in 1990 and remained so in 1991. In the latter year, the amount of capital committed to the market rose for the first time since the start of the new trading arrangements in October 1986.

The Bank of England keeps the capital position of all GEMMs under observation and also monitors their fulfilment of their trading obligations. As part of this on-going process of supervision, each GEMM is required to furnish details of its market position to the Bank at the close of business each day.

In return for accepting these obligations – obligations which, it should be recalled, are additional to the normal requirements as to conduct and to financial reporting imposed on all members of the London Stock Exchange[12] – gilt-edged market makers have the right to certain privileges. These consist of: (i) a direct dealing relationship with the Bank of England; (ii) borrowing facilities at the Bank; (iii) access to IDBs; (iv) facilities for borrowing and lending stock; and (v) the right to submit bids slightly later than others at auctions of new government stock.

The dealing relationship with the Bank enables GEMMs to bid for stock that the Bank holds, to offer stock to the Bank for sale and to propose switches between different stocks. The Bank of England is, of course, free to respond as it chooses to any such bids or offers but, as well as being concerned to finance the government's borrowing needs on the best possible terms, the Bank has a publicly-expressed interest in the liquidity of the gilt-edged market. In view of this, it is prepared, on occasions, to buy particular stocks for which there is little demand otherwise; for instance, the Bank was a net purchaser of index-linked stocks during certain periods in 1990 when demand for these stocks was low.

Access to the inter-dealer brokers in gilts (to be distinguished from the different IDBs that act in a similar capacity in the equity market) is restricted to GEMMs. Intra-market business is large and, as is shown by Table 3.3, has in recent years been averaging over £2 billion per business day. It is an important part of the market as at present constituted that market makers be able to deal freely with each other so that each can eliminate undesired surpluses or shortages of stock arising from past or prospective business with clients. But there will frequently be considerable advantages in being able to deal anonymously. If, for example, a GEMM has acquired an unusually large amount of a particular stock and is known to be keen to sell, other market makers may cut dealing prices; conversely, if a GEMM is known to want to buy large amounts of stock, other market makers may raise prices. By dealing through brokers who have access to market-wide information and who are continually matching buying and selling offers, GEMMs can adjust their positions in the knowledge that prices will only move in response to generalised market shortages or surpluses of stock and not in anticipation of any particular deals of their own.

The ability to borrow and lend stock is an important facility and enables market makers more easily to take long positions (large holdings) and short positions (low or negative holdings) of stocks. Borrowing and lending stock is officially regulated as there are both prudential and tax considerations: GEMMs are approved lenders and approved borrowers. Other approved lenders include many of the large institutional investors. Borrowing and lending of stock is facilitated by eight (at end 1991) Stock Exchange Money Brokers (SEMBs) who, as well as acting as brokers in the actual loan of stock, make loans to GEMMs to finance long positions and stand ready to borrow from them any surplus funds arising out of short positions.

Stock Exchange money brokers finance themselves additionally by short-term borrowing from banks but, in the event that funds are not forthcoming on normal market terms, they like the GEMMs have individual borrowing rights at the Bank of England.

Settlement of transactions in government securities is now carried out largely through the Central Gilts Office. This is discussed further below.

3.1.5 New issues

All new issues as well as all redemptions of government stock are carried out on behalf of the government by the Bank of England. Gross new issues of gilt-edged stock are made in order to finance (i) new borrowing needs of the government; (ii) the redemption of maturing government stock; and (iii) net payments in sterling made by the Bank of England to acquire foreign currency. During the period from late-1988 to early-1991, when the government had a budget surplus, there were no new issues of stock and, at times, the Bank was an active net buyer of outstanding stock.

New issues of stock are now made in three distinct ways. Firstly, there is the traditional method of the offer for sale by tender where the Bank of England offers a large amount (usually not less than £1 billion) of newly created stock for sale at or above a specific minimum price. Bids to purchase stock have to be submitted by 10 a.m. on an appointed day and the Bank then decides how many of the bids to accept. If the offer is under-subscribed, all valid bids will be accepted; if the offer is over-subscribed, it will be the highest bids that are accepted. In each case, all bids are accepted at a common price, either the tender price or the minimum bid price accepted. When an offer is under-subscribed, the unsold stock is taken on to the books of the Bank of England and used as a tap stock for sale to the market over time as and when demand develops or can be created.

Secondly, new stocks are issued by auction. This method is relatively new in Britain and was first used in May 1987. As with sales by tender, the Bank offers a large amount (not less than £1 billion) of newly created stock for sale and invites bids to be submitted before 10 a.m. on the appointed day. But here there is no minimum price specified and stock is sold to the highest bidders and sold at the price that each has bid. To date, all seven offers of stock for sale by auction have been oversubscribed and, on each occasion, all stock on offer has been sold. After each auction, the Bank publishes details of the average yield on accepted bids and the yields on the highest and lowest accepted bids.

Three auctions were held between May 1987 and January 1988 and four were held during 1991. In the earlier series of auctions, there were large differences (in terms of yield) between minimum and maximum accepted bids but market operators appear to have learned by experience and, with the four auctions of 1991, the difference was never more than three basis points. Individual small bids (up to £100,000) may be submitted on a non-competitive basis and the bidder receives stock at the mean accepted price. Such bids are regularly submitted but only account for a very small amount of stock allotted. Large investors may bid directly but many choose to acquire stock directly from GEMMs by buying on a 'when issued' basis in the period between the announcement of an auction and the date of the auction. At all four auctions in 1991, the GEMMs built up substantial short positions prior to the auction through 'when issued' trading.[13]

The Bank of England reserves the right to decline to accept bids that it judges to be out of line with market conditions even if this should mean that it does not sell all stock on offer. But the Bank has always indicated that it would only take such a step in exceptional circumstances and continues to stress its awareness of the need to avoid actions which could be seen as capricious if it is to retain the confidence of market makers and investors in gilt-edged stock.[14]

The third method of issue involves the Bank of England taking stock on to its own books and then selling this as a tap stock over a period of time in day-to-day dealings with GEMMs. This method is very flexible and can be used equally to make large new issues of stock or to sell comparatively small extra tranchettes of an existing stock.

Table 3.4 provides details of new issues of government stock between 1 October and 31 December 1991. Prior to this period, the Bank had been funding actively and, during the preceding six months, had made issues of stock by all three methods amounting to £8.5 billion and including both conventional stocks and index-linked stocks. The pattern, which continued into the last quarter of 1991, was one of large periodic issues by tender or by auction and frequent and usually small issues of tranchettes of tap stock.

During October 1991, the bond market was subdued and the Bank of England sold only modest amounts of previously issued tap stocks but also received payments in respect of a stock sold earlier by auction but with payment by instalments. During November, the Bank took advantage of rising bond prices to sell what was left of its tap stocks and to announce the auction of £1.5 billion of 9% conversion 2011. The auction was successful with bids received amounting to 2.28 times the amount of stock on offer and the following day the Bank announced the issue of three new tranchettes of tap stock. Gilt-edged prices continued to rise strongly, all three tranchettes were quickly sold out and, shortly afterwards, the Bank announced the issue of a much larger tap stock: £1 billion of 8½% Treasury 2007.

As the government's manager of the marketable national debt, the Bank of England plays a predominant role in the gilt-edged market. It is usually in the position of seeking to sell new debt in the short term but it is also concerned to promote efficient trading mechanisms and to sustain the demand for government debt in the long term. It is primarily such long-term considerations which have led the Bank to adopt a particular approach to the issuing and selling of new government securities.

Both holders of government stock and dealers in it know that prices fluctuate and that capital losses can be expected as well as capital gains. They also know that fluctuations in bond prices (the obverse of changes in interest rates) are frequently the result of monetary policy conducted by the Bank of England. The operations of the latter in the money markets are frequently designed to move short-term rates of interest up or down; and movements in short-term rates usually affect medium- and long-term rates, albeit not necessarily in a one-to-one manner. So the Bank of England is in the situation that it usually wishes to sell government securities; it invariably wishes to sustain long-run demand for such securities but it periodically has to take action which inflicts losses on the holders of such securities.

Faced with this ambiguity, the Bank has sought to make a clear distinction between its money-market operations (for purposes of monetary policy) and its bond-market operations (for purposes of meeting the government's borrowing requirement). In the bond market, the Bank does not actively try to sell at a time when prices are falling; indeed its spokesmen have often asserted that it cannot sell in such conditions, that the views of investors in the short-term are predominantly extrapolative and that few will wish to buy stock when the price is falling. This is a view which goes back a long way, at least as far as the time of the Radcliffe Report in 1960.[15]

The strategy of the Bank of England is to bring forward auctions and offers for sale by tender at times when it thinks market demand will be strong and not at times when prices are falling. Further, from the time of an announcement of an auction until 28 days after it has been held, the Bank observes a fallow period during which it does not sell stock of a similar type to that being auctioned so as not to be seen to be depressing the price. With tap stocks, the Bank seeks to sell to the market when bond prices are rising and does not actively try to sell when prices are falling. Ideally, the Bank would like to sell all tap stock at or above the published issue price – minimum tender price or certified price at which it acquired the stock – but this is not always possible; inevitably there are occasions when the Bank is holding unsold stock and when rates of interest rise and bond prices fall. In such circumstances, if the Bank wishes to sell the stock it is holding over a reasonable time period, it will often be unable to avoid reducing its price. But the Bank is keen to avoid suggestions that – in its bond-dealing – it leads prices down or in any way operates to impose losses on existing holders of government bonds: at times of falling prices, it follows the market and does not lead it.

3.1.6   Redemptions

With a stock of government bonds outstanding of over £120 billion and an average maturity of around 10 years, it follows that stock falling due for redemption will average about £12 billion per annum. The Bank of England has, for many years, sought to make this a continuous operation and it seeks to buy stock approaching maturity rather than waiting for legal redemption dates. The Bank stands ready to buy from market makers, and at a price of its own choosing, any stock with three months or less to maturity; it is also usually prepared to quote a price for stocks with between three and twelve months to maturity. In this way the Bank avoids the potential disruption to the money markets due to its having to make large payments to private-sector bond-holders all at once.

3.1.7   Secondary trading

Secondary trading in the government bond market is dominated by the gilt-edged market makers (GEMMs) of which at the time of writing there are eighteen. As explained above, each is committed to making, within normal business hours, a continuous market in all existing government stocks. The market is an over-the-telephone market and prices are quoted on demand by telephone. Most market makers also display prices for the most widely traded stocks on screen on SEAQ.[16]

During the two years 1990 and 1991, business with customers averaged around 2,000 deals per day and intra-market business (between GEMMs) averaged around 600 deals per day. The average size of transactions, it was noted above, has been rising over time and now amounts to about £1 million for transactions with customers and about £4 million for intra-market business. This means that total market turnover per day is now of the order of £4,400 million on average.

Market liquidity depends not just on average figures of turnover but on the size of transactions that are possible. At present, it is usually possible to undertake deals in widely traded stocks of from £5 million to £10 million on best terms, and deals can be done for £30 million or even more albeit at higher margins.[17]

Dealing costs have declined since the restructuring of the market in 1986. Under the old system, commission payments for transactions of £1 million in widely traded stocks would have varied between £80 and £500, depending on the maturity of the stock. These have now largely disappeared. In addition, the spread between buying and selling prices quoted by market makers has roughly halved. The spread is measured in 'ticks' with each tick equal to $\frac{1}{32}\%$ and whereas, prior to October 1986, a typical spread for short-term bonds would have been 2-4 ticks (the lower for the more liquid stocks, the higher for the less liquid) it is now 1-2 ticks. For medium- and long-term bonds, spreads which used to be of the order of 4-8 ticks are now more likely to be 2-4 ticks.[18]

It is worth making explicit that $\frac{1}{32}\%$ equals £312.5 for a transaction of £1 million. It is then clear by just how much dealing costs on large transactions have fallen. Taking into account both the virtual disappearance of explicit commissions and the shrinking of spreads, it is evident that dealing costs, for the most part, are now appreciably less than half of what they were prior to the reforms of October 1986.

Dealing takes place between GEMMs and investors in gilt-edged; between GEMMs themselves, usually but not invariably through one of the three inter-dealer brokers (IDBs); and between GEMMs and the Bank of England. Deals with investors tend to be direct in the case of large institutional holders of government stock but will often be through agency brokers in the case of personal customers. A number of GEMMs provide a small-business service.

Table 3.5 shows the main categories of holders of government stock as at end-March 1991. It is apparent that the dominant holders are the insurance companies and pension funds who together accounted for around 50% of all holdings. Foreign holders, including overseas central banks and monetary institutions, held around 12% and UK official holders, including the Bank of England, accounted for nearly 13%. Persons and private trusts held somewhat less than 10% of the total and the combined holdings of the banking sector and the building societies were around 5.5%. Almost all of the holdings shown as belonging to the banking sector were held by banks; discount houses have, in recent years, ceased to be significant holders of gilt-edged securities in their own names. A number of the houses are still actively involved in the market through their ownership of GEMMs or (in one case) of a SEMB.

Table 3.5: Holders of government stock 31st March, 1991

(% of total market value)	
Banking sector	2.9
Building societies	2.5
Insurance companies and pension funds*	52.7
Investment trusts and unit trusts	0.7
Persons and private trusts	9.2
Foreign central monetary institutions	5.6
Other foreign holdings	6.4
Other non-official holdings**	7.1
Official holdings***	12.9
Total	100.0

Notes:
*Figure partly estimated. As a consequence other non-official holdings are also affected.
**Includes industrial and commercial companies, local authorities, public corporations, the public trustee, various non-corporate bodies and a residual item.
***Includes government departments and the Bank of England. The Issue Department of the Bank of England accounts for over 60% of the holdings under this heading. (Authors own estimate.)
Source: Bank of England Quarterly Bulletin, The net debt of the public sector: end-March 1991, November 1991.

Holdings of persons and private trusts although small compared to those of the large institutional investors remain significant. As was noted above, the Bank of England provides special facilities for small bidders when offering stock for sale by auction and a number of GEMMs provide a retail service, i.e. they are prepared to buy and sell stock in relatively small amounts.

Dealing between GEMMs plays an important part in the maintenance of an efficient and liquid market. For each individual GEMM, it is improbable that daily transactions with customers will leave it holding the desired amounts of all the different stocks in which it deals. On the contrary, it is to be expected that sales to and purchases from customers will leave individual market makers holding more or less of particular stocks than they would choose. In this situation each market maker can seek to adjust its own holdings of different stocks by trading with other market makers and can do this anonymously by dealing through the IDBs. The IDBs, who are in constant contact with all GEMMs, will be able to match offers to buy and to sell and so localised shortages and surpluses of particular stocks will be quickly ironed out. And if shortages or surpluses are general across the market this will be immediately apparent and indicate to GEMMs a need to adjust quoted prices.

Further room for manoeuvre is provided by GEMMs' ability to borrow stock from approved lenders, typically large insurance companies and pension funds. This is facilitated by the Stock Exchange Money Brokers (SEMBs), described above in Section 3.2.4, and enhances the ability of GEMMs to supply large amounts of stock on demand without having always to hold large inventories of stocks or without having to offset large sales by matching purchases in intra-market business. But also the ability to borrow stock provides a means whereby GEMMs can choose to take short positions when they think that prices will fall.

The existence of well developed facilities for borrowing and lending stock can be seen as an alternative to the 'repo market' found in the USA and in a number of other countries. This is a market for the sale and repurchase of government bonds and serves much the same function as the lending of stock in the UK.

Such position-taking obviously involves risks and if expectations were incorrect and bond prices rise rather than fall then market makers with short positions will incur losses. There are analogous risks with long positions; those with net holdings of stock lose when bond prices fall. There are a number of ways of dealing with these risks when they are unwanted as opposed to being deliberately chosen in the hope of making capital gains.

Market makers can aim to run only modest positions in any group of similar stocks or they can run large but offsetting positions, i.e. being long on certain stocks and short on others such that capital gains and losses can be expected to cancel each other out. A further means of risk management is provided by the derivative markets in futures and options in which GEMMs can broadly offset spot positions by dealing in bond futures or options. The use of derivative markets is discussed further below.

3.1.8   The Central Gilts Office (CGO)

During the 1980s, the Bank of England and the London Stock Exchange developed jointly a computerised settlement system for transactions in gilt-edged securities. It is managed from an office located within the Bank of England which has direct computer links to over 100 firms including all GEMMs, IDBs, SEMBs, the large banks and many of the large institutional investors in government stock. Member firms hold stock in accounts with the CGO and same-day transfers can be made between accounts on receipt of instructions via computer terminals. Member firms can also have nominee accounts in which stock owned by their clients can be held.

Following agreement with a number of settlement banks, payment for gilt-edged stock transferred within the CGO is guaranteed.

Use of the CGO has decreased settlement costs for members, reduced the number of paper transfers by means of stock transfer forms and eliminated the credit risk involved in delivering stock against a promise of payment. The system, which is also used for the borrowing and lending of stock and for the pledging of stock as collateral for short-term loans, has proved popular and, by late-1991, some 70% of all outstanding gilt-edged stock was held in accounts with the CGO.

3.2   Other sterling bonds

3.2.1   Issuers and types of security

The main issuers of sterling bonds, other than the Uk government, are British companies, British local authorities, foreign public authorities, international agencies, and foreign companies. During the nineteenth and early twentieth century foreign issues were the most important but, for many years during and after the Second World War pervasive exchange controls excluded all such issues. Of the domestic borrowers, local authorities issued, in the years between the mid-1950s and the early 1980s, a large volume of stocks (over five years to maturity) and negotiable bonds (from one to four years to maturity); but in recent years it has been government policy to centralise most public-sector borrowing and as a result public issues by local authorities have all but ceased. On the other hand, bond issues by

British companies which, during the 1970s, had dwindled due to high and volatile nominal rates of interest have increased markedly in recent years. As foreign issues have also grown rapidly following the abolition in 1979 of exchange controls, it is no exaggeration to see the 1980s as a period of renaissance for the sterling bond market.[19]

A wide variety of bonds exists. An important distinction is between bonds which carry a fixed (coupon) rate of interest and floating-rate notes (FRNs) where the rate of interest varies in line with movements in a designated short-term rate. Then one must distinguish between 'straights' which are bonds which just earn interest until maturity and 'convertibles' which are bonds which give the holder the right to convert, on specified terms, into another security, usually the equity of the issuing company. Some bonds are secured on the assets of the issuer (known as debentures) while others are unsecured but invariably carry a negative pledge to the effect that the company in question will not subsequently issue bonds which have any greater security or degree of preference. Bonds may be registered or they may be issued in the form of bearer securities. Terms to maturity vary widely and so also do coupon rates.

A major difference of form exists between domestic bonds and sterling eurobonds, although the differences of substance have tended to decline in recent years. Domestic bonds traditionally are registered securities, usually issued in the form of debentures; they are listed on the London Stock Exchange and they pay interest net of UK income tax. Issues are managed by domestic security dealers or by merchant banks and are largely sold to investors resident in the UK. Sterling eurobonds, which are a part of the international eurobond market described in Chapter 5 below, are normally issued as bearer securities and are usually unsecured but with a negative pledge; they are listed on an exchange but not necessarily the London Stock Exchange and they pay interest gross. Issues are managed by large banks or security traders and sold to both domestic and overseas residents.

In recent years, more and more borrowers have chosen to make issues in the form of sterling eurobonds and the volume of domestic issues has declined. This trend would appear to be an inevitable consequence of the internationalisation of bond trading and, in the absence of unexpected changes in regulation, is unlikely to be reversed. More specifically, there are a number of reasons why it should have come about.

Foreign investors are better acquainted with customs and practices in the eurobond market and they are also widely believed to have strong preferences for the anonymity of bearer securities and for the receipt of interest payments without deduction of tax. It would appear to be due to the strength of these preferences that prime borrowers have frequently been able to raise funds more cheaply by making a eurosterling rather than a domestic issue. At times during the 1980s, yields on short-dated eurosterling bonds even fell below those on gilt-edged stocks of similar maturity.[20]

Issues of eurobonds are limited to highly rated and usually well known borrowers so investors do not require additional security in the form of specific claims on assets provided by domestically issued debentures. Furthermore for those borrowers who have eurobonds outstanding, it is no longer possible to issue bonds with such security in view of the negative pledge on the eurobond. Such borrowers now include a growing number of large British companies. And as both issues and potential issuers of traditional domestic bonds have declined, so British institutional investors have had to overcome some initial reluctance and look to eurosterling issues as a source of non-gilt fixed-interest assets.

Another important reason for the trend to eurosterling bonds has been the growth in interest-rate swaps. As is explained in Chapter 5 below, the formalities of issue of eurobonds are somewhat less than with domestic bonds and issues can be arranged more quickly. This allows borrowers more scope to time issues so as to take advantage of temporarily favourable patterns of interest rates such as would permit profitable swaps. Notable among issuers of sterling eurobonds who have swapped their resultant fixed-rate obligations for floating-rate payments have been British and foreign financial institutions. They have been able to take advantage of their good standing internationally to raise funds on fine terms which could then be converted into floating-rate liabilities suitable for financing the acquisition of floating-rate sterling assets. Among the counterparties to these swaps have figured a number of British companies that were too small to issue bonds in their own name but were happy to acquire an equivalent fixed-interest liability in exchange for floating-rate obligations.

3.2.2 The size of the market

During the 1950s and 1960s, the debenture market was an important source of funds for domestic British companies. Over the two decades, according to Midland Bank statistics, sums raised averaged nearly £200 million per annum.[21] While this single figure conceals sharp year-to-year fluctuations as well as a secular upward trend, it is noteworthy that sums raised over this period by bond finance (including convertible bonds) exceeded those raised by the issue of ordinary shares and also exceeded the sums raised for the government by the sale of gilt-edged securities.

But during the 1970s, inflation rose to levels unprecedented in peacetime and in consequence nominal interest rates rose to very high levels. This discouraged companies from issuing fixed-rate securities to such an extent that, over the years 1973–1980, redemptions exceeded gross issues and net issues were negative. At the same time, exchange controls continued to prevent foreign issuers from raising bond finance in London and the eurosterling market was still in its infancy. The sterling bond market apart from gilt-edged had all but ceased to exist.

But the picture changed sharply in the 1980s. Inflation, if still a problem, was much lower than in the previous decade and nominal rates of interest were also lower. Issues of government stock declined and this may have contributed to the lower trend in rates of interest. It also meant that financial institutions put less of their funds into gilt-edged stocks and, in consequence, were more ready to purchase other fixed-interest securities. This combination of lower interest rates and a ready demand for their debt securities meant that British companies increased markedly their issues of sterling bonds. At the same time, following the ending of exchange controls, both foreign companies and foreign public authorities were once again able to issue sterling bonds in the British market (the so-called 'bulldog issues'). Both domestic and foreign borrowers also increased their usage of the eurosterling market.

Table 3.6 provides details of sterling bond issues, excluding those of the UK public sector, for the years 1980–1991. It shows the remarkable rise in total issues over the period in question and also shows the rising share of eurosterling issues in total issues. It would however be unwise to assume too easily that volumes will continue to grow rapidly. British government finances deteriorated in the early 1990s and the prospects are for a return to large net sales of gilt-edged securities. Some 'crowding-out' of private-sector bond finance may occur.

Table 3.6 Gross sterling bond issues other than by the UK public sector* 1980–1991 (£ million)

	Domestic issues			Eurosterling fixed rate			Total fixed rate	Eurosterling FRNs
	British	Foreign (Bulldog issues)	Total	British	Foreign	Total		
1980	219	75	294	52	295	347	641	70
1981	7	440	447	0	249	249	696	0
1982	880	725	1,605	85	375	460	2,065	0
1983	300	595	895	145	688	833	1,728	505
1984	640	1,040	1,680	345	1,265	1,610	3,290	1,548
1985	597	710	1,307	522	1,450	1,972	3,279	2,275
1986	2,339	838	3,177	1,787	1,540	3,326	5,850	3,700
1987	2,030	0	2,030	3,544	4,413	7,957	9,987	1,247
1988	2,499	185	2,684	4,080	3,219	7,299	9,983	6,500
1989	5,280	645	5,925	3,292	3,303	6,595	12,520	5,150
1990	1,344	0	1,344	4,282	2,404	6,686	8,030	5,933
1991	996	0	996	6,520	5,051	11,571	12,657	4,285

* including convertibles
Source: Bank of England

An idea of the size of the secondary market in non-gilt sterling bonds is given by Table 3.7 which shows outstanding amounts of such bonds listed on the London Stock Exchange at end September 1991. The main gap in Table 3.7 is that it does not show the amount of sterling eurobonds not listed on the London Stock Exchange. However, from comparisons of Stock Exchange statistics and those compiled by the Bank for International Settlements, it can be inferred that between 70–75% of all sterling eurobonds are listed in London. This would suggest that sterling eurobonds not listed in London would, at end September 1991, have amounted to a figure between £14 million and £19 million.

Table 3.7 Sterling bonds, other than gilt-edged, listed on the London Stock Exchange 30.9.1991

	No. of securities	Nominal value (£m)	Market value (£m)
UK local authorities and public corporations	108	362.9	290.2
Overseas public sector	166	4,242.1	4,074.3
Company securities			
UK	800	13,068.9	13,890.4
foreign	25	134.7	384.3
Total company securities	**825**	**13,203.6**	**14,274.7**
Sterling eurobonds			
UK	362	34,635.5	33,688.6
foreign	236	9,679.6	10,046.5
Total sterling eurobonds	**598**	**44,315.1**	**43,735.1**

Notes:
Overseas public sector and company securities include small amounts of bonds denominated in foreign currencies. The table excludes nine company securities listed on the USM which had a market value of £14.5 million at end September 1991.
Sterling eurobonds not listed on the London Stock Exchange are not included in this table. It may be noted however that the Bank for International Settlements estimated the total nominal amount of sterling eurobonds outstanding, at end 1990, to be £55.25 billion.[22]
Source: Stock Exchange Quarterly, July–September 1991.

Turnover in secondary market trading has traditionally been low, both for domestically issued bonds and for eurosterling bonds. Many issues are relatively small and liquidity is low. As far as most outstanding bonds are concerned this is still true but the picture has become more varied. Some large issues were made in the 1980s and turnover of eurosterling bonds has increased as has turnover of eurobonds in general.[23] Turnover in all sterling bonds listed on the London Stock Exchange has, in recent years, been averaging around £50 billion per annum, split more or less evenly between client business and intra-market business.

3.2.3 New issues

The methods of issuing new sterling bonds in the domestic market, whether for UK borrowers or for foreign borrowers, are broadly the same as those for new issues of equity shares. Issuers can choose a public offer for sale, either at a fixed price or by tender or alternatively they can opt to issue bonds by means of a placing. In recent years, virtually all domestic issues of bonds have been by means of a placing. These methods of issue are described in detail in Chapter 2 above.

Eurobond issues are managed by international banks and security traders and are invariably in the form of a placing. The method of issue is described in detail in Chapter 5 below.

3.2.4 Secondary trading

Prices are quoted for non-gilt bonds by market makers but, due to the small size of many fixed-interest issues, quotations are often only indicative. Under the classification of stocks which existed prior to January 1991, fixed interest securities were virtually all classified as gamma or delta stocks. But liquidity has increased for a number of the larger issues of recent years and certain gilt-edged market makers are now active dealers in a range of non-gilt securities.

Secondary trading in eurosterling issues follows the pattern of secondary trading in the eurobond market in general and is described in Chapter 5 below.

3.3 Financial futures and options

Financial futures and options, discussed fully in Chapter 4 below, are now used widely by market makers and investors in the sterling bond market as a means of managing risk. The important contracts are the long gilt future (£50,000 nominal value, notional gilt with 9% coupon) and the option on this future; both traded on LIFFE. As can be seen from Table 4.1 (p. 94), they are among the most important of the derivative contracts traded in London. To a certain extent turnover follows that of the cash market in government securities: it rose in 1987 following the start of the new trading arrangements for gilt-edged securities and it fell in 1988 and 1989 when government accounts moved into surplus and there was a cessation of new issues.

The derivative markets are useful to both market makers and to investors. Market makers, GEMMs notably but also dealers in sterling eurobonds, are continually buying and selling large volumes of bonds and their risk exposure is continually changing. And at times of new issues, they will often be committed to purchasing very large amounts of stock which they can only expect to sell over a period of weeks; during which period they are exposed to the risk of capital loss if prices fall. The use of futures and/or options offers a quick way of hedging this and other risks by creating future positions which offset those in the cash market.

The large institutional investors may also choose to hedge positions. If they fear a fall in prices, selling a future or acquiring a put option are alternatives to selling the underlying securities. Or alternatively if cash has been allocated for a later purchase of, say, an expected new issue of bonds and the fear is of prices rising, an investor can hedge by buying a future or by acquiring a call option. The evidence is that institutional investors in Britain were initially wary of financial futures and options and were also concerned about the uncertain tax treatment of gains and losses arising from dealing in such derivatives. The 1990 Budget clarified the tax position and a recent survey of pension fund managers reported in the *Financial Times* appears to confirm a growing use of derivative products.[24]

3.4 International comparisons

The Bank for International Settlements has published detailed figures on the volume of publicly issued bonds outstanding by currency of issue and covering issues denominated in twenty-one different currencies. Table 3.8 draws on these figures to show the sizes of the largest bond markets in the world and to give an international context to the sterling bond market. It should be borne in mind that there are always problems of definition and of classification in compiling figures such as these and also that all the figures for currencies other than the US dollar have had to be converted to dollars and hence depend upon the exchange rate used. But even allowing for such problems and treating the figures with due caution, they do give a dramatic picture of the relative sizes of different currency segments of the world bond market.

Table 3.8 shows the complete dominance of the US dollar in all sectors of the market: government bonds, domestic private issues and eurobonds. The value of US dollar bonds outstanding exceeds that of the combined total of bonds outstanding from the other six currency segments put together.

The sterling bond market is not only small compared to those denominated in dollars and in yen, it is also much smaller than those denominated in marks, lira and French francs. Not only has the British government and its agencies borrowed less in recent years than other European governments, it is also the case that, until recently, the private bond market was narrow. Sterling issues expanded dramatically in the 1980s but increasingly in the form of eurosterling bonds and Table 3.8 shows the important share that such bonds now have in the total sterling bond market.

Notes

1   For a detailed historical account of the growth of the market in government securities, see E.V. Morgan and W.A. Thomas (1962).
2   Several different terms are used to describe UK government securities. They are referred to as government stock or government bonds or as gilt-edged, the latter term stemming from the days when the stock certificates actually did have a gilt edge. All three terms will be used interchangeably in this chapter.
3   This is the correct title of the Exchange which now organises security trading in Britain and Ireland (see Section 2 of Chapter 2 above). Trading is concentrated in London and (for Irish securities) in Dublin. For brevity, the term London Stock Exchange will be used throughout the remainder of this chapter.
4.   See Bank for International Settlements (1991), Chapter VI.
5   See Bank of England (1991).
6   UK government securities are priced in pounds and fractions of pounds; the smallest price movement is £$\frac{1}{32}$.
7   There was also a small volume of business carried out on a dwindling number of exchanges in provincial cities.

Table 3.8 The largest bond markets by currency of issue (nominal values outstanding, US$ billion)

Currency	Public sector issues		Provincial and local	Domestic private sector issues	International issues		Total publicly issued
	Central government	Government agencies			Foreign	Euro	
US dollar	1,653.4	1,413.5	596.0	1,714.4	81.7	525.9	5,984.9
Japanese yen	1,163.6	387.2	143.3	714.8	52.1	115.9	2,576.9
Deutschmark	295.3	49.3	27.0	604.8	147.4		1,123.8
Italian lira	594.0	23.1	–	127.8	0.5	14.0	759.4
French franc	152.5	213.6	4.4	87.8	1.5	27.5	487.3
Pound sterling	225.7	–	0.5	28.0	9.5	106.6	370.3
Canadian dollar	119.5	–	145.4	48.9	1.1	46.8	361.7

Notes: Local currency figures converted at end 1990 exchange rates.
Source: Bank for International Settlements quoted in Benzie (1992).

8   See Chapter 2 above.
9   See Bank of England (1985).
10   See Chapter 2 above and also Foley (1991).
11   See Bank of England (1992).
12   See Section 2.3.1 of Chapter 2 above.
13   See Bank of England (1992).
14   See for instance Townend (1992).
15   This view was put forward in evidence given by Bank of England officials to the Radcliffe Committee in the late-1950s and is discussed in Chapter 7 of the report of that committee. See Committee on the Working of the Monetary System (1960). For subsequent statements of this view, see Bank of England (1966) and Townend (1992).
16   See Chapter 2 above.
17   See Townend (1992).
18   The figures in this paragraph are taken from Bank of England (1989).
19   For a detailed discussion of the development of the sterling bond market in the 1980s see Bank of England (1988). See also Plenderleith (1989) and Townend (1992).
20   See Bank of England (1988).
21   Figures on corporate finance were published annually in the *Midland Bank Review* (February or Spring issues) since 1987. For a detailed historical look at corporate finance in Britain, see Thomas (1978).
22   See Benzie (1992).
23   See Chapter 5 below and Chester (1991).
24   See Corrigan (1992).

Bibliography

Bank for International Settlements (1991) *61st Annual Report.*
Bank of England (1966) Official transactions in the gilt-edged market, *Bank of England Quarterly Bulletin,* **6**, 141–9.
Bank of England (1985) The future structure of the gilt-edged market, *Bank of England Quarterly Bulletin,* **25**, 250–82.
Bank of England (1988) Recent developments in the corporate and bulldog sectors of the sterling bond market, *Bank of England Quarterly Bulletin,* **28**, 62–8.
Bank of England (1989) The gilt-edged market since Big Bang, *Bank of England Quarterly Bulletin,* **29**, 49–58.
Bank of England (1991) The net debt of the public sector: end-March 1991, *Bank of England Quarterly Bulletin,* **31**, 538–45.
Bank of England (1992) The gilt-edged market: developments in 1991, *Bank of England Quarterly Bulletin,* **32,** 56–9.
Benzie, Richard (1992) *The development of the international bond market,* BIS Economic Papers, No. 32.
Chester, A.C. (1991) The international bond market, *Bank of England Quarterly Bulletin,* **31,** 521–8.
Committee on the Working of the Monetary System (the Radcliffe Committee) (1960) *Report,* HMSO.
Corrigan, Tracy (1992), Diversification is the spur, *Financial Times,* 19 March.
Foley, Bernard J. (1991), *Capital Markets,* Macmillan.
Morgan, E.V. and **Thomas, W.A.** (1962) *The Stock Exchange,* Elek Books.

Plenderleith, I. (1989), The development of the sterling bond market, *Bank of England Quarterly Bulletin,* **29,** 383–7.

Thomas, W.A. (1978), *The Finance of British Industry 1918-1976,* Methuen.

Townend, J. (1992) Recent developments in the gilt-edged market, *Bank of England Quarterly Bulletin,* **32,** 76–81.

4   Futures and options

by James Leslie and Geoffrey Wyatt

The end of the era of stable exchange rates in 1972 coincided with the birth of a whole new class of financial instruments designed to accommodate the uncertainties of the new era. The birthplace of this new industry was Chicago, and Chicago is still the global centre of the financial futures and options industry, though by the 1990s virtually all respectable financial centres have local access to at least one derivative assets exchange. London's exchanges, the London International Financial Futures Exchange (LIFFE) and the London Traded Options Market (LTOM), are among the most important outside of the United States.

4.1   The hedging demand for derivative assets

Futures and options are known as derivative assets because they are based on other 'underlying' assets which have volatile prices. It is the volatility of price of the underlying asset which makes it worthwhile to create the derivative asset. A fluctuating asset price exposes holders of that asset to uncertain future returns. While the average return may be acceptable, the element of variability could imply a risk of financial loss that is unacceptable. People who need to hold the asset in question for trading purposes may therefore be prepared to pay for a device that guarantees a stable price. Futures and options are such devices.

Individuals and corporations hold portfolios of assets, the precise composition of which depends both on the characteristics of those assets and on the asset holder's attitude to risky outcomes. The characteristics of an asset include both its financial properties and the uses to which it can be put. A ton of wheat is an asset just as is a house. But if wheat prices fluctuate more widely than house prices, an investor who had no particular interest in either wheat or houses would not be indifferent between them.

We thus turn to investors' attitudes to risk and return. All investors prefer a greater return, other things equal. In particular, if all assets were equally risky, then everyone would choose the one with the greatest expected payoff to holding it. Equally, we expect that if all assets have the same expected (average) payoff, then most people would choose the one with the lowest variability, that is, the smallest risk. But, largely for that very reason, assets do vary in both their expected returns and their riskiness. These financial characteristics of return and risk are, in fact, positively correlated across assets. Investors must therefore choose and, given the same menu, not all will choose the same combination of return and risk. Their choice will depend on both their objective circumstances and the strength of their subjective aversion to risky prospects.

An investor who needs to hold a particular asset in his portfolio for trading purposes may wish to exchange some of its expected return for a reduced variance in its return. He could do a deal with another investor who wishes to achieve a greater return, even if that means accepting a greater risk. The problem is to find the other party to the deal, which requires a 'double coincidence of wants'. In normal economic life such bartering is made unnecessary by the use of money. In the world of finance the need to barter is avoided either by using a financial intermediary, such as a bank, or by the use of an impersonal medium of exchange such as a derivative asset.

Someone who wishes to reduce the risk involved in holding an asset which is essential to his business, and takes steps to do so by purchasing a future or a call option, is referred to as a 'hedger'. His counterparty could be someone who is prepared to take on that extra risk by selling a future or writing a call option. If that person has no real exposure as a concomitant of trading activity but takes on the risk as a means of generating income, he is referred to as a 'speculator'. In essence, hedgers as a group buy insurance from speculators who take calculated gambles.

The distinction between hedging and speculating is somewhat blurred in practice. It is of course difficult to appraise peoples' motives for buying or selling derivative assets, so mere observation is insufficient. Furthermore, a pure hedge is almost impossible to achieve, so even if hedging were the main motive for acquiring a derivative asset, the transaction would almost invariably involve an element of speculation. A 'pure hedge' refers to a situation in which the derivative asset exactly offsets the price risk involved in holding a real asset, but this can only be attained if the real asset is identical in specification to the underlying asset on which the derivative is based. It is seldom so in practice.

Despite these caveats, the essential point is that the buying and selling of derivative assets is a process by which risk bearing is transferred between individuals.

4.2   Futures and options: what are they?

4.2.1   Futures

A futures contract is an obligation on one side to deliver, and on the other side to take delivery of a precisely specified quality and quantity of some commodity on a specific future date. The only aspect of the contract that can vary is the price at which the exchange is made, which is determined at the time of the transaction. The obligation to make or take delivery can be avoided by an offsetting purchase or sale before the settlement date, and normally only a small proportion of all contracts are settled by delivery. The concept of 'delivery' is a carry over from commodity based futures. In view of the near perfect fungibility (i.e. financial interchangeability) of financial instruments, modern financial futures exchanges sometimes specify settlement by cash. Thus stock index instruments and short term interest rate instruments based on bank accounts, which are difficult or impossible to deliver physically, are settled by cash.

A futures contract is distinguished from a forward contract by the fact that it is traded anonymously as a homogeneous product on an exchange, whereas a forward contract is one whose specification is determined in direct negotiation between a particular seller and a particular buyer, and is therefore not normally tradeable. Futures and forward contracts have the common feature that the agreement to transact and the transaction itself are separated in time: both payment and delivery are made in future, unlike in the spot market where the the agreement is simultaneous with the exchange. Most people have, perhaps unwittingly, made forward contracts – for example when ordering some good for future delivery, with an immediate down payment of a non-refundable deposit and payment of the balance by cash on delivery.

Clearly, someone who wishes to hedge his exposure to variations in the price of an asset in his portfolio could do so either by purchasing an appropriate forward contract – from a bank perhaps – or by purchasing exchange traded futures. In this sense, as alternative ways to meet the same need, the two markets can be thought of as being in competition. However, the relation between the forward and futures markets is more complex than this.

The set of actively traded futures contracts is very limited in comparison to the almost infinite variety of forward contracts that are struck. It is therefore very unlikely that any particular uncertain prospect can be completely offset by purchasing a future. There will always be some residual risk due to the fact that the specification of the future does not correspond exactly to the exposure in question. Thus the forward market – also referred to as the 'over the counter market' – has the advantage, from the point of view of the hedger, that a better match to the uncertain prospect can be obtained. The counterparty to this forward contract, let us say it is a bank, may for its part be willing to transact because it has a wider, more diversified portfolio than the hedger, within which it can to some extent offset the risky prospect. However, the bank can also use an exchange traded futures contract to further reduce its risk in taking on the forward contract. It could do so if price fluctuations in the asset underlying the futures contract are highly correlated with the risky prospect that is the subject of the forward contract. Thus there are elements of both substitutability and complementarity in the services provided by the futures and forward contracts, and the two markets, while competing up to a point can also synergistically reinforce each other.

Markets in exchange traded futures are much more 'transparent' than the corresponding over the counter markets: the prices at which a future can be purchased are publicly available, and are the same for everyone. Thus the inconvenience of negotiation can be avoided and a decision to purchase can be made at any time and immediately put into effect. But to achieve these advantages, derivatives exchanges have had to devise institutional arrangements to ensure the absence of default risk. In over the counter deals the transactors can appraise such counterparty risk and take steps to avoid it, for example by writing conditions into the contract. The institutional arrangement by which futures exchanges eliminate counterparty risk of default, and preserve the anonymity of dealing, is the establishment of clearing houses. The clearing house may or may not belong to the exchange, but it is the counterparty to all exchange based futures and options contracts. All exchanges ensure that the integrity of their clearing house is beyond question so that people may invest in their derivative products without fear of default risk.

The clearing house holds accounts for all the clearing members of the exchange. When a future is bought or sold, both buyer and seller deposit a sum of money called 'initial margin' into a clearing member's account at the clearing house. The size of this deposit varies by contract, and from time to time depending on trading conditions. It should be sufficient to cover one day's price movement, perhaps between one and five per cent of the face value of the contract. The open position of each investor is then 'marked to market' every day by paying into the account, or collecting from it, any losses or profits from that day's price movement. These daily payments or receipts are called 'variation margin'. Since the cash outlay on initial margin is only a small fraction of the value of the futures contract, price movements in the underlying asset have a magnified effect on this investment compared with a straight purchase of the underlying asset. This effect, called 'leverage' or 'gearing', increases the investor's exposure to price fluctuations.

Exchange traded futures have their origins in the markets for agricultural products, and existed in some form already in the seventeenth century in Amsterdam and in Osaka. The modern form of futures exchange, with a clearing house to settle contracts, is however a development of the American commodities exchanges of the nineteenth century, and the leading centres worldwide are still Chicago and New York. Financial, as opposed to commodity, futures were innovated in currencies by the Chicago Mercantile Exchange (CME) in 1972 and in bonds by the Chicago Board of Trade (CBOT) in 1976.

In many countries there is no legal recourse to defaults on gambling debts, and a futures contract may be considered to be a kind of gamble. Clearly, the development of futures markets in such countries has to wait until futures contracts are legally enforceable. The need to change the law has been an important source of delay in the establishment of futures exchanges in several countries. An example is the Deutsche Terminbörse (DTB) in Frankfurt.

To be successful, a futures contract must have a liquid market with low transactions costs associated with trading in the contract. One of the salient features about this process is a phenomenon that might be described as endogenous economies of scale: more business is attracted to contracts with low bid-ask spreads (i.e. high liquidity), and that attracts more market makers and more arbitrage and speculative activity on the exchange, and this increased competition drives down bid-ask spreads and so on in a virtuous circle. As a consequence, an exchange that establishes a highly liquid contract can drive away competitors and create a monopoly position for itself. Other exchanges have to rely on niches that are impervious to the competition from the low cost exchange – they compete by innovating such niches.[1]

One consequence of the process generating endogenous economies of scale is the virtual monopolisation of global markets, for example, futures contracts in currencies, eurodollars and US T-bonds[2]. These were innovated in the United States, where the innovating exchanges quickly built up a form of 'first mover advantage' via endogenous economies of scale, which gave them an impregnable position in the market for their respective instruments within a very short span of time. Thus the main business of futures exchanges outside the US, which were not the first movers into the global markets, is in contracts for local bonds and share indexes.

4.2.2 Options

An option is a contract that gives its holder the right, but not the obligation, to buy or sell a specific quantity of a specific quality of a specific asset at a specific price (the 'exercise price' or 'strike price') on or before a specific day (the settlement day). An option contract giving a right to buy is a 'call' option, while one that gives a right to sell is a 'put' option.

Traditional options are contracts written by stock exchange market makers entitling their clients to buy or sell quoted shares in some stock in the future at a price fixed at the time the option contract is purchased. Such tailor made option contracts should be distinguished from the traded options we consider here.

Another distinction is between so called European type options which can only be exercised on the settlement day, and American type options which can be exercised at any time up to and including the settlement day. Despite the terminology, some European type options are traded on US exchanges, and many American type options are traded on European exchanges. The European variety has the advantage of a simpler and better understood theory of pricing,[3] but it is a less flexible instrument.

An investor who holds a European call option in a stock thus has a guaranteed price at which he can buy the stock on the settlement day, if he so wishes. Compare this with the position of an investor who holds a forward contract in the same stock, which requires him to take delivery at the prearranged price on the settlement day. On the settlement day the value of the forward contract could be negative since it equals the current price of the stock minus the prearranged forward price. In contrast, the value of the option contract cannot be negative since it is only exercised if it has a positive value. It thus has a value on the settlement day which is either zero or the difference between the current price of the stock minus the option's exercise price, if that is positive.

The seller of an option contract, or option writer, has a set of possible returns which is the exact opposite of that of the buyer of the contract. In particular, the option writer's possible gain is restricted to the price at which he sells the option, the option premium, while his potential exposure to loss is unlimited so long as the contract remains open. He can however close out the position by simply buying an option of exactly the same description as the one he had previously sold.

Like futures contracts, options require cash guarantees in the form of margin, but unlike futures such margin arrangements differ from one exchange to another. On many exchanges, it is just the seller of the option who puts up initial margin, with the buyer simply paying the option premium at the outset. The system operating at LIFFE, called 'delta based margining', is more complex. It involves both buyer and seller putting up an initial margin based on the estimated sensitivity of the option price with respect to the price of the underlying asset (the option 'delta'), with subsequent marking to market on a daily basis via variation margin. The actual payment or receipt of the option premium is effected when the position is closed, at the rate prevailing at that time, with the difference between that and the option price at the outset having been made up by payments of variation margin. As with futures contracts, in most cases options are not actually exercised. Instead they are normally closed out by an offsetting sale or purchase beforehand.

The option premium fluctuates over time as a function of the price of the underlying asset, its volatility and the rate of interest. When the current spot price of the underlying asset exceeds the exercise price of a call option, the option is said to be 'in the money' (a corresponding put option would be 'out of the money'). The markets in options that are deeply in or out of the money tend to be rather thin, and such options are not actively traded. Most of the arbitrage and speculative activity on the floor of an options exchange tends to be in options that are 'at the money' – i.e. those whose exercise price is approximately the same as the current spot price of the underlying asset.

Options are more sophisticated than futures as instruments for hedging and speculation. Combinations of options allow investors to create a huge variety of contingent contracts: paper assets whose returns depend on the change in price of the underlying asset in very particular ways. However, to benefit from the range of choice in the trade-off between risk and return that options offer, rather more is required of somebody who invests in options than is required of an investor in futures. He must know not only about the risks he wishes to avoid, or to take, and the price at which he is prepared to transact, but also more about the characteristics of the underlying instrument such as its volatility and the degree to which its price is correlated with the risky prospect against which he seeks a hedge (or upon which he plans to speculate).

The recent proliferation of financial options contracts and options exchanges was led by the Chicago Board Options Exchange (CBOE), which was established in 1973 to create a market in share options. Two years later, the Philadelphia Stock Exchange (PHLX) also began to trade share options, and the next wave was in 1982 when CBoT introduced options on US T-bond futures and PHLX introduced options on dollar denominated currencies, followed smartly by the CME with options on its stock index future and on currency futures. Outside of America, the European Options Exchange (EOE) in Amsterdam and LTOM both introduced stock options in 1978, while options on bonds appeared on LIFFE in 1985. There has been less enthusiasm for options in the Far East where the Singapore International Monetary Exchange (SIMEX) introduced options on its CME-linked contracts in 1987.

As indicated above, it is possible to have an option on a future – indeed all of the options traded on LIFFE are of this variety. LIFFE followed the lead of the CME in this, but it is by no means a universal practice. Of course, in order to be able to establish an option contract on an underlying futures contract, the futures contract must have a prior existence. But, given this condition, such options then have the advantage of a transparent, and often highly liquid, market in the underlying which is traded on the same exchange. Why then, it may be asked, aren't such contracts more widespread? Partly, it seems, because of the inherent time delay in innovating such contracts. This produces a trade-off between the quality of the contract and the first mover advantage that accrues to the innovator of a derivative contract.

It is typical of options that if a particular contract does not exist in a ready made form for trading directly on an exchange, it can be manufactured from existing tradeable instruments. Thus the purchase of a put option is exactly equivalent to purchasing a call option at the same exercise price and simultaneously selling the underlying asset and investing a sum equal to the exercise price in a riskless bond.[4] Nevertheless, we often find that both put and call contracts are available on the same exchange. This illustrates the importance of providing investors with products that meet their requirements at low costs. However, the simultaneous availability of both calls and puts may have the effect of diminishing the depth of the market in both types of instruments, and thereby reducing their liquidity. As a consequence, the sequence of development of a contract on an options exchange is initially to offer just a call option on the underlying, and when that is established to supplement it with a put contract. Option contracts, however, tend to have thinner markets than futures contracts. This is partly due to the greater sophistication of the instruments, but it is also due to the variety of contracts brought about by the range of exercise prices, which adds an extra dimension to contract specification.

Just as with futures, an over-the-counter market in non-traded options exists in parallel, and synergistically, with the exchange traded products. Banks play an important role in providing such tailor made contracts to their customers. But intermediaries are often not required at all. The finance departments of many companies are able to create the financial options appropriate as hedging instruments to protect against adverse price movements in their trading commitments. For them, the attraction of standardised exchange traded options is mainly due to the low transaction cost, flexibility and ease of trading of this type of instrument.

4.3   London's futures and options exchanges

In London the exchanges trading financial derivative assets, namely LIFFE and LTOM, are distinct from those trading derivatives based on commodities. At the time of writing there is a plan to merge these two exchanges to create a single London financial derivatives market, and we consider its implications.

4.3.1   London International Financial Futures Exchange (LIFFE)

LIFFE was the first pure financial futures exchange to be established outside of North America. It started from scratch without the prior existence of an exchange of any kind and was modelled on the successful Chicago Mercantile Exchange, which had introduced financial futures to the world a decade earlier. It opened for business in September 1982 with three interest rate futures contracts (eurodollar, Long Gilt and Short Sterling) and four currency futures contracts. Subsequently in 1985, option contracts were introduced on the interest rate futures, and in 1986 new futures contracts were introduced in US T-bonds and in the FT–SE 100. By this time it was apparent that LIFFE had become a firmly established feature of London's financial markets.[5]

a) Contract innovation

LIFFE has pursued a policy of aggressive innovation of new derivative instruments and now has one of the most comprehensive product ranges of financial futures and options of any derivatives exchange in the world. This policy has been international in scope, as was presaged by LIFFE's early attempt to use its niche in the European time zone to create a market in US T-bond futures, for which the CBoT had established the world's most successful futures contract in the US time zone. However, the policy has not been unequivocally successful, and it is interesting to note which contracts have turned out to be successes and which failures.

The first notable failures were the currency futures – this despite the huge global demand to hedge currency risk and the fact that London has the most important cash and forward markets in currencies. LIFFE simply could not establish a sufficiently liquid market in its currency futures to compete with the global centres for this business, in Chicago (CME) and Philadelphia: LIFFE's European time zone advantage was not sufficient to offset the higher cost of trading in its less liquid markets. This experience might have caused LIFFE to evaluate more carefully what the value of its time zone advantage actually is. However, the time zone niche was also the basis for LIFFE's introduction of US T-bond futures in 1986 and Japanese bond futures in 1988. The latter was never able to attract sufficient business to create a liquid market, and the contract in effect became moribund and had to be relaunched in April 1991 with different contract specifications, trading and settlement procedures. For US T-bonds the situation looked a little more optimistic for a couple of years after the launch, but the volume of contracts traded has fallen steeply since 1988 although there has been no such decline in their home base on the CBoT, and despite the fact that LIFFE invested much effort in internationalising this contract – establishing a fungible link with the Sydney Futures Exchange (SFE) in 1986 to allow global trading in US T-bonds for 19 hours a day, and reaching an understanding with the CBoT for fungible contracts in the US T-bond and the UK Long Gilt. Both international links have so far come to nothing – the SFE link having been effectively abandoned for the time being, and the CBoT accord never having been implemented. We must conclude that the time zone niche has not delivered the benefits that were held out for it when LIFFE was established.

By contrast, LIFFE has introduced new contracts on European interest rates, the German Government Bond ('Bund') and the eurodeutschmark, which have become highly successful. This has been achieved despite direct competition for the German Government Bond contract from the recently created Deutsche Terminbörse (DTB) in Frankfurt, which has had considerable support from the German financial community. LIFFE scored here by exploiting the first-mover advantage achieved by introducing the contract two years ahead of the DTB. This lead time allowed LIFFE's contract to exploit the process generating endogenous economies of scale and become sufficiently liquid to attract substantial hedging demand in German long term interest rates. No doubt this success encouraged LIFFE to introduce other European products in 1991, including three month euro ECU and euro Swiss franc interest rate futures and an Italian Government Bond future. However, the competition was not asleep, and LIFFE was pipped to the post on Italian bond futures by the Paris MATIF exchange, more on which later.

b) Trading systems

The bulk of LIFFE's trade is conducted by 'open outcry' in pits, each of which is specific to a particular type of instrument which is traded in it only during the recognised hours laid down by the Exchange. A large electronic price board displays current in-house information in the Exchange, which is relayed to outside agencies. In order to deal with increased turnover, LIFFE introduced a computerised trade registration system for all its contracts in the late 1980s. This provides for the rapid matching, allocation and confirmation of all trades, and at the same time supports a range of client accounting systems.

Like other pit trading exchanges, LIFFE hosts a number of floor traders who are individual members of the exchange and who conduct business on their own account rather than on behalf of clients. These individuals, known as locals, are vital for the liquidity of the markets in the contracts traded in the pits. Their normal activity is a particular form of arbitrage, called 'scalping', in which they trade off the bid-ask spread: buying at the bid-price and selling at the ask-price. Of course they can only make a living in this way if they are faster than other dealers in the market. That is why their presence enhances liquidity. Locals on LIFFE may account for 20 to 25 per cent of turnover, considerably less than on the main US exchanges which tend to have more individual members than LIFFE. In November 1989 LIFFE commenced live operations with its Automated Pit Trading (APT) system which simulates the principles of open outcry trading on a screen after the Exchange floor has closed for trading until approximately 6 pm.

In April 1991 LIFFE launched a new version of the Japanese Government Bond

(JGB) futures contract which trades exclusively throughout the day (7 am to 3 pm London time) on the APT system. This contract enables international market participants to hedge their positions during the European trading day. Unlike other LIFFE futures contracts, all open positions at the end of a trading day are automatically closed out at the first subsequent opening price for the respective delivery month on the Tokyo Stock Exchange's JGB futures contract. In this manner the TSE's JGB future can in effect be traded on LIFFE without actually being fungible between the two exchanges. LIFFE believes the APT system will provide an efficient and cost effective market for this new contract. Members have direct access to the contract from their offices, which is particularly attractive to those with a limited presence on the trading floor but an active interest in the Japanese bond market.

c) Clearing, regulation and membership

LIFFE uses an independent clearing house to register, clear and guarantee (via margins) all trades whether generated in the pits or by the APT system. The London Clearing House (LCH) performs this role. It is a division of the International Commodities Clearing House Limited (ICCH) which is owned by six major UK clearing banks and provides clearing facilities to a number of UK and foreign exchanges. The banks which own the ICCH have provided an explicit guarantee of £150 million to cover the LCH's clearing activities. All LIFFE's clearing members of the LCH must satisfy strict standards as regards their ownership, management control and tangible net worth.

Both LIFFE and its members are regulated under the provisions of the Financial Services Act, 1986. LIFFE is authorised as a Recognised Investment Exchange by the Securities and Investments Board (SIB), the chief regulator of the UK financial services industry. To satisfy the requirements for authorisation, LIFFE must ensure that its rules and market practices are such that business is conducted in an orderly manner and affords proper protection to investors. Daily supervision is the responsibility of LIFFE's Board of Management. Its Market Supervision Department is charged with ensuring an orderly market for contracts at all times. This department monitors the financial position of Exchange members and requires them to report daily on their aggregate open positions in each contract. In addition, it is authorised to inspect members' accounting records. The LIFFE Board has the authority to raise margin requirements and to close out positions on all or specific contracts in the event of a market emergency.

The Securities and Futures Authority (SFA) which is the Self Regulating Organisation (SRO) for the securities and derivatives industries, takes on most of the responsibility for authorising which firms can carry out futures and options business in the UK. In particular it monitors each firm's conduct and capital adequacy.

LIFFE's membership is widely representative of the financial services industry. It includes banks, stock exchange firms, commodity brokers and discount houses, together with experienced individual traders, locals, who trade on their own account. Overseas firms make up a significant proportion of the membership. Financial deregulation, with its resultant mergers and reconstructions, has reduced LIFFE's membership to under 200 firms which between them own shares in the Exchange. Each share enables the holder to have one trader on the floor. Anticipating the merger, four classes of shares have been issued: A shares permit full futures contract trading; B shares permit restricted futures trading in specific contracts; C shares permit options trading; and D shares permit trading in equity (share) options. A secondary market exists for these shares, and they fluctuate in value according to demand, which is of course determined by the profitability of the trading on the Exchange. Exchange turnover and the commission income it generates are key factors in the determination of profitability and hence share prices.

d) Assessment

Table 4.1 provides information on trading volumes for the futures and options contracts listed on LIFFE between 1987 and 1990. In addition to these, the following contracts were introduced in 1991: a euro-Swiss franc interest rate future, an ECU bond future, a 'Eurotrack 100 Index' future, and an Italian Government Bond future. It is evident from this spate of new product launches that LIFFE sees an important European role for itself in the future.

We judge the success of a contract by the volume of trades conducted in it. This is correlated with both the profitability for members of the Exchange who trade in that instrument, and the liquidity of the instrument, which is the relevant criterion for the hedgers and speculators who are the exchange's ultimate customers.

Table 4.1 Trading history on LIFFE

Contract	Size	Volume traded ('000s)				
		1987	1988	1989	1990	1991
Interest rate						
Futures						
ECU (3 month)	ECU 1 million	..	..	16	64	115
Eurodollar (3 month)	$ 1 million	1739	1648	2064	1249	994
Eurodeutschmark	DM 1 million	..	..	952	2660	4784
German govt. bond	DM 250,000	..	315	5330	9582	10112
Gilt (UK govt. bond)	£50,000	7036	5631	4065	5643	5639
Sterling (3 month)	£500,000	1510	3538	7131	8354	8064
US T-bonds	$100,000	1571	2042	967	756	463
Options						
Eurodollar (3 month)	$ 1 million	40	77	82	65	31
Eurodeutschmark	DM 1 million	..	..	..	248	514
German govt. bond	DM 250,000	..	..	469	1804	2453
Gilt (UK govt. bond)	£50,000	1045	1141	727	790	844
Sterling (3 month)	£500,000	16	445	824	1377	1594
US T-bonds	$100,000	56	84	76	88	40
Stock Index						
Futures						
FT–SE 100	£25 × Index	470	465	1028	1444	1727
TOTAL		13500	15402	23741	34124	37374

Source: LIFFE
Note: .. = not trading

The very strong growth of 1989 and 1990 enabled LIFFE to regain from the MATIF its position as the busiest futures and options market in Europe. In 1987 the Long Gilt future accounted for more than half the trades on LIFFE but, while still trading strongly, it had been relegated to third place by 1990, having been outstripped by both the new German Government bond ('Bund') contract and the Short Sterling contract in importance. The three-month euro D-mark interest rate future, which was introduced in 1989 has been an important source of trading activity from its inception.

These developments can be explained by the factors affecting the underlying hedging demand for these products. Thus the Long Gilt suffered a mild setback in 1988 and 1989 as the public sector finances moved from deficit to surplus and the Treasury instituted a 'buy-back' programme for long-dated gilts. Partly due to this, the long end of the yield curve has been rather stable in the UK, and the need to hedge at this end of the term structure was diminished. However, turnover increased in 1990 due to UK entry into the European Exchange Rate Mechanism, which implied a shift in longer term inflationary expectations and *a fortiori* long rates of interest, combined with the fact that the public sector finances had moved back into deficit.

The German Bund contract was strong from the outset, probably due to the previously unsatisfied demand for derivatives based on German bonds, but this has been strengthened considerably by the reunification of Germany and the resulting uncertainty about long term yields on German paper. The volume of trading of this contract was hardly affected by the introduction of an identical contract on the DTB in November 1990. The screen traded DTB Bund contract achieved only one tenth the volume of trading of LIFFE's pit traded equivalent up to October 1991. Thereafter the DTB received 'official' support from the German banks which have re-routed Bund futures contract business through their own domestic exchange. This notwithstanding, LIFFE's Bund contract volumes have remained healthy at over 900,000 contracts per month and it remains LIFFE's most important contract.

At the short end of the term structure of interest rates are the three month Sterling and the three month euro D-Mark futures. Both have had a strong hedging and speculative demand due to the volatility of short interest rates, and they are connected by the fact that the authorities in the UK, as well as the market participants, keep a close eye on the differential between short rates in the two countries. As a consequence there is considerable scope for 'basis trading' on the interest rate differential by simultaneously adopting positions in both contracts.

LIFFE's other international products, based on US T-bonds and eurodollars, have been markedly less buoyant than its European products since 1988 and 1989 respectively. These contracts complement their Chicago equivalents in the European time zone, and the trends on LIFFE to a certain extent mimic those in Chicago. But in addition, the time zone advantage is, as has been noted earlier, less valuable than was originally thought. It is also vulnerable to an extension of trading hours in Chicago, either in the pits or from new electronic trading systems. It is certain that LIFFE could not match the CBoT's or the CME's liquidity in these contracts if it came to head on competition.

The FT-SE 100 index future is LIFFE's only foothold in UK equity derivatives. Its initial growth was interrupted by the subdued stock trading that followed the 1987 stock market crash, though it has since resumed to trade in reasonable volumes. Since February 1991 the contract has been traded on LIFFE's screen-based APT system after 4.32 pm, when share dealing on the International

Stock Exchange (ISE) stops. Thus, the APT system allows investors to react to market sensitive news released late in the afternoon and also to movements of New York share prices that might affect the direction of the following day's trading on the ISE. This contract may be strengthened by the fact that deregulation now permits the use of futures and options by pension funds and unit trusts, and also by recent changes in the tax regime as regards profits from derivative trading.

e) Innovation competition

The dynamic process generating endogenous economies of scale leads exchanges to compete by being first off the mark in a particular contract so as to achieve a sufficiently high level of trading, and consequently liquidity, and thereby low transactions costs for the traders in that contract. Once that has been achieved it is very difficult for a competitor to come from behind. We have compared this process to a gold rush[6] – it is an example of the more general phenomenon of 'first mover advantage' that can be found in the economics literature on innovation competition.

The need to steal a march on the competition when introducing new contracts is illustrated by the recent history of product innovation on LIFFE. The German Government Bond contract was the first example of really aggressive product innovation in Europe. LIFFE was aware of plans to set up the DTB, and moved quickly to pre-empt its business in German long interest rates. It then had the good fortune of lengthy bureaucratic delays in setting up the DTB in Frankfurt, which enabled LIFFE to establish a very liquid Bund contract market.

The lesson has not been lost elsewhere in Europe, where the competition to launch new products has become very intense. Thus, in February 1991 LIFFE launched a euroswiss franc interest rate contract, recognising the Swiss franc's important role as a eurocurrency and its non-ERM status. But SOFFEX (Swiss Options and Financial Futures Exchange) responded promptly by launching an identical contract in March 1991. The competition between LIFFE and SOFFEX for this business is not yet resolved. It will probably turn on the relative importance of being close to the cash market (SOFFEX) as against the synergistic presence of other contracts on the same exchange (LIFFE).

LIFFE launched an ECU bond contract in March 1991, in direct competition with a contract with slightly different specifications that the MATIF had launched in October 1990. LIFFE had the advantage of a pre-existing ECU interest rate contract so that the pair could provide a fuller coverage of the ECU interest yield curve. But this synergy was not sufficient to overcome the early liquidity advantage established by the MATIF. In late 1991 LIFFE revised its ECU bond contract specifications in an attempt to increase its liquidity and make it a viable product rather than delisting it. Both exchanges are looking ahead to increased used of ECU debt instruments as the single European financial space becomes a reality.

It was hardly a coincidence that the MATIF launched an Italian Government Bond future contract a few weeks ahead of LIFFE's similar product in September 1991. The attraction of this product for both exchanges is the hedging and speculative demand for a derivative product from holders of long term Italian national debt. The Italian national debt is the third largest in the world, but until recently the short maturity and floating rate nature of its debt has prevented the provision of a suitable futures contract.

On 26 June 1991 LIFFE launched a futures contract on the ISE's new Eurotrack-100 Index. This is a GNP-weighted index of 100 European stocks, excluding UK stocks. The contract is denominated in deutschemarks and is expected to be used by fund managers managing their mainland Europe portfolio exposures. A complementary option on this index was launched by LTOM in September 1991. However, these novel contracts face stiff competition from the Euro-Top 100 Index contracts, which include UK equities and were launched simultaneously on 6th June 1991 by EOE and SOFFEX and later by MATIF. These latter are denominated in ECUs, Swiss francs and French francs, respectively, but are otherwise equivalent.

4.3.2 London Traded Options Market (LTOM)

LTOM was established in 1978 as one of the component markets within London's International Stock Exchange (ISE). It provides a market for trading in two types of options – UK equity stock options and Index options. All ISE members are entitled to trade on LTOM, where they can undertake a variety of different functions ranging from broking through to market making and clearing.

The initial low volume of stock option deals gave rise to doubts as to whether demand existed in the UK for a traded options market. However, tax legislation changes and vigorous marketing overcame the investor hesitancy. An American style cash settled traded option contract on the FT–SE 100 Index was launched in May 1984, more than two years before LIFFE's complementary futures contract. In February 1990 a European style option was made available on the FT–SE 100 Index, and this has generated a fair degree of interest among the investing public. More recently in September 1991 LTOM launched a FT–SE 100 Eurotrack Index option contract which complements LIFFE's similar futures contract. The European style option is denominated in deutschemarks. It is the first joint product venture undertaken by the two exchanges in the lead up to merger.

Dealing in traded options is by open outcry on the once busy floor of the Stock Exchange. When a bargain has been struck the TOPIC ('Teletext Output of Price Information on Computer') price displays are altered to show the last trades made. No off-floor or out-of-hours dealings are permitted. All bargains are registered and settled at the London Options Clearing House (LOCH) a wholly owned ISE subsidiary. The amount of margin needed is calculated by reference to both the price of the underlying security or index and the exercise price of the traded option. A limited number of ISE member firms are registered market makers in options, which means that they are required to make a market in classes of ISE listed traded options.

The volume of contracts traded on LTOM reached a peak of 12 million in 1987, since when the annual volume has declined to 7 million. To boost business and enhance the market's appeal to retail investors LTOM introduced firm price quotations on screen for retail orders of up to ten contracts (10,000 shares) while at the same time providing volume as well as price information.

A major problem for LTOM is that it derives only 30 per cent of its turnover from retail investors unlike the average of 70 per cent achieved at other pure options exchanges such as the CBOE and the EOE. The retail business, which is essential for the maintenance of adequate market liquidity, declined after the 1987 stock market crash. The lack of such participants has been aggravated over the years by high commission costs and clearing fees. The decline in overall volume encouraged the proposed merger with LIFFE. Daily turnover in options has been regularly less than the 30,000 contracts per day which it is estimated the LTOM needs to cover its costs. Some large securities firms have withdrawn from options market making due to inadequate returns thereby reducing market liquidity further, leading to less competitive quotes and irregular updating of prices.

This is all in marked contrast to the DTB and SOFFEX, both of which operate screen based trading systems. The merger with LIFFE, and the use of a single trading floor, must result in the LTOM contemplating its own Big Bang (i.e. switching to screen trading, just as its ISE parent did in October 1986). Despite some resistance from independent options traders, only the index contracts are likely to be traded via open outcry on the new trading floor. Unless volumes pick up, stock options are destined for screen based trading as a means of cutting costs, improving market transparency and boosting overall liquidity.

4.3.3   London International Financial Futures and Options Exchange

In July 1990, after behind the scenes prodding from the Bank of England, LIFFE and LTOM agreed to merge into one financial derivatives market. A similar proposal failed in 1987 due to vested interests in both exchanges. Three years later competitive pressures from abroad overrode their concerns. By the end of 1991, all outstanding issues between the two exchanges as regards rights, clearing arrangements and operational aspects were resolved, thus making it possible to finalise the new exchange's rulebook and receive SIB/OFT approval to commence business. The government also helped to resolve outstanding tax problems by announcing that members of the new exchange would have stock lending relief and exemptions from stamp duty and stamp duty reserve tax. On 23 March 1992 the new merged market became operational under a single administration and membership with unified exchange systems and clearing arrangements.

The new market, which preserves the LIFFE acronym, will be the most comprehensive financial futures and options exchange outside the USA. The operation and development of the equity derivatives market is no longer split between two exchanges, and unit operating costs may be further reduced, as enhanced economies of scope come into play. The move of equity options trading onto the LIFFE trading floor in the new premises at Cannon Bridge should generate trading synergy within an environment which accommodates substantial potential for growth.

4.4   London's overseas competition

4.4.1   United States

Overseas competition for London's financial derivatives exchanges comes from the United States and Europe. Some of LIFFE's products were designed to be complementary with existing and successfully established instruments in the United States: in particular currency futures and options, and interest rate derivatives based on US T-bonds and eurodollars. The thinking behind this was to use London's time difference to enable trading in these instruments while the Chicago and Philadelphia exchanges were closed, the aim being to offer complementary products rather than direct competition. As it turned out, the time zone advantage was insufficient to compensate traders for the higher cost of doing business in LIFFE's less liquid markets, so the bulk of the global business has thus remained in the USA. The upshot is that London currency derivatives have completely disappeared, currency futures are now a monopoly of the CME while currency options are split between the CME and Philadelphia. Meanwhile, LIFFE still trades derivatives in US T-bonds and eurodollars, but these account for less than 5 per cent of the exchange's total business.

London is therefore not competing directly with US exchanges. However, the situation could change if the latter introduce electronic trading systems which would enable them to do business 24 hours a day. Such technology once in place may signal a new era of competition: for example, it might allow the Chicago exchanges to try to wrest some of the specifically European interest rate and index derivatives away from the Europeans.

Within the United States the exchanges sometimes complain of over regulation by Federal agencies and excessive tax burdens. This combined with the common threat of over-the-counter futures and options, i.e. off-exchange activity, has encouraged cooperation between exchanges. The CBoT and CME, once deadly rivals, are now cooperating over the development of a screen based electronic global trading system called Globex. Officials from all US exchanges have thwarted further derivatives industry regulation which might have entailed higher costs and lost business to overseas exchanges. This cooperation has also served to strengthen the sole regulatory powers of the Commodity Futures Trading Commission (CFTC), and has reinforced the opposition to a transaction tax proposal on futures transactions.

We now profile the main Chicago exchanges as potential future competitors for London's, and Europe's, derivatives business.

a) Chicago Board of Trade (CBoT)

The CBoT is the world's largest physical and financial commodities derivative exchange. In 1975 it launched the world's first interest rate futures contract on Government National Mortgage Association (GNMA) mortgage backed certificates. For the first time cash market traders could hedge interest rate sensitive investments with a near comparable futures equivalent. In 1977 the US T-bond futures contract was launched; it is now the world's most successful futures contract. Another CBoT innovation was options on futures contracts, which were initiated in 1982 with options on the US T-bond futures contracts. Since then the CBoT has launched various bond and stock index futures contracts though many have been delisted due to insufficient trading volumes. It is worth noting that only one in twenty new products introduced by US exchanges have been successful. By 1981 financial futures accounted for one third of total CBoT turnover, while in 1990 the 120 million financial futures contracts traded were over three quarters of total CBoT business.

Trading is carried out in pits. No futures trading is permitted outside the official time. Throughout the trading session completed trades are cleared through the CBoT Clearing Corporation which as a separate legal entity provides a counterparty guarantee for all trades. US regulation of the futures industry is carried out by the

CFTC which sanctions new contracts or changes in trading practices. The CBoT Directors are responsible for all aspects of the Exchange's activity. CBoT members with access to all or some of the listed contract markets include banks, securities firms, producers and independent traders, or locals, whom the CBoT recognises as playing a particularly important role in maintaining the liquidity of its various contract markets. Membership is sold through a bid-ask system when a seat becomes available for sale.

The CBoT has internationalised its futures contracts and lengthened its trading day. In April 1987 it introduced evening trading sessions in US T-bond contracts to enable Japanese investors to hedge their cash market positions before Tokyo opened for business. This strategy was an alternative to trading fungible contracts.

Table 4.2 Recent trading history on the CBoT, main contracts

Contract	Size	Volume traded ('000s)				
		1987	1988	1989	1990	1991
Interest rate						
Futures						
Municipal Bond Index	$1,000 × Index	1,613	1,274	1,068	697	549
US T-Bonds	$100,000	66,841	70,308	70,303	75,499	67,887
US T-Notes	$100,000	5,254	5,708	7,891	8,698	10,013
Options						
US T-Bonds	$100,000	21,720	19,509	20,784	27,315	21,928
US T-Notes	$100,000	1,422	1,012	1,168	1,024	1,020
Stock Index						
Futures						
Major market Index	$250 × Index	470	465	1,028	951	703
TOTAL		97,320	98,276	102,242	114,184	102,100

Sources: IMF: International Capital Markets: Developments and Prospects, May 1991; Chicago Board of Trade.

Table 4.2 provides an indication of the main contracts traded and their volumes on the CBoT. Though the CBoT achieved a record volume of contracts traded in 1990, it is heavily dependent on derivatives based on the US T-bond which accounted for over two thirds of total turnover. This situation has encouraged the CBoT to seek working arrangements with other exchanges and launch new contracts.

Since 1988 it has had a working arrangement with the Tokyo Stock Exchange (TSE) which allows the TSE's Topix stock index and Japanese Government Bond futures contracts to be traded on the CBoT. So far both have traded in low volumes. Despite this setback to the diversification of its product range, the CBoT has received CFTC permission to trade German Government Bond futures and options contracts, and contracts on other foreign cash instruments are planned for the future.

b) Chicago Mercantile Exchange (CME)

The CME is the world's second largest and most diversified financial futures exchange. It trades over 30 futures and options on physical and financial commodities. Its financial derivative contracts are distributed between two divisions: the International Money Market (IMM) trades currency and interest rate futures; and the Index and Option Market (IOM) trades stock index futures and options on a variety of futures contracts.

The IMM commenced business in 1972 when it listed seven foreign currency futures contracts. These were the first exchange traded financial derivatives. In 1981 the IMM introduced a eurodollar interest rate futures contract, its most successful contract to date. In November 1991 the CME's eurodollar futures contract was the first one to exceed the one million contracts open interest, i.e. number of contracts outstanding. This had a dollar value of $1,000 billion, roughly one fifth of US GNP. As the first US cash-settled contract its success enabled the US futures industry to introduce a new array of cash settlement stock index futures contracts. In April 1982 the IOM commenced trading in the S&P 500 stock index futures contract, with an associated option contract in 1983. Foreign currency option contracts were introduced in 1984.

With approximately one third of the CME's business generated by non-US residents, the exchange was quick to recognise the international scope of the futures market. It established the first international trading link with the Singapore International Monetary Exchange (SIMEX) in 1984. This mutual offset system involving identical contracts was a major step toward a 24 hour trading day in derivative instruments. The CME and SIMEX also obtained the exclusive licence to trade Nikkei stock index futures contracts outside Japan, but while this has been fairly successful on SIMEX, it has been less so in Chicago (881,000 contracts on SIMEX as against 61000 on the CME in 1990).

The CME has extended its currency product range by launching six currency cross-rate futures such as DM/£ and ¥/DM. The cost of taking a position in such cross rates will be reduced if the contracts can achieve the necessary volume and liquidity.

CME trading is by open outcry and all trades are cleared and guaranteed by the CME clearing house. Exchange membership, seat acquisition and regulation are similar to the CBoT.

Table 4.3 provides an indication of the main CME contracts traded and their volumes.

c) Chicago Board Options Exchange (CBOE)

In April 1973 the CBoT established the CBOE for the sole purpose of trading options on a limited number of New York Stock Exchange (NYSE) listed equities. Now totally independent of the CBoT, the CBOE is the world's largest options exchange. With options now available on over 160 NYSE-listed stocks, the CBOE accounts for almost 45 per cent of all US share options trading.

In 1983 the CBOE introduced two index options: the S&P 100 and 500. The former is an American option, and the latter a European option. Both are cash settled contracts. Options on various component indices, e.g. telecommunications, oil, etc., have been introduced but the lack of activity has resulted in some being delisted.

CBOE index options are traded in the same manner as traded equity stock options via market makers and floor brokers. Options are issued and guaranteed by the Options Clearing Corporation.

Table 4.3 Recent trading history on the CME, main contracts

Contract	Size	Volume traded ('000s)				
		1987	1988	1989	1990	1991
Interest rate						
Futures						
Eurodollar (3 month)	$1 million	20,416	21,705	40,818	34,696	37,244
Options						
Eurodollar (3 month)	$1 million	2,570	2,600	6,002	6,860	7,875
Currency						
Futures						
Deutschmark	DM 125,000	6,037	5,662	8,186	9,169	10,929
Japanese yen	¥12.5 million	5,359	6,433	7,824	7,437	6,017
Pound sterling	£ 62,500	2,592	2,616	2,518	3,410	3,746
Swiss franc	SwF 125,000	5,268	5,283	6,094	6,525	5,836
TOTAL		19,256	19,994	24,622	26,541	26,528
Options						
Deutschmark	DM 125,000	3,126	2,734	3,795	3,430	5,643
Japanese yen	¥12.5 million	2,251	2,945	3,127	3,116	2,397
Pound sterling	£ 62,500	569	543	406	501	651
Swiss franc	SwF 125,000	1,053	1,070	1,489	1,130	998
TOTAL		6,999	7,292	8,818	8,177	9,689
Stock Index						
Futures						
S&P 500 Index	$500 × Index	19,045	11,354	10,560	12,139	12,340
TOTAL		68,286	62,945	90,820	88,413	93,676

Sources: IMF: International Capital Markets: Developments and Prospects, May 1991; Futures Industry Association Inc., Washington, D.C.

4.4.2 Europe

The most intense competition that the London derivative exchanges face is from the other 23 European exchanges. Recently this competition has intensified as all the main exchanges introduced new products, often competing head on with London's new contracts.

The competition between exchanges sometimes reflects official support for the 'national champion'. A classic example is the tussle between the LIFFE and the MATIF for the ECU interest rate derivative market. The apparent failure of LIFFE's ECU bond contract brought about a review of the product's specifications to make it more attractive to hedgers, speculators and arbitrageurs. The MATIF secured a higher contract volume and more liquid market in the initial phase of this competition, but it is not clear whether this was due to more appropriate contract terms, or a larger underlying cash market, or whether it was due to a commitment by French banks to support their own derivatives market, perhaps with official support. By contrast, LIFFE has not received comparable backing, either moral or financial, from UK banks or the UK government.

LIFFE is also involved in a tussle with the electronic DTB in Germany which is seeking to divert DM contract volumes from London to Frankfurt. SOFFEX has also entered the fray by launching a euro-Swiss franc interest rate contract in competition with LIFFE's equivalent product. And with the expectation of a single European capital market, LIFFE and LTOM have launched futures and options contracts on the FT–SE 100 Eurotrack Index as a direct challenge to the Euro-Top 100 Index contracts launched by EOE, SOFFEX and MATIF. The main point of contrast relates in these contracts to the composition of the underlying indices used. The Eurotrack index excludes UK equities which can be hedged with London's established FT-SE 100 index contracts.

Competition also exists between European exchanges on what is the most appropriate trading technique. Longer established exchanges such as LIFFE and MATIF use the traditional outcry method in a pit for most deals whilst more recent exchanges such as DTB and SOFFEX use electronic trading. Electronic trading has a number of distinct advantages: the screen price is the one at which the transaction is concluded; a large number of banks, customers and market makers have direct access to the trading system irrespective of their location; and all transactions are confirmed immediately with positions being automatically recorded. This notwithstanding, it is doubtful that pit culture is on the brink of extinction. Electronic exchanges can experience a complete collapse, sometimes for several days, which necessitates a return to open outcry trading or the creation of a telephone market. Furthermore, it appears that electronic exchanges have wider bid-ask spreads, which might be a reflection of inadequate liquidity due to the lack of locals (although there seems to be no inherent reason why individuals trading on their own account could not use an electronic system so long as it enables the scalping and other arbitrage trading practices typically carried out by locals).

On LIFFE's APT system a high speed communications network links APT trader workstations in LIFFE members' dealing rooms to a central processing system based at the Exchange. As its name implies, the distinctive feature of this automated trading system is that it emulates physical pit trading on the screen; other electronic screen systems are order matching systems only. So far the APT system has proved to be a highly effective way of extending trading hours until approximately 6pm, which enables LIFFE to increase its overlap with the North American time zone. The APT has recorded an average turnover of 5,000 contracts per day, roughly 4 per cent of daily volume. It had a peak of over 31,000 contracts on 5 October 1990 when sterling joined the ERM, the announcement of which had been delayed until the main London cash markets closed. As traders attempted to hedge their positions that evening, the Short Sterling contract traded nearly 40 per cent of its daily turnover, and the Long Gilt futures contract 20 per cent, in just one hour on the APT system. This was an important demonstration of its ability to cope with high volumes.

At the end of the day success will go to the system and the exchanges which are able to deliver the lowest costs to traders. That is, those able to win the battle for contract liquidity.

At present twenty-three futures and options exchanges exist in Europe trading about 250 different contracts in either physical and/or financial derivatives. The European exchanges have witnessed a rise in trading volumes from one million contracts in 1980 to about 120 million contracts in 1990. The real danger for European derivative exchanges in the 1990s is, perhaps, not the perennially threatened Globex electronic trading system from Chicago, nor the Japanese, but the existence of too many similar products with inadequate levels of liquidity. Each new financial futures exchange initially concentrates on local cash market instruments as a basis for its product range. But they have realised that there may be no safe national niches in the looming common European capital market, so each sooner rather than later tries to enhance turnover by introducing euro or international contracts. This has been the strategy of LIFFE, MATIF, EOE and SOFFEX.

This glut of contracts can also be partly explained by the actions of some banks supporting their national exchanges, and by some governments' policies through their tax legislation and regulation actions which are aimed at establishing a presence in what is thought to be an essential requirement for each country's financial centre. Nationalistic sentiment may for a while distort commercial viability. It may even have a permanent effect due to the dynamic process generating economies of scale. Intervention of this kind has occurred in most countries. The danger is that in the ensuing artificial competition it may not be possible to establish some markets at all, and traders would then be forced to use less efficient over-the-counter markets, which are conceivably harder to regulate and thus more prone to fraud.

However, not all interactions between exchanges are rivalrous. Where externalities and jointness are perceived, exchanges have begun to cooperate. In the UK a Joint Exchanges Committee (JEC) was established in 1982 by London's futures and options exchanges. It discusses matters of mutual concern and puts forward an industry view in discussions with the SIB, the SFA etc. It has issued papers on relevant EC Directives. The lobbying of MPs and Euro MPs is also undertaken to influence legislation and regulation affecting the UK derivatives industry.

Pan-European cooperation is also evident. In October 1988 the European Community Options and Futures Exchanges (ECOFEX) was established to act on behalf of EC derivative markets. ECOFEX's prime role is the presentation of a coordinated view on regulatory matters affecting the futures and options industry. It has held extensive meetings with EC officials on proposed Investment Services and Capital Adequacy Directives. A commonality of interest ensures such cooperation takes place: the creation of a single financial space must create an environment which engenders the growth and development of derivative market activities. ECOFEX has shown particular concern about proposed minimum levels of capital for market members. If set too high these could damage the competitiveness of European exchanges by threatening the position of locals who are vital for liquidity on each exchange.

A long term aim of ECOFEX is to unify market trading, order routing and clearing systems within Europe. This would enable each exchange to trade its own local products, with international or pan-European contracts being traded perhaps on screens within the EC. Such a development would avoid the unnecessary replication of contracts, but to implement it requires the necessary political will to exist in Europe. It might be that the intensity of competition at present is partly an attempt by individual exchanges to improve their bargaining positions prior to the creation of a quasi-unified European futures and options market.

We now briefly examine the four main European rivals to the London derivative exchanges: the MATIF, the EOE, the SOFFEX and the DTB.

a) Paris: Marché à Terme International de France (MATIF)

French financial markets have benefited from deregulation in the 1980s, and the last few years have witnessed an acceleration in financial innovation in France. This has been encouraged by developments in the international financial markets and by French aspirations to establish Paris as mainland Europe's prime financial centre. At the same time, an enlarged domestic bond market with monetary policy implemented through interest rate changes rather than quantitative credit controls has encouraged cash market investors to use financial futures and options to manage their interest rate risks.

The circumstances were therefore propitious for the MATIF's establishment in 1986. It commenced trading with a Notional Government Bond contract in 1986. Traded options on this contract followed in 1988. Thereafter a French stock index ('CAC 40') future, a short interest rate ('PIBOR') future and option and a eurodeutschmark future and option have been introduced onto the MATIF's trading floor.

MATIF trading takes place in a pit. All trades are channelled through clearing house members and are guaranteed by the clearing house, the MATIFSA. Any individual or corporation, French or foreign, may deal in financial and physical derivative contracts on the MATIF. The MATIFSA is owned by stockbrokers, banks and insurance companies. It is also charged with a regulatory function in cooperation with the principal regulatory body, the Conseil du Marché à Terme (CMT). The CMT regulates the MATIF, ensures its proper functioning, approves new contracts or the deletion of existing ones, and lays down the conditions that clearing house members must meet.

To become a clearing house member a MATIF applicant must be in stockbroking, banking, money brokerage, or portfolio management. At present non-French institutions make up nearly one third of the MATIF's membership. Each clearing house member deals on the MATIF's floor for its clients and also on its own account. In January 1989 locals or 'Nips',[7] as they are called, were introduced onto the exchange in order to enhance the overall liquidity of the various derivative product markets. New seats are made available on the MATIF as required but unlike on the US exchanges, there is no market for seats.

Table 4.4 provides an indication of turnover growth on the MATIF.

Table 4.4 Recent trading history on MATIF, main contracts

Contract	Size	Volume traded ('000s)				
		1987	1988	1989	1990	1991
Interest rate						
Futures						
French Govt Bond	FF 500,000	11,911	12,357	15,004	15,996	21,088
Options						
French Govt Bond	FF 500,000	..	3,431	7,150	7,410	8,412
PIBOR 3 month	FF 5million	..	..	..	710	1,374
Stock Index						
Futures						
CAC 40	FF 200 × index	..	64	581	1,642	2,311
TOTAL		12,018	16,321	25,730	28,246	36,902

Source: MATIF

The Government Bond futures and options contracts account for the bulk of trading on the MATIF. But their success may also be due to the fact that MATIFSA appointed five designated market makers to ensure sufficient liquidity and tight spreads in the option contract. They must maintain a permanent presence in the pit at all times, provide continuous bid-ask quotes on the strike prices traded and be committed to buy or sell on request up to 20 contracts based upon current displayed prices.[8] Out-of-hours trading is permitted by the clearing house and can account for up to a third of on-exchange trading. These trades are recorded the following day. All these factors have made the Government Bond's futures and option contracts the most heavily traded in Europe.

The MATIF's other French products, namely the Paris Interbank Offer Rate (PIBOR) contracts and the CAC 40 index future,[9] trade at adequate volumes, though by no means as vigorously as the Government Bond derivatives. The index future is complemented by traded CAC 40 Index options on the Paris Bourse which also trades stock options on over 25 companies' shares.

The MATIF's eurodeutschmark future trades at much lower volume, and is presumably less liquid, than LIFFE's equivalent product, even though the latter is not yet supported by an option. Nevertheless, the MATIF sees its niche in the development of more European contracts, such as the Euro-Top Index and the Italian Government Bond futures, where again it will be vying with LIFFE for liquidity.

b) Amsterdam: European Options Exchange (EOE)

The EOE, which is modelled on the CBOE, began trading stock options in 1978 and interest rate options in 1981. It is one of the largest option exchanges outside the USA. Nearly two thirds of the EOE's clients are private investors who account for about half of the trading volume. The EOE responds flexibly to investors' needs, with new options being introduced to replace those with insufficient open interest.

At present the EOE trades options on approximately 30 Dutch stocks, Dutch Government Bonds, Dutch florins (guilders), various stock indices and gold. Trading is by open outcry on the exchange floor. Domestic trades are cleared by the European Stock Options Clearing Corporation (ESCC), a wholly owned EOE subsidiary, which guarantees contract obligations and holds margins. Seats on the exchange, which carry varying rights, are owned by companies and individuals registered as EOE members.

In August 1987 the EOE launched its most successful contract: an American style option on the Major Market Index (MMI) of US blue chip stocks. Fungible trading in the option is linked to a similar contract on the American Stock Exchange in New York, where the MMI is the second most actively traded index option in the US after the CBOE's S&P 100 index option. The MMI was the first US index option to be traded outside the US, and is specifically designed to enable European investors to deal in US stocks before Wall Street opens. Trading in this fungible option contract takes place for ten hours each day, with a one hour overlap between Amsterdam and New York. The contracts are priced in US dollars and clearing is handled by the Options Clearing Corporation in Chicago.

A US$/DFL option is listed but volumes are disappointing, as might be expected with the Netherlands in the Exchange Rate Mechanism and liquid D-mark contracts available in Chicago and Philadelphia.

The overall trading volume on the EOE, which is mainly in stock options, has fluctuated around a plateau in recent years, and in 1990 was about one third that on LIFFE.

c) Swiss Options and Financial Futures Exchange (SOFFEX)

SOFFEX opened for business in May 1988 as Europe's first fully computerised (automated trading/clearing system) exchange. It was established by the Basle, Geneva and Zurich stock exchanges together with five major Swiss banks to trade options on eleven Swiss stocks. SOFFEX also launched an options contract on the Swiss Market Index (SMI) in 1988 which has proved to be highly successful and accounts for over half of the exchange's annual turnover. An SMI index futures contract was introduced in November 1990, and is trading healthily.

In 1990 SOFFEX traded over 9 million contracts, of which SMI options were 4.7 million. Thus after just two years' trading SOFFEX's turnover exceeded that of LTOM. A euro-Swiss franc interest rate futures contract, competing directly with LIFFE's equivalent contract, was launched in March 1991. So far its trading volumes and liquidity have been lower than LIFFE's. No long interest rate future or option contract exists at present due to the lack of liquidity in the underlying cash bond market. The short interest rate contract was followed up by the launch of a Euro-Top Index futures contract denominated in Swiss francs in June 1991.

d) Frankfurt am Main: Deutsche Terminbörse (DTB)

The DTB became operational on 26 January 1990 with traded options on fourteen German stocks. It is a fully computerised exchange which enables dealers to conduct their business via display screens linked to a central computer rather than by open outcry on a trading floor. Market entry is thus possible from any location in Germany. The DTB adapted the SOFFEX's computer software to suit its own needs. This computerised derivatives market guarantees a high level of market transparency and a rapid handling of clients' transactions. An electronic trading system was adopted for two reasons. Firstly, the absence of any kind of derivative exchange in Germany meant that it lacked the financial culture to guarantee the successful operation of a one centre open outcry market. Such a market might have lacked adequate liquidity for success. Secondly, the DTB system was born out of the political necessity to involve the small regional stock exchanges in Germany.

The DTB is operated by a private company, DTBGmbH which is owned by seventeen major German banks, with the board of directors consisting of seven selected bank representatives. In 1990 the exchange had 59 members, including 13 foreign banks. The DTB acts as a counterparty to all trades on the exchange. Most of the DTB's terminals are located in Germany, as the banks have discouraged the use of trans-frontier terminals for fear of losing broking business to non-German firms.

In November 1990 the DTB listed a Bund interest rate future and a DAX index future. The Bund future is in direct competition with LIFFE's identical contract. This situation has not arisen by chance; it represents a desire of the German financial community to see Frankfurt established as the centre for trading DM derivative products.

Despite such 'official' backing and aspirations, the DTB's Bund contract only averaged 2,500 contracts per day, about one-tenth of LIFFE's turnover, in its first few weeks of trading. To boost this low volume of activity the German banks who

107

invested over DM 10 million in the exchange announced their intention to give the DTB preference in Bund derivative trading in 1991. In August 1991 an option contract was launched on the Bund future. By mid-November 1991 Bund futures contract volumes on the DTB were matching those at LIFFE. However, some market participants suggested that volume had been boosted by cross-trading, that is, the to-and-fro trading of contracts between market makers to create volume artificially. Open interest on LIFFE, perhaps a truer indicator of contract success in such circumstances, considerably exceeds that of the DTB.

Meanwhile the DAX 30 index contract, which faces no competition from a similar product on other exchanges, developed steadily after its launch. Stock options business has also expanded rapidly during 1990 and 1991, with regular monthly volumes exceeding those achieved on the LTOM and the EOE.

The DTB's total contract volume in 1990 was approximately 6.7 million. However, over three quarters of this business was initiated by market makers and banks rather than on behalf of clients. The DTB needs to educate German investors in the benefits of futures and options trading.

As regards international linkages, the DTB is not seeking to become a partner in the Globex system. Instead, its officials believe that the unification of Europe's financial markets after 1992 puts electronic link-ups between European derivative markets higher up the agenda.

4.4.3   Global electronic trading

If the main US exchanges put their 24 hour trading system in place, they might consider launching products in direct competition with the European exchanges. It is therefore worth considering the potential of global electronic trading.

In September 1987 the CME announced an agreement with Reuters to introduce a global electronic transaction system for trading futures and options before and after regular US business trading hours. The Globex system, as it became known, is to complement rather than replace the open outcry system.

The CME hopes to entice more foreign users to its product range and thus enable it to globalise its contract markets without the need for linkages or extending pit trading hours. In August 1988 the CME and Reuters agreed to open up Globex to other exchanges, MATIF, etc. This did not imply an end to the CME's fungible link with SIMEX, but it did signal the realisation that regulatory complications made it unlikely that the mutual offset system could be extended around the globe. In 1989 the CME suspended negotiations with other exchanges and began discussions with its local rival, the CBoT, about the latter abandoning its own automated exchange proposal (Aurora) and adopting a modified Globex system. Despite CBoT/CME cooperation thereafter, several launch dates for the new electronic global trading system have been missed and as a result other exchanges have lost interest in the concept or decided to develop their own in-house electronic system.

Many industry experts have severe reservations about the Globex system. Firstly, it is an order matching system and thus tends to have a slower response rate than, say, LIFFE's APT system. Secondly, the transaction fees will need to be quite high if the investment made by Reuters and the CBoT/CME of between 40 and 50 million dollars is to yield a positive return. Thirdly, Globex must be accepted by non-US futures industry regulators in order to be successful, and Japanese involvement will be a key factor in the system's success. Perhaps ominously, the Japanese have been absent from all discussions. Any lengthy dispute with the

Japanese regulatory authorities could undermine the entire *raison d'être* for developing the system. Fourthly, the CME's independent traders (locals) who make up nearly three quarters of the membership feel threatened by this new technology. They fear an end to the open outcry system and a lack of arbitrage opportunities on the new system. Only when Globex becomes operational will it be seen whether an open outcry system can be successfully linked to global screen trading.

4.4.4   Assessment

The main threat to London's share of global futures and options business is likely to come from existing exchanges on mainland Europe. The world's other main exchanges are outside the European time zone. Only a truly successful 24-hour electronic trading system, like Globex, could compete directly for the European derivative markets. In the first instance this would threaten the eurodollar and US T-bond contracts. However, these contracts are not essential for the survival of European exchanges.

Within the European time zone we expect competition to intensify with the creation of a single EC capital market and the possible advent of a single currency, the ECU. The main exchanges are already competing to establish their stake in pan-European futures and options contracts such as the ECU bond and the euro-index contracts. After a first phase of innovation competition to establish liquid niches in interest rate and share index markets, there is likely to be a phase of consolidation and rationalisation. The winners will be those that establish the most liquid markets with the lowest transaction costs, but at present the crystal ball is clouded by the coexistence of very different trading systems across Europe. The merged LIFFE will, however, start from a strong position with established products and an apparently successful toehold in new electronic trading. When the regulatory playing field is levelled after 1992, the mist should clear somewhat and the pattern of derivative trading for the rest of the decade may begin to emerge.

Notes

1   For more analysis of the organisation of futures markets and the processes of competition within them and between them, see Anderson (1984) and Dale *et al.* (1987).

2   A eurodollar is a US dollar held in a bank account outside the United States. A US T-bond, that is 'Treasury bond', is a unit of long term debt of the US government – compare US T-bill, which is a unit of short term debt of the US government.

3   The theory of option pricing, including the well known Black-Scholes formula, is well set out in Cox and Rubinstein (1985).

4   This protects the holder of the asset against the risk of a fall in its price while allowing him to realise a gain from a rise in its price. See Brealey and Myers (1988, Chapter 20) for more details.

5   For details on the development of interest rate futures and currency options see Bank of England (1989a and 1989b).

6   See Dale *et al.* (1987) for development of this idea and several examples.

7   Négociateurs individuels de parquet.

8   Similar arrangements exist for up to 50 PIBOR option contracts and 30 ECU Bond futures contracts.
9   CAC 40 is a capitalisation weighted index composed of France's most liquid blue chip stocks. CAC 40 Index options are traded on the Marché des Options Négociables Paris (MONEP) which is a division of the Bourse.

Bibliography

Anderson, R.W. (editor) (1984) *The Industrial Organization of Futures Markets.* D.C. Heath & Co.

Bank of England (1989a) The market in currency options, *Bank of England Quarterly Bulletin,* **29**, 235–42.

Bank of England (1989b) A survey of interest rate futures, *Bank of England Quarterly Bulletin,* **29**, 388–98.

Brealey, R.A. and **Myers, S.C.** (1988) *Principles of Corporate Finance,* 3rd edn, McGraw-Hill.

Chicago Board of Trade, *CBOT Financial Instruments Guide,* CBoT.

Chicago Mercantile Exchange, *The Merc at Work,* CME.

Cox, J. and **Rubinstein, M.,** (1985) *Options Markets,* Prentice Hall.

Dale, R.S., Leslie, J. and **Wyatt, G.** (1987) *Futures and Options: Winners and Losers.* Financial Times Business Information Ltd.

Deutsche Terminbörse, *Annual Reports,* DTB.

European Options Exchange, *Annual Reports,* EOE.

London International Financial Futures Exchange, *Annual Reports,* LIFFE.

Marché à Terme International de France, *Meet the MATIF,* MATIF.

Swiss Options and Futures Exchange, *Annual Reports,* SOFFEX.

5   The eurobond market[1]

by Phil Davis

The eurobond[2] market is a key component both of the international capital markets *per se* and of the financial activity of the City of London. The market has grown rapidly since its inception, to a size comparable to or in excess of domestic currency markets. (Total outstanding eurobonds at end-1990 were valued at $1142 bn). This chapter seeks to offer a broad description of the eurobond market; an economic analysis of its behaviour, microstructure and reasons for location in London; and an assessment of certain key issues relating to prospects for the eurobond market and its location in London.

5.1   An overview of the eurobond market

5.1.1   Origins

The origins of the euromarkets lie in the late 1950s and early 1960s. Although geopolitical factors (desire of East Europeans to hold dollars outside the US) and the US current account deficit (which led to an accumulation of dollar holdings in Europe) played a role, the development of the euromarkets is largely explicable in terms of various fiscal and prudential regulations applied to domestic financial markets.

Thus, in combination with the above factors, the imposition of maximum rates of interest on US based deposits (Regulation Q), as well as the US withholding taxes, led to the development of the offshore eurocurrency deposit market in London in the late 1950s and early 1960s. Depositors in the eurocurrency markets sought to diversify into dollar bonds, the main source of which was the New York based 'yankee' foreign bond market. But this was expensive for borrowers in terms of commissions (partly because bonds had to be lead managed by US firms, who formed a cartel), and suffered from listing, rating, registration and disclosure requirements. In addition, since US banks had limited placing power in Europe, European banks played a major part in distribution. Such a situation offered an opportunity for European firms – often based in London – to profit by lead managing offshore dollar issues themselves. Their comparative advantage was compounded by further US regulation. First, the 1963 US interest equalisation tax, designed to stop the capital outflow from the US, effectively raised the cost of foreign borrowing in the US. Second, the 1965 US 'voluntary restraint programme' (made mandatory in 1968) imposed limits on outward direct investment (unless US multinationals could show offsetting balance of payments earnings), and discouraged loans by US banks of over one year to international borrowers including subsidiaries of US multinationals. While the IET mainly encouraged supranationals and European multinationals to issue eurobonds (partly at the expense of yankee issues), the mandatory VRP led to a sharp increase in use of the eurobond market by US firms.

More generally, the development of eurobond markets in a variety of currencies (see section 5.1.4 below) can largely be attributed to the imposition of withholding taxes, listing, disclosure and other regulatory requirements in domestic markets, all of which made development of an offshore market attractive (although another factor was the increased importance of currency considerations in balance-sheet management, with the end of fixed exchange rates). For example, the German authorities in the 1960s sought to offset upward pressure on the deutschmark; as a result they took a relaxed view of the development of a foreign deutschmark bond market and German residents' purchases (which entailed a capital outflow). And more decisively, they imposed a withholding tax to deter foreign residents from buying domestic deutschmark bonds.

Although some of these factors proved temporary (for example IET was abolished in 1974), the initial stimulus was enough to provide the eurobond market with sufficient critical mass (size and diversity of issuers and investors, reputation, relationships and expertise of intermediaries) to survive their abolition. And some of the identified regulations – notably regulations on domestic bond markets such as listing and registration requirements – remain widespread. Meanwhile, as discussed in section 5.2.1, the eurobond market's development in London can be attributed to prior development of the eurocurrency market, London's overall infrastructure as a financial centre, the innovative merchant banks with a long tradition of intermediating financial flows, and the comparatively relaxed regulatory and fiscal regime.

5.1.2 The straight eurobond

A eurobond may be defined as an international bond issue underwritten by an international syndicate of banks, and sold principally in countries other than that of the currency of denomination.[3] Eurobonds are generally bearer bonds (i.e. there is no register of holders), pay interest free of tax, and are usually unsecured but offer a negative pledge.[4] Besides entailing bearer form (hence attractive to some types of investor) lack of registration, disclosure and prospectus requirements also makes eurobond finance more flexible, and so allows borrowers both to take advantage of temporary shifts in relative yields, and to respond quickly to market demand. The basic form of eurobond is the straight fixed rate bond, having bullet[5] repayment. As discussed in detail below, eurobonds are issued by a variety of entities (companies; banks; sovereigns; international organisations), the common feature being high reputation (credit quality and name recognition). The main unknown feature is the nature of the investor base. Anecdotal evidence, however, suggests a relative shift from retail investors attracted by tax advantages to institutional investors such as life insurers and pension funds. Eurobonds may either be public issues or private placements – issues sold direct to investors and not traded. The latter are typically transactions specially structured to meet specific requirements of issuer and investor.[6]

5.1.3 Innovations

Besides the straight eurobond, the market has been the location of a number of key product innovations, many of which have since been adopted in domestic markets.

For example, the *Floating Rate Note* (FRN) differs from the straight eurobond described above in having a variable coupon set in relation to a reference rate such as the London interbank offered rate. Such issues have been particularly popular with banks (partly for reasons of asset matching) and sovereign issuers. *Equity warrant* bonds, developed from the traditional convertible bond, offer warrants giving the right, but not the obligation, to buy the issuer's equity at a prespecified price and future date. After syndication, these warrants can be split off from the bond and traded separately. Such warrants offer the potential for sizeable capital gains if equity prices rise. The development of interest rate and currency swaps has offered a further fillip to the eurobond market, by increasing borrowers' flexibility in issuance, as well as enabling them to profit from comparative advantage in borrowing in different markets (see Hammond, 1987). *Asset backed bonds*, usually secured against pools of illiquid loans, offer financial institutions a means of removing assets from their balance sheets and thus reducing capital requirements; but such securitisation can also be seen as a tool which facilitates the separation of the loan origination and funding function of banks. Besides these major product innovations, the eurobond market has seen a plethora of subsidiary innovations, many of which have been one off or flourished only for a time. For example, in the FRN market there have been perpetual (i.e. non-redeemable) FRNs, and variable rate notes[7] – stimulated in part by banks' capital needs following the Basle agreement on capital adequacy. (Mason, 1986, offers details of a variety of such innovations.)

Market innovations have also been common. Among the most important have been the development of the *grey market* and the *bought deal* (see section 5.1.7), together with the ECU (European Currency Unit) market. This developed from a first issue in 1982 to being the fifth largest sector in the euromarket by issuance in 1990. The ECU proved attractive as a hedge against currency movements, as realignments became less common in the late 1980s, while yields remained above those on the deutschmark. Issues by the Italian, French and UK governments have become among the most widely traded issues, and created a basis for ECU based futures contracts.[8]

5.1.4 Patterns of issuance in the eurobond market

The growth of the international bond market is evident from Table 5.1, which shows that issuance has increased over ten times in nominal terms since 1975. Most of the growth has been in issuance of eurobonds, but there has also been significant growth in issuance of foreign bonds, largely in Swiss francs.

Table 5.1 Volume of international bond issues ($ billion)[9]

	Eurobonds	Foreign bonds	Total
1975	9.9	12.1	22.0
1980	25.6	11.3	36.9
1985	137.2	27.3	164.5
1988	183.7	43.1	226.8
1989	223.7	39.0	262.7
1990	212.4	50.8	263.2

As outlined above, the traditional international bond issue has been a straight fixed rate bond with bullet repayment. However, for a period from 1982-6, and again more recently, the floating rate note has become a popular form of fund raising. The hiatus after 1986 relates to a crisis arising from a large volume of issuance in relation to demand at excessively tight spreads, although it was triggered by concerns regarding regulation of banks' issues (see Davis, 1989). Meanwhile, largely due to the rise in the Japanese stock market over 1986-9, bonds with equity warrants attached became an attractive means of finance for Japanese industrial companies. However, the decline in the Tokyo stock market, which has rendered many warrants worthless, may seriously damage the market.

Table 5.2 Volume of international bond issues by type ($ billion)

	Straight	FRNs	Equity related
1975	21.0	0.5	0.4
1980	28.7	4.7	3.5
1985	97.0	55.9	11.6
1988	161.1	23.8	41.8
1989	150.5	27.1	85.1
1990	172.6	57.6	33.1

The pattern of issuance in the bond markets has varied considerably over time, although there has generally been a predominance of banks, industrial companies and supranational organisations (such as the World Bank). As noted, eurobond issuers need to be of good reputation, whether in terms of credit quality or name recognition.

Besides its inherent flexibility – avoiding the need to file prospectuses and accounts for example – the attraction of borrowing in eurobond markets can be related, first, to desire on the part of borrowers to diversify sources of funding and, second, to desire to minimise uncertainty in international contracts by issuing claims denominated in the currency specified by the contract (e.g. a UK firm issuing eurodollar bonds to finance trade or direct investment in the US).

Table 5.3 Borrowers in the international bond markets ($ billion)

	Industrial companies	Banks	Supranationals	Other financial	Public sector
1975	9.2	1.3	4.5	1.7	5.3
1980	13.8	5.0	6.6	3.6	7.9
1985	58.0	40.7	18.8	22.6	24.4
1988	91.7	50.8	20.5	28.4	35.4
1989	119.1	55.7	23.1	36.0	28.8
1990	92.9	63.0	30.3	42.9	34.1

As for the nationality of issuers, abstracting from supranational institutions, the market has tended to be dominated by borrowers from OECD countries. Table 5.4 shows that US borrowers, dominant until recently, have partly withdrawn leaving

Japanese and to a lesser extent UK institutions as the main issuers.[10] Ldc (less developed country) borrowers have never been active in the international bond markets, as they lack the required credit quality and/or reputation.

Table 5.4 International bond issuance by nationality ($ billion)

	US	Japan	UK	Canada	France	Germany	Other	Ldc	Supra-nationals
1975	0.5	1.7	0.6	4.6	2.3	0.3	7.2	0.3	4.5
1980	5.1	3.8	1.7	3.2	3.2	0.1	14.2	0.5	6.6
1985	40.7	20.0	14.4	9.5	11.8	2.9	44.4	2.0	18.8
1988	17.1	50.8	26.8	12.9	16.2	11.8	69.0	1.7	20.5
1989	15.9	97.7	24.7	13.3	13.4	9.7	62.4	1.3	23.1
1990	21.9	58.0	23.4	13.1	20.4	7.8	87.5	0.7	30.3

The currency of issuance in the international markets has traditionally been the dollar, but its dominance has been eroded recently, particularly by increases in deutschmark, sterling and yen issuance and the rise of the ECU market.

Table 5.5 International bond issuance by currency ($ billion)

	US dollar	DM	Yen	Sterling	ECU	Other
1975	11.2	3.2	0.1	0.1	0	7.6
1980	17.9	7.8	1.6	1.2	0	10.1
1985	99.4	11.3	12.3	7.6	7.0	27.6
1988	83.4	23.6	20.6	24.4	11.1	63.7
1989	129.9	16.0	24.2	21.5	12.3	58.8
1990	87.5	32.8	32.2	22.3	20.5	67.8

5.1.5 Investors

Because eurobonds are bearer instruments, data are not available on the investor base. However, two main types of investor can be identified, namely private individuals (often seeking to avoid tax), and institutional investors holding eurobonds as part of a normal diversified portfolio. Note that eurobonds are unlikely to attract tax exempt investors such as pension funds, given the lower yield associated with bearer status. In addition, many institutions are restricted from holding foreign securities (e.g. German life insurers)[11] and many have restrictions on acceptable credit ratings.

Besides these general points, market professionals suggest that holders of dollar eurobonds fall into five categories, namely: (i) UK money managers managing funds for US captive insurance companies, whose tax liabilities are not known in advance and who therefore have a preference for euro-issues. These form a stable investor base; (ii) Swiss investors, generally buying eurodollar bonds on a US$ currency view; (iii) domestic US investors, especially of US corporate name issuers; (iv) Japanese domestic investors, especially of equity-warrant bonds of Japanese issuers; (v) central banks and supranationals. Although it is still true that *most* dollar eurobonds are held by non-US residents, US residents now form an important group. In particular, they enjoy: (i) a different variety of instruments in the eurobond market; (ii) arbitrage opportunities between domestic and euro-issues – e.g. GMAC euro/domestic spreads might widen out to 30 basis points, generating arbitrage opportunities; and (iii) a tax advantage.

Also, investors in countries without a double taxation agreement prefer euros. This preference might endure after the establishment of a double tax treaty (e.g. the Central Bank of Taiwan still has a preference for euros). Euroyen issues have been very attractive to Japanese investors because of the tax break/investment structure. US holdings of FRNs increased after the market collapse as US investors were generally happier with the credit quality of the names involved.

5.1.6 Intermediaries

The behaviour of eurobond intermediaries is the principal focus of section 5.2.3, which seeks to provide an economic analysis of market behaviour and microstructure. Suffice to say that the main intermediaries active in the eurobond market are commercial banks, investment banks and securities houses. Their activities can be distinguished between primary markets (launching of new issues) and secondary markets (trading of existing issues). Salient features of these activities are discussed below.

5.1.7 Primary market issuance procedures

Prior to the early 1980s the issuance procedure (*traditional syndication*) was as follows. A prospective borrower would approach a number of investment banks, one of which would be invited to act as the lead manager of an issue. The lead manager would in turn invite a small additional group of banks to aid it in organising the issue (the managing group). Two other categories, the underwriters and the selling group, would be invited to participate in later stages of the issuance. Once the syndicate was formed and terms agreed, the borrower would sell the bonds to the managing group, which in turn would sell them direct to the underwriters or the selling group, who in turn would distribute the bonds to the public. The price would only be fixed at the end of the selling period, generating some uncertainty for the issuer. The function of underwriters was to commit themselves before the issue to buy the bonds at a set minimum price, if they could not be sold by the managing group at a price above this minimum. The roles were not necessarily distinct; the lead manager may also be an underwriter and a seller.

Since the early 1980s, the principal issuance method has been the *bought deal*, wherein the lead manager buys the entire issue at set terms from the borrower prior to announcement. Syndication of the deal is arranged after purchase (transferring risk from the issuer to the intermediary). The role of underwriters and selling groups in this process is considerably reduced. An important feature of both the bought deal and traditional syndication is the lack of discipline over the price at which members of the syndicate sell bonds. As a result of intense competition, bonds are often sold at a discount to attract investors (the 'reallowance') or else banks would sell their bonds in the grey market (a market for bonds on which the issue price or syndicate allocations has not yet been determined, where quotes are set in relation to the unknown final price), which may oblige the lead manager to buy the bonds back in order to support the price.

In the late 1980s it was felt that low profitability, partly arising from discounting of bonds by syndicate members in the grey market, necessitated a reform of primary market procedures. This led to the introduction of the *fixed price reoffer technique* (the main technique in the US domestic market). Under this method, banks in the syndicate have a contractual obligation not to discount fees by selling bonds cheaply to investors until issuance is complete. Control numbers on bonds have often been used to reinforce the discipline (as they allow any violations to be detected). This innovation has been widely adopted, and has helped intermediaries to rebuild profitability. It is particularly attractive to firms with strong institutional placing power; retail firms prefer to sell at issue price, retaining full fees as profit, rather than selling at the lower fixed reoffer price set by the lead manager.[12] However, some have suggested that coordination of fees by the major players amounts to an anti-competitive practice.[13]

Note that the description above assumes the issue is a straight fixed rate bond. In many cases complex financial engineering (structuring) is needed during primary issuance to provide a package which satisfies the borrowers' funding needs. A discussion is provided in section 5.2.3.

5.1.8   The secondary market

Most secondary market transactions in eurobonds occur in over the counter (OTC) trading, i.e. not on a recognised exchange (partly for historical reasons but also due to the non-standardised nature of the instruments). Although they are often listed in London or Luxembourg, this is largely in order to comply with regulations which bar some institutional investors from holding unlisted securities. Settlement occurs through one of the two international clearing systems known as Euroclear and Cedel, who maintain a system of book entry transfers. The volumes involved are large; turnover of straight bonds in recent years, for example, has typically amounted to $500 bn per quarter.

Eurobond trading is centred on intermediaries acting as reporting dealers, who make markets in securities for customers. Reporting dealers have the privilege of access to screens operated by inter-dealer brokers (IDBs) which facilitate the unwinding of unbalanced positions by market makers. IDB screens display price quotations by reporting dealers anonymously; when another market maker is located and securities sold, the IDB receives commission. In addition, reporting dealers display their price quotes for customers on screens (prices are usually 'indicative' rather than 'firm' – i.e. final prices must be agreed by telephone). Reporting dealers are also obliged to submit daily to the International Securities Market Association (formerly the Association of International Bond Dealers) details of the securities in which they deal and prices and quantities in which they are ready to buy and sell them. The ISMA offers the lists of quotations publicly.

The secondary market tends to suffer from a lack of liquidity relative to domestic markets; often even the lead manager of an issue is unwilling to quote two way prices. This is partly a result of the small sizes of international bond issues, but also a consequence of the long holding periods typical of such bonds. Most turnover is concentrated in large issues by sovereigns and supranationals. Low liquidity for publicly issued eurobonds is one feature underlying development of international private placements.

One aid to liquidity is provided by stock lending facilities organised and guaranteed by the main clearing systems (Euroclear and Cedel). Typically the lender is a passive investor seeking to make a turn on his portfolio, while the borrower is an active investor or trader seeking to finance temporary shortages of securities and avoid the risk of settlement failure. However, the market is not very active, with typically only 0.2% of outstanding bonds being lent at any one time. This may relate to transactions costs and limits on proportions of issues that can be lent.

A recent development has been the introduction of trade matching and reporting systems (which replaced a highly fallible system of telexes to reconcile details regarding agreed trades). The TRAX system was developed by the ISMA in an attempt to provide up to date information on transactions (which are supposed to be reported in 30 minutes) to allow matching inconsistencies to be resolved quickly. The system was required under the UK Financial Services Act (FSA) to enable an audit trail to be made for trades transacted in London – and hence its use is compulsory for London based secondary market traders who are members of ISMA. The ACE system was set up by the ISMA, Euroclear and Cedel to satisfy pre-settlement matching requirements of the two clearing systems, and is offered to all participants in them.

5.1.9   The role of London

For those currencies in respect of which the home authorities allow bonds to be issued out of foreign centres, most structuring of issues and about 65% of primary issuance have taken place in London in recent years. For example, most eurodollar, euroyen, Canadian dollar and Australian dollar eurobonds are issued out of London. ECU bond issues are now also mostly made in London. (In contrast most European authorities – including the UK – insist on lead management occurring in their own market.) As noted, structuring does not merely involve routine tasks but also often requires complex financial engineering, in which houses based in London have developed considerable expertise over the years. The development of the market for eurodollar bonds with equity warrants attached has proved a particular spur to activity in London recently, while the rapidly growing swaps market, the outstanding value of which was $1,500 billion at end-1989,[14] is located principally in London and New York.

Most secondary market trading of eurobonds also takes place in London. As a rough indicator of the location of market making, it may be noted that 73 out of 97 dealers reporting prices daily or weekly to ISMA in September 1990 were located in London. Market estimates suggest that approximately three quarters of secondary market turnover in dollar eurobonds (which amounted to $358 billion in the first half of 1989)[15] occurs in London. One influence is the fact that eurobonds cannot be sold into the United States before the end of a 90-day seasoning period and must be registered. Trading in other centres tends mainly to be driven by local customer needs. Market estimates suggest that about 30% of the turnover of German government bonds (bunds), 50% of the turnover in international deutschmark straight issues, and 80%-90% of the turnover of deutschmark FRNs occur in London. Several German banks have in recent years set up capital market units in London to trade deutschmark bonds. Until its abolition in 1990, trading took place in London partly to avoid Germany's turnover tax on corporate bonds. Trading of euroyen bonds (which totalled $70 billion in the first half of 1989[16]) is concentrated in London. In contrast, trading in London of straight Swiss franc issues is minimal, partly due to the limited investor base outside Switzerland.

5.2 The economics of eurobond issuance

This section seeks to probe more deeply the nature of London's eurobond markets by addressing three issues; first, linking to the previous section, a discussion of the economic factors underlying London's role; second, an econometric assessment of determinants of eurobond issues at a macro level; and third, an analysis of the structure and performance of the market for primary issuance.

5.2.1 Economic factors underlying the development of London

The eurobond market fits well into the more general paradigm describing the development of financial centres developed in Chapter 1 (see also Davis, 1990). Thus, for eurobond firms London has offered a pool of suitably trained labour; in recent years, low levels of personal and corporate taxation; a reasonable tax regime for financial instruments (e.g. ability to issue bearer eurobonds that effectively pay interest gross and absence of turnover taxes – a particular handicap for the Swiss); a supply of suitable premises; the absence, since 1979, of exchange controls (although initially exchange controls were seen as an advantage, since eurobonds did not interfere with onshore sterling markets); prudential and monetary regulations that have not historically tended significantly to raise the cost of funds, distort or prevent competition among domestic or international intermediaries; English law (widely accepted as a basis for international financial business); the English language; and political stability. There has also been a degree of confidence among eurobond firms that regulations will not be altered without good reason and appropriate consultation. Finally, London's time zone position offers a natural complementarity with New York and Tokyo for trading of securities such as eurobonds as well as forex.

As noted in Chapter 1, among the most important factors supporting London's position have been external economies of scale – the mutual benefits arising from the concentration of financial firms in one location. Eurobond firms participate in markets whose liquidity (enabling rapid execution of large orders with minimum disturbance to prices or margins) and efficiency (in establishing prices which reflect all available information) increase with the number of participants. Groups of different markets (as well as different firms in the same market) are sufficiently interrelated also to benefit from location in London (for example futures markets to cover eurobond exposure, or the different currency sectors of the eurobond market). Firms can diversify their activities by operating in several markets (e.g. eurobonds and UK equities (after Big Bang)). Firms, whether in the same or related activities, need and benefit from close business contacts with each other: for example, the lead manager and other participants in a eurobond issue require close links. A group of trades and professions has grown around the core financial institutions to provide other services, such as lawyers (of particular importance to primary eurobond issuance), accountants, actuaries, security printers, computer programmers and consultants. Customers of eurobond houses such as industrial and commercial companies and fund managers often find it convenient to be represented in the financial centre too. A supply of skilled labour with established expertise in bond markets is readily available to newcomers. Bodies such as the International Primary Markets Association (IPMA) and the largest regional ISMA groupings are located in London.

In such an environment London's share of eurobond business has grown in a self-sustaining manner, as by the mid-1980s the origination activities of all the leading firms had become centralised in London. The benefits arising from contacts and participation in markets increased progressively with the number of firms in the locality, and firms continued to be attracted to the centre because of the numbers already there. Business became concentrated and competing centres find it hard to become established. And London developed reputation and prestige to keep firms there. The continuing shift e.g. of ECU bond activities to London, shows the continuing potency of these mechanisms. But the process could also go into reverse if key aspects of the environment such as relative regulatory burdens deteriorate (see section 5.3).

5.2.2   Determinants of issuance

Estimates were made in Davis (1988) of the nature of the determinants of gross eurobond issuance. It was assumed that the following variables would influence issuance (bearing in mind that the level of issuance observed results both from demand and supply influences).

– the yield on eurodollar bonds
– the yield differential with US domestic bonds[17] (net of withholding tax)
– the yield curve relationship in the euromarkets (eurobond yield less 3-month eurodollar rate)
– the yield differential with Swiss franc eurobonds
– the US$ effective exchange rate
– US industrial production (as a proxy for economic activity).

Seasonal dummies also proved to be necessary – eurodollar issuance follows a seasonal pattern, with a marked trough in December. The data period was August 1983–February 1988 (monthly) and was mainly determined by the availability of data on eurobond yields. Equations were estimated for eurodollar straights, all eurodollar bonds and all eurobonds. The specification used was in error correction format (Hendry *et al*, 1983) which by specifying variables in both differences and lagged levels enables one to separate out long and short run influences on the dependent variable. Due to the simultaneity between the dependent variable and the current eurobond yield, the equation was estimated by instrumental variables.

Table 5.6 shows estimates of the equations, after a specification search from a more general equation. As noted, there are few long run effects given the negligible size of the lagged dependent variables – a point which shows in itself the instability of demand for issuance – the market tends to be subject to 'feasts and famines'. Very high elasticities with respect to changes in yields and differentials are apparent. In general, an increase in eurobond yields decreases eurobond issuance, while a steepening of the yield curve leads to an increase in issuance, as does a decline in the dollar/Swiss franc bond differential in the case of US dollar bonds. A widening of the euro/domestic differential leads to increased issuance – an effect likely to be feeding from the lender side of the market rather than the borrower. Meanwhile, a depreciation of the dollar tends to reduce eurobond issuance, especially for dollar issues, suggesting that depreciation leads to expectations of further falls and hence losses for non-dollar based investors. This effect also obtains for total eurobonds, in which case it is likely to proxy the uncertainty and adverse interest rate expectations caused by a falling dollar.

Table 5.6 Eurobond issuance equations (dependent variable: difference of the log of real gross issuance) Estimation method: IV. Period: 1983/8–1988/2 (t-statistics in brackets)

	US$ straights	US$ eurobonds	All eurobonds
Lagged dependent	−0.93	−0.83	−0.91
	(5.5)	(5.0)	(5.2)
ΔRED	−1.4	–	−0.59
	(2.2)		(2.5)
Δ(RED-RDB)	0.3	0.25	–
	(1.7)	(1.5)	
Δ(RED-REC)	0.91	0.75	0.43
	(4.4)	(4.0)	(5.4)
Δ(RED-RSF)	–	−1.2	n/a
		(2.8)	
Δln EER	12.5	6.1	3.4
	(2.8)	(1.8)	(1.9)
Δln IP	–	–	–
RED$_{-1}$	−0.7	−0.49	−0.32
	(3.8)	(3.2)	(4.1)
(RED-RDB)$_{-1}$	0.46	0.34	0.11
	(2.9)	(2.6)	(2.1)
(RED-REC)$_{-1}$	–	–	–
(RED-RSF)$_{-1}$	–	–	n/a
ln EER$_{-1}$	8.3	5.8	2.5
	(3.9)	(3.2)	(3.3)
ln IP$_{-1}$	17.7	13.6	5.7
	(3.2)	(2.8)	(2.9)
Constant	−116.1	−86.0	−32.1
	(3.4)	(2.9)	(2.7)
Seasonals	Significant	Significant	Significant
$\bar{R}^2$	0.67	0.52	0.81
DW	2.3	2.3	2.3
se	0.50	0.43	0.19

Key: RED: yield on eurodollar straights (secondary market)
 RDB: yield on US AAA corporate bonds
 REC: 3-month eurodollar rate
 RSF: yield on Swiss franc straights
 EER: US$ effective exchange rate
 IP: US industrial production

Less attention should probably be paid to levels than difference effects, as it seems likely that the levels are partly illustrating the long run trends (largely upward) in eurobond issuance. On the other hand, it is economically reasonable for borrowers that issuance should be higher, the lower the eurobond yield demanded by investors. A high level of industrial output, too, is likely to entail higher real levels of bond issuance. The positive levels effect of the exchange rate, on the other hand, probably illustrates more a coincidence with the trend of eurodollar issuance, as does the level of the euro/domestic differential. Seasonal variables were significant in each of the equations, generally showing a sharp decline in issuance every December. The statistics indicate a reasonable level of explanation for a difference equation. The DW does indicate a degree of autocorrelation, however.

5.2.3   Structure of the primary eurobond market: an industrial analysis

The analysis of the microstructure of the eurobond market is in four sections. In the first, the main features of the market are introduced; the second and third focus on market structure and profitability more closely; and the final section interprets behaviour in an industrial economics framework.

a) The nature of competition

In characterising the primary eurobond market as an 'industry' it is useful first briefly to define the price and the product in question. The product is taken to be intermediation of eurobonds on behalf of borrowers. This always includes management, underwriting and selling of a bond issue, but may additionally entail arrangement of a swap, initial support for the price of the issue and an implicit commitment to make markets at a later stage. It is thus evident that secondary market trading cannot be entirely divorced from primary issuance. (Firms may also feel the need to set up secondary market operations to build up relationships with investors, and to have an investor base for distribution of new issues.) The price of eurobond intermediation is composed largely of commission or fees, which are divided between lead managers, underwriters and sellers. However, since managers can also offer a coupon for the bonds – and hence a yield – which is more or less competitive by taking a higher risk, the overall price must also contain elements of the deviation of the yield from that which would be obtained from other competing intermediaries. A third cost element is the cost of ancillary services such as the swap fee. Finally, features such as initial market support will be reflected in fees and yields.

In this context, eurobond houses typically compete for mandates in various ways. For straight bonds, they may try to offer the most attractive swaps, low spreads over domestic bonds, low commissions (including underwriting fees) and primary and secondary market support. The locus of competition may change over time; however, in general the interest cost, gross of fees, may be defined as the price of a eurobond issue to the borrower, and is the continuing obligation in relation to the bond issue. The level of general interest rates is clearly beyond the control of intermediaries, but commissions can be trimmed and, as noted, yields at issue can be varied by an increase in the risk taken by underwriters. The cost of a swap may also be varied. Out of pocket issue fees, including legal, printing and fiscal agents' fees, tend to be small; in extreme cases differences in them can sway deals, but in general the yield, commission cost and cost of the swap (if included) remain primary factors. Of course, cost is not the only factor; ability of the investment bank to maintain a secondary market is important to the extent that repeat borrowing will tend to be priced on the basis of the yield on outstanding issues; ability to structure and innovate may be important where there are specialised funding requirements; the investor base and banking relationships can also be important, as discussed below.

Offered prices will not necessarily always cover fixed costs – firms may often sacrifice short run profit maximisation to lead manage or to be included in a deal. Or intermediaries may be prepared to offer deals at times when other firms are unable to do so, taking the risk of putting a deal on their own books. Alternatively, they may cross subsidise deals with their profits in other markets such as swaps. Such behaviour results from the importance of 'league tables' in attracting further primary eurobond business and 'relationships' with issuers, the existence of 'joint demand' for different products from the same firm – and possibly also joint costs in the production of different services. Cross subsidisation will be particularly common when firms are trying to penetrate new markets or attract new clients. Indeed, primary eurobond operations are often categorised as 'loss-leaders', making low or negative profits to attract clients to other operations (equity issuance, financial advice, bank lending, etc.) or to penetrate new markets.

To some extent, the nature of competition described above is similar to other financial markets. But there are also important features for industrial structure which differentiate the eurobond market from most other financial markets. First, the market is *globalised*, i.e. issuers and investors may be from any country (subject to regulation), while intermediaries may be from third countries. It thus differs from most domestic banking markets and many domestic securities markets where savers, borrowers and intermediaries are typically also domestic. Second, the market is relatively unregulated. For example, there are no barriers preventing activity by commercial or investment banks; indeed the eurobond market is characterised by a wide variety of types of firm and ownership structures (divisions of a firm, wholly-owned subsidiaries). In addition, there are no regulatory restraints against entry to the market, and until recently there were no regulations for dedicated specific capital or prudential controls on players' activities, except (in the case of universal banks) to the extent that banking supervision of a company impinged on a eurobond operation. (Some tightening of regulation has resulted from the recent introduction of the Financial Services Act in the UK: see section 5.3). The absence of regulatory constraints has resulted in many financial firms in the eurobond market being *multiproduct* (financial conglomerates). The firms involved are often multinational in a way that is atypical of most other financial markets. Such a structure is much more typical of industrial markets such as those for cars and pharmaceuticals. The globalisation of the market and the absence of regulatory restraints are among the factors behind this tendency.

Like many industrial markets, the eurobond market has featured a variety of innovations as firms have sought actively to increase market share or create new markets by the introduction of attractive new financial products. Lack of regulations is clearly an important permissive factor. Profitability of successful innovations has, however, typically been competed away as the product becomes a simple standardised product or 'commodity'. The eurobond market has featured rapid growth and new entry of intermediaries, though also periods of consolidation.

Certain other general features of the eurobond market are important for understanding its behaviour. As noted above, regulatory barriers do not constrain new entry to the market, and rapid entry suggests that any other constraints to establishment in the market are weak. The distribution of successful firms, which includes various 'niche players', suggests that entry at a low level of activity need not entail losses. As a result of these tendencies, the market structure of the eurobond market has generally been categorised as competitive – although such aspects as product differentiation, growth maximising strategies and the inability of a firm to gain infinite demand for its services if it sells at below market prices[18] suggest *imperfect* rather than perfect competition (firms do not compete on price alone). However, despite rapid entry, there has been relative stability in the market share of the large established firms (see section (b) below). This suggests that there may be barriers, which, while not restricting entry *per se*, do restrict the ability of firms to become sizeable participants in the market.

What are the *barriers to growth*? First, capital needs are sizeable if firms wish to become major players, to invest in technology, to be able to handle underwriting and distribution, notably of 'bought deals', to hire expertise[19] and to be able to trade and make markets. An institution which is already well capitalised or faces a low cost of capital will thus have an advantage. Among the other barriers to growth beyond a low level of activity appear to be the investor base and hence placing power of established firms, which influence the ability to win mandates. This partly depends on factors such as the strength of demand in the firm's country of origin for securities as opposed to deposits, together with restrictions on entry of foreign firms. Strength of local demand for international securities will also often be correlated with the balance-of-payments surplus/deficit position of the country in which the firm or its parent is based, as well as the strength and internationalisation of the currency. Given that these change over time, the dominance of the industry by a certain nationality of institutions may be transitory. The expertise and capitalisation of the dealing desk, and the ability to innovate are also important factors though these may stem from the knowledge of the investor base. A more intangible barrier, partly a function of the other factors, is 'franchise' or reputation of existing firms, the perceived ability in the mind of the client to deliver top quality services.

Many commentators have suggested that eurobond market intermediaries have at least historically been characterised by a managerial objective of *growth maximisation*, rather than short run profit maximisation. As a result of strong growth, firms hope to become sufficiently large to make a 'name' and thus attract new issuers and build placing power, an objective that may be felt to be consistent with long term profit maximisation. The relative lack of entry barriers and large number of firms appear to lead firms to believe that growth maximisation is a feasible objective, although the barriers to growth outlined above mean that, in practice, the objective is difficult to attain. These tendencies have entailed certain structural problems – the market suffers from excess capacity (see section 5.3), with many eurobond operations unable to make profits on turnover averaged over the interest rate cycle. Firms are often poorly capitalised, relative to their needs, as shown elsewhere by the difficulties of some securities firms resulting from their equity operations after the stock market crash and the need for injection of capital from parent banks. Undercapitalisation entails risks when such firms carry out eurobond 'bought deals' or take on large positions in secondary market trading.

Finally, it is emphasised that conditions in the eurobond market are subject to change over time, secularly as well as cyclically.[20] Important long term developments include the change of the customer base from individuals to institutions, and the increasing receptiveness of the latter to new currencies and instruments, the increase in volatility of exchange and interest rates, the advent of bought deals, deregulation of national securities markets, the declining segmentation of the different currency and instrument sectors of the euromarkets, the growing sophistication of corporate customers, financial innovation and unbundling of financial services. These changes – in particular the increasing size and sophistication of counterparties – have tended to increase competition between firms and hence the need for adaptability on the part of players, as well as reducing profitability.

To summarise; among the most important 'stylised facts' of eurobond market competition are the following: apparently highly, albeit imperfectly competitive market conditions; low profitability; periods of rapid entry with little effect on concentration (barriers to growth); growth maximising strategies by firms (long run profit maximisation); a high level of innovation; and periodic changes in the nationality of the dominant firms. The following sections focus more closely on market structure and trends in profitability, before an attempt is made to interpret behaviour in the light of the theory of industrial economics.

b) Concentration and market structures

The market has undergone the evolution shown in Table 5.7 (as recorded by 'league tables' of lead managers[21] in the primary market for all international issues, ranked by the value of issues lead managed in dollar terms). The five firm concentration ratio has varied around an average of 41% over this period, rising to a peak of 53% in 1978 before falling to 34% in 1980, rising to 47% in 1983 before declining to 30% in 1990. Broadly, the declines in the concentration ratio have tended to occur

Table 5.7 Primary eurobond market concentration

	5-firm proportion	Nationality of top 5	Issues $ bn	Issues (1987 prices)	Annual real percent increase
1975	40	G,US,B,G,S	18.1	35.8	–
1976	46	G,S,US,UK,N	29.6	55.1	+53.9
1977	47	G,S,G,S,G	29.3	51.3	–6.9
1978	53	G,G,N,G,S	31.2	50.9	–0.8
1979	36	S,G,G,G,US	37.3	55.6	+9.2
1980	34	S,G,UK,US,F	38.1	52.2	–6.1
1981	38	S,UK,US,G,US	48.3	60.4	+15.7
1982	44	G,S,US,US,US	74.3	87.3	+44.5
1983	47	S,G,UK,US,G	73.9	83.5	–4.3
1984	43	S,US,G,US,US	108.4	118.3	+41.7
1985	37	S,US,US,US,G	164.5	173.9	+47.0
1986	36	S,JP,G,US,US	221.5	228.1	+31.2
1987	36	JP,S,G,JP,JP	175.6	175.6	–23.0
1988	35	S,JP,G,S,US	226.8	217.8	+24.0
1989	43	JP,US,JP,JP,S	262.7	241.7	+11.0
1990	30	JP,S,G,S,US	263.2	228.1	–5.6

Key: G: Germany; F: France; S: Switzerland; N: Netherlands; JP: Japan; B: Belgium; US: United States.

125

during periods of market growth, while the rises have corresponded to recessions, suggesting that high levels of bond issues lead to a more even spread of issues between firms as well as new entry, while in slack periods the dominant houses tend to take a larger proportion of issues, smaller houses being squeezed out.[22]

The nationality of the top five lead managers in the eurobond market has changed significantly over this period – in itself an indicator of the intense competition prevalent in the market. German and Swiss lead managers were dominant between 1975–79, but US houses became increasingly important during the 1980s, and by 1984–85 three US houses and the US/Swiss CSFB were included in the first five. The dominance of the US houses was, however, broken by the entry of the Japanese, with one in the top five in 1986 and three in 1987. More recently the Japanese hegemony has weakened. Comparison with Table 5.4 shows a strong relationship with patterns of issuance by nationality.

New entry to the industry has been frequent (Table 5.8); the total number of bookrunners has risen sharply since 1980 and 54 firms have entered the top 50 issuers since 1975, while 15 firms have gained positions in the top 10 lead managers for the first time (see Table 5.8). However, very few have been able to maintain these positions: only 5 in the top 50 and 3 in the top 10. This suggests that while entry to the eurobond market is easy, it is more difficult for a firm to establish itself as a dominant player.

Table 5.8 Industrial dynamics of the eurobond market

	New entry to top 50 (of which durable[b]	New entry to top 10 (of which durable)[b]	Memo: Total number of bookrunners
1976	(a)	(a)	n/a
1977	9	0	n/a
1978	10	3	n/a
1979	2	1	n/a
1980	5	1	93
1981	5	4	88
1982	3	2	84
1983	2(1)	1(1)	88
1984	1(1)	0	98
1985	0	0	108
1986	1	1(1)	123
1987	4(2)	1	121
1988	5(1)	0	119
1989	2	1(1)	116
1990	5	0	132

(a) Omitted
(b) i.e. always in the relevant section after entry

There have been 125 firms in the top 50 since 1975, but of these only 14 (11%) have been consistently in the top 50 (see Table 5.9). To these one can add the five new entrants who have established themselves, to give a set of 'core players' amounting to 19 (15%). Obviously, there are others on the fringes of this group who have dropped out for 1–2 years (an extra 13 firms) but this leaves a large number who are at most transient players. Of these two sets of firms, 12 have never been in the top 10, and can be classified either as niche operations or unsuccessful major players. In addition, 25% have managed only one issue in the relevant period, and no less than 38% have been in the top 50 for less than four years, excluding those who have established themselves in the last four years. These data suggest that there is a durable core of banks and securities houses whose position is hard for other banks to challenge.[23]

Table 5.9 Summary of market structure 1975–90

		No	%
(i)	Always in top 50	14	11%
(ii)	Successful new entrants	5	4%
(iii)	Only dropping out 1–2 years since entry	13	10%
(iv)	Firms in groups (i)–(iii) never in top 10 – niche players or unsuccessful entrants	12	10%
(v)	Only one appearance	31	25%
(vi)	In top 50 for less than 4 years, not there in 1990	48	38%

c) Indicators of pricing and profitability

An assessment of *commissions* in international bond markets in the early 1980s shown in Davis (1988) suggests that in general, commissions in the eurobond market (2%) were higher than in the US domestic market (1%), but rather lower than in the various European domestic markets (2.5%). Levich (1985) suggested that large selling commissions were required to induce European banks to participate in deals. On the face of it, such high commissions suggest a lack of price competitiveness, but as noted above, large institutional buyers are able to force distributors to share all or part of the selling concession, and prices may thus be lower than they appear. For example, Hanna and Staley (1983) quoted 'reallowances' of 1–1.5% against average commissions of 1.95%, making a net commission of 0.45–0.95%. This is shown by prices in the 'grey market' which are often reported to be so low as to negate all of the gross fees, thus absorbing all of the underwriters' risk premium. Firms are then only able to make money by stockpiling inventories and reselling when (if) prices rise. The shift to fixed price reoffer primary issuance attempts to offset these patterns (see section 5.1.7), although Jeanneau (1989) suggests it will not be effective as long as excess capacity remains.

Average commissions on eurobonds have declined, albeit irregularly, since 1980 (see Table 5.10). Although a parallel shift in average maturities[24] means that part of the fall is not accounted for by increased competition, comparison of years with similar average maturities does show a decline in gross fees. Over 1980–83 the average level of gross fees for supranational issuers (i.e. controlling for credit quality) was 1.84 while over 1984–87 they were 1.8 and over 1988–90, 1.57. Commissions in the eurodollar market as a whole (not illustrated) obviously depend on maturities and the quality of the issuer, but similar trends in fees are observable.

Table 5.10 Commissions on eurodollar fixed rate bonds by supranationals (percent)

	Total	of which Selling	of which Management/ Underwriting	Maturities (years)
1980	1.85	n/a	n/a	9.1
1981	1.86	n/a	n/a	7.1
1982	1.78	1.25	0.53	7.1
1983	1.87	n/a	n/a	6.9
1984	1.83	1.1	0.73	6.4
1985	1.80	1.26	0.54	9.2
1986	1.81	1.29	0.52	10.8
1987	1.77	1.23	0.54	12.1
1988	1.74	1.21	0.53	7.9
1989	1.66	1.12	0.54	9.4
1990	1.30	n/a	n/a	6.2

Margins or spreads, for example over domestic government bonds, are typically influenced by a wide variety of factors, including default risk of the issuer, call risk that bonds may be liquidated early, tax exemption, maturity, and expected market liquidity. Given these factors, in particular the fact that default premia tend to vary over the trade cycle, it is not a trivial task to isolate factors related to competition in the new issue market. Clearly, spreads can only be compared in one currency sector. However, it may be indicative of increased competition that in the case of dollar issues for supranationals the average margin over US T-bonds in 1980–83 was 17 basis points while in 1984–87 it was –11 basis points.

To summarise, results drawn from grey market activity and from spreads and commissions indicate an increasingly competitive market, relatively independent of changes in concentration. However, the end result of the degree of competition in a market can only be observed in *profitability*. Various complications arise, notably the fact that eurobond activities are typically only one business entered into by a conglomerate, the results of which may be hidden in its balance sheet (though, given the importance of joint demand for fixed income business in general, total profits on the balance sheet may reflect the underlying profitability of eurobonds). Losses on eurobond activities may be cross-subsidised by profits from other markets.

Given these caveats, the state of the euromarket, with declarations from all sides of low profitability and a rapid shakeout in the market, does suggest that current profitability is low. For example, *The Economist* (1987) noted[25] that 'banks lose money in the eurobond market because it is the most competitive capital market...compete to underwrite bonds at rates so cheap they can only be sold at a loss, often exceeding fees (1⅛%)...some institutions subsidise borrowers by providing money at below market rates...In 1985 UBS, in 1986 the Japanese.' These tendencies are at most tangentially in line with changes in concentration, suggesting a need to look elsewhere for causal factors.

Turning to company data, the fact that five leading US investment banks had post tax returns on average equity of 26% in 1982 does suggest high profitability (Table 5.11). However, the decline in profitability since then, when concentration has changed little and output has grown strongly, contradicts any suggestions of low competitiveness.

The decline partly reflects factors relating to US domestic activity, although similar forces are at work in the eurobond market. As regards the US domestic market, these changes in profitability are opposite to those of concentration, which rose over the period. Similarly, the decline in profits in the eurobond market has not been accompanied by a particularly marked decline in concentration since 1982.

Table 5.11 Profitability of US investment banks active in eurobond market (return on average equity)

	1982	1983	1984	1985	1986	1987	1988	1989	1990
First Boston	26.5%	35.1%	23.1%	18.8%	19.3%	10.4%	n/a	n/a	n/a
Merrill Lynch	22.4%	13.9%	4.8%	9.9%	13.1%	11.6%	14.0%	n/a	5%
Morgan Stanley	33.8%	27.1%	27.4%	38.4%	32.0%	25.3%	33%	28%	14%
Salomon Bros	21.2%	23.5%	9.1%	20.8%	16.1%	4.0%	8%	15%	8%
Shearson Lehman*	n/a	27.6%	12.7%	18.9%	24.9%	7.0%	8%	7%	n/a

* Partially withdrew from eurobond market in 1987.
Source: Salomon Bros.

d) An interpretation

These stylised facts and structural factors can be interpreted in the light of the theories of modern industrial economics. On the face of it, the market appears to have many of the features of a contestable market, that is, one where competitive conditions are maintained regardless of the market structure, due to the threat of new entry. This requires the absence of sunk (irrecoverable) costs to entry. Capital costs, in terms of dealing rooms, finance for underwriting, expertise, etc., may be high, but those specific to eurobonds are rather low, because they can be adapted from other sectors such as domestic corporate bonds. There are a wide variety of well-capitalised firms and investment banks ready to contemplate entry. Entry can be rapid, as can withdrawal. It is thus clear that contestable market features help to explain some of the behaviour of firms in the eurobond market, i.e. that it is highly competitive, especially within the individual currency sectors, despite the market structure.

It should be added that contestability may have changed over time, especially within individual currency sectors. In the 1970s eurobonds were typically placed in managed accounts, international investors had few alternatives to eurobonds, and there was high demand for bonds, all these factors suggesting ease of entry. On the other hand, except for eurodollars, most currency sectors were the preserve of a few domestic institutions owing to regulatory barriers and cartels. In the 1980s, the increasing dominance of capital markets by institutional investors and the lower excess demand for eurobonds has made placing of bonds more difficult, adding to entry barriers for firms lacking an institutional investor base. Capital costs have risen as a result of increasing use of bought deals, and the need to set up research and secondary market trading operations (to satisfy institutional investors' liquidity requirements and to gain an investor base to complement primary activities), although capital requirements as such do not prevent a market being contestable. On the other hand, entry by intermediaries to currency sectors has been facilitated by the advent of swaps and improvements in technology. Bought deals are costly in terms of capital, but do not require development of a wide range of relationships with other banks. On balance contestability has increased, partly explaining the decline in profitability. It is, however, harder to explain purely in the context of the theory of contestable markets why some firms' eurobond operations have continued to be successful while others have been unable to establish themselves, why there has been no significant decline in market concentration over time despite continual new entry, and why profitability has declined so steeply.

Certain features of eurobond market structure, interpreted in the light of other aspects of the new industrial economics, may help to explain these tendencies. There may be significant entry barriers to the upper echelons of the industry, resulting from intertemporal dependencies on the demand and cost side, and from strategic competition, both of which create sunk costs. Dealing first with intertemporal dependencies, the advantages of established firms may include accumulated expertise, reputation and relationships, summarised above as 'franchise'. Offered the same price for an issue, borrowers will choose an existing firm, given their reputation for successful launches, to avoid all the disadvantages in terms of future borrowing costs should an issue fail. Similarly, investors tend not to deal with a new house if they are doubtful about its tenacity – and skilled market staff will not join a firm even for high salaries if they are unsure that it will remain in the market.

Recent experience suggests that these advantages of existing firms can only be offset if there is a large savings surplus in the home country, where entrants have strong relationships with investors and issuers, where there is a desire and ability to invest in euromarket instruments and/or a lower cost of capital, as is the case for Japanese firms. These enable such entrants to charge a lower price than incumbents, cross-subsidising competitive deals (e.g. in straight bonds) from markets (such as equity warrants) where they have market power. Implicitly, there are two types of new entry, one with a secure customer base, and one assuming 'speculatively' that business can be taken from other houses or that a suitable share of any incremental business can be obtained. This would explain the pre-eminence of various investment banks over the years and the inability of many new entrants to gain profitability. Implicitly, exit costs exceeded costs of entry, largely due to the sunk costs of contacts, reputation and privileged access to information on market movements[26] (on the demand side) and expertise (on the cost side) built up over time.

In addition, incumbent firms have actively carried out *strategic moves*. They have, in effect, invested in excess capacity, though whether this was deliberate or accidental is harder to judge.[27] Predatory pricing has been widely used by both incumbents and entrants to the eurobond markets.[28] Development of specialised expertise, for example in swaps, is a further form of strategic investment. Established firms are tending to scoop up the talent in the market which is still in second-tier houses – without which they will not survive.

It may be suggested that competition in provision of market analysis and in research and development has also been aimed at increasing market share and discouraging entry.[29] Strong and timely market analysis may enable a firm to retain its investor base. Such analysis by some firms obliges others to gather similar information to protect themselves, or attempt to enter the market. Meanwhile, the invention of new financial instruments may enable an institution both to make initial gains by charging high fees and, by virtue of its developing expertise, to make longer term excess profits. Even if high prices are not charged, an innovation may give an investment bank an advantage in gaining mandates, which may enable losses to be converted into 'normal' profits. From an economic point of view, the private benefits to the successful innovator are likely to exceed social benefits even if the latter are positive[30] because many innovations, particularly on the product development as opposed to the process/new technology side, do not offer strong benefits to investors aside from existing instruments. In some cases they may worsen the situation for market participants by reducing liquidity in an unanticipated way[31] which offsets any benefits arising from a closer 'fit' to investment needs. The large potential private benefits to innovation lead to a high and perhaps excessive level of such innovation[32] – including duplication of effort to the same end, at considerable resource cost.

The decline in profitability can also be explained by factors relating to *the nature of trade* in the eurobond market between borrowers and intermediaries. Which side bears the larger sunk costs? Borrowers may find it in their interests not to break a relationship with an investment bank, as the latter may stabilise the bond price and maintain an orderly aftermarket, ensuring a good reception of future issues. If it seeks too low a spread, its issue may fail, thus damaging its chances of making further issues. On the other hand, rules of the ISMA require firms to make markets to some extent and other firms may be ready to make markets in the relevant issue. Borrowers are increasingly sophisticated and thus have less need of information that the intermediary can offer, particularly as lead manager performance can be monitored in the grey market, i.e. information asymmetries are becoming less important. Borrowers are increasingly ready to deal with several firms rather than merely a 'house' bank. The investment bank wishes to maintain relationships in order to ensure future business,[33] to preserve its reputation, and to maintain the value of any information it has gathered about the firm in question – which is obviously unsaleable. Once these factors are taken into account, together with the tendencies to rapid new entry, intense competition and the high elasticity of demand for eurobonds, it is evident that the balance of advantage is increasingly to the borrower. The investment bank is unlikely to be able to squeeze monopoly rent from a relationship. Similarly, the investor base of the market has tended to change from private account holders to institutional investors. They have considerable countervailing power against intermediaries, as placing power is an essential part of dealers' strength to win mandates and again institutional investors' sophistication entails symmetric information. It is more in the investment banks' interest to maintain relationships.

e) Summary

To summarise this section, the structure of the primary eurobond market features rather high concentration despite a rapid increase in the number of bookrunners; a degree of fluidity among a limited number of leading firms, often related to the nationality of borrowers or investors; and a large number of peripheral firms. As regards conduct, firms appear frequently to use strategies such as innovation, predatory pricing and cross subsidisation of deals in pursuit of relationships with borrowers and investors. Last, in terms of performance, the outturn for most intermediaries has been rather poor in terms of profitability, while borrowers of funds have gained from lower commissions and margins. It is suggested that these observations can be reconciled by appeal to contestable markets theory – where potential competition restrains the profitability of intermediaries, together with shifts in bargaining power towards end users of funds. However, there also appears to be a degree of strategic competition in the market, which in combination with advantages for incumbents that develop over time (relationships, reputation and expertise) form a barrier to growth for second line firms.

5.3 Prospects for the eurobond market

This final section identifies some key issues relating to the future of the eurobond market – patterns of borrowing and the issue of convergence – and its location in London – regulation and excess capacity.

5.3.1 Borrowers

Benzie (1991) outlined a number of doubts over the general prospects for international bond issuance. For example, for US borrowers the balance of advantage appears now to favour the domestic market. One reason is the low credit quality of US corporations following the wave of takeovers and leveraged buyouts and associated issues of 'junk bonds'. Issues hence no longer meet the high standards of credit quality required by the eurobond market. And the advent of 'event risk' (i.e. the threat to credit quality, arising from the risk of leveraged takeover which would reduce the value of outstanding bonds) has also harmed the standing of US borrowers in general. Longer-term factors favouring the US domestic market are the abolition of withholding tax and introduction of shelf registration (which allow bonds to be registered prior to issuance, thus enabling flexibility in taking advantage of market opportunities). Moreover, in Japan the fall in the stock market has cast a shadow over the equity warrants market, the mainstay of Japanese issuance in recent years. However, Benzie felt that issuance by important European issuers such as banks, industrial companies, mortgage institutions and to a lesser extent governments could make up for these. Easing of issuance queues and limitations on use of proceeds from euroissues could have a particularly favourable influence.

5.3.2 Convergence

A more general factor influencing the future prospects of the eurobond market is convergence between domestic and eurobond markets, which has been a strong feature of recent years. For example, abolition of exchange controls has reduced the usefulness of direct restrictions on bond issuance such as issue queues and other limits. Even where restrictions are still important, as in the yen market, the swap market has facilitated circumvention. A second trend has been abolition of withholding taxes in countries such as the US, Germany and (for non-residents) France and Spain. Third, issuance of 'global bonds' simultaneously in domestic and international markets is increasing integration. Such reforms increase substitutability of euro and domestic bonds and raise the issue of the future viability of the eurobond market, if there are no distinctions with domestic markets. At least, it will need to maintain a high level of competition and innovativeness in order to survive. Not that convergence should be exaggerated. A number of countries retain withholding taxes, such as the UK and Belgium; issuance queues remain in a number of markets, as do limits on the extent to which certain types of borrowers can make euroissues, constraints on use of such funds and restrictions on institutional investors' freedom to acquire foreign securities.[34]

5.3.3 Regulation

Despite the volume of complaints about the Financial Services Act, the regulation of the eurobond market in London is relatively light. The ISMA, the main trade body of eurobond dealers was made a recognised overseas exchange under the Act and is overseen by the Securities and Futures Authority. Use of the TRAX system is now compulsory as noted above, but this has been seen as a benefit as much as a burden. The greater difficulty is that eurobond houses are active in other markets where the regulatory requirements are more severe. Complaints focus particularly on the setup costs of reporting systems and more general costs of management time in meeting regulatory requirements. Moreover, accounting fees that even the smallest bank has to face amount to a considerable additional cost. As well as regulation *per se* there is the problem of legal risk (e.g. the House of Lords decision that swaps entered into by UK local authorities were unlawful).

In the context of international bond markets, such difficulties are of particular importance given the efforts at deregulation made by other centres in recent years, which could attract euromarket intermediaries to the relevant financial centres. For example, the French have been steadily deregulating the international French franc bond market, relaxing listing and authorisation requirements, reducing minimum maturities and allowing French subsidiaries of foreign banks to lead issues. The Dutch have abolished turnover tax and fixed minimum commissions on securities transactions. In Germany turnover taxes have been abolished and the Bundesbank has dismantled the remaining restrictions on issuance and underwriting of foreign currency bonds by borrowers domiciled in Germany (until then issuance in foreign currency required a non-resident financial subsidiary). In the US the SEC rule 144a and Regulation S effectively liberalised the US private placement market, by waiving registration requirements and allowing immediate resale to qualified investors. Such measures could lead to more sales of euroissues in the US as well as enabling issuance to take place there. A longer term issue could be the abolition of US and Japanese laws separating commercial and investment banking, which could entail repatriation of eurobond business to New York and Tokyo.

5.3.4 Excess capacity

As noted in section 5.2, the emergence of excess capacity in bond (and equity) markets located in London has been a notable feature of recent years. With hindsight, it is apparent that new entrants experienced difficulty in predicting customer demand, and may in the event have overestimated the sustainable level. A number of firms may also have had problems in achieving the synergies expected of newly formed structures. Those that sought to grow organically may have faced fewer problems of this type. Firms also had to face the challenge of creating and managing new systems of risk control and of exploiting new developments in information technology.

For a while after the emergence of excess capacity, a number of firms, particularly some large domestic and international conglomerates with diversified operations, appeared willing to continue loss-making securities operations. It has become increasingly evident, however, that few institutions are content continuously to cross subsidise loss-making operations for the sake of customer relationships. They have responded to excess capacity in a variety of ways, but generally by seeking to concentrate on their perceived areas of expertise. Some are focussing on areas such as swaps and derivatives, which can give them an edge in the primary bond market. Another response has been to withdraw from 'commodity' type financial markets (such as commercial paper, foreign exchange and government bonds), where profitability is low, in favour of more specialised activities[35] which generate fee income, and require less capital then does trading or issuance. Examples are fund management and corporate finance. Firms that remain in commodity type business are under particular pressure to contain their costs, given that success in such markets typically flows to the lowest cost producer. As noted, eurobond firms are seeking to reform issuance procedures in a bid to reduce the current pressures on profitability, one underlying cause of which has been excess capacity. A further motive for rethinking organisational structures has been the growing awareness of potential conflict of interest. Conglomerates can find themselves faced with contentious negotiations involving clients of different parts of the same institution. A return to specialisation reduces this risk.

Withdrawal from some types of business and geographical retrenchment may reduce representation in London markets. However, Davis and Latter (1989) concluded that such developments are not necessarily to the benefit of any other centre, and orderly removal of excess capacity should be seen as a normal component of London's evolution.

Notes

1   The views expressed are those of the author and not necessarily those of the Bank of England. The author thanks A. Chester, H. Melandri and P. Temperton for helpful comments, R. Pryor for research assistance and S. Friend for typing.

2   The prefix euro is commonly applied to a type of transaction whose distinguishing feature is the participation of lenders, intermediaries or borrowers from countries other than that of the currency of denomination, and which is conducted offshore.

3   The other type of international bonds are *foreign bonds*, issued by borrowers from other countries on the domestic market of the currency of issuance.

4   That the borrower will not issue debt in the future that is senior to the bonds in question.

5   I.e. all principal is repaid at once, at the final maturity date.

6   For general references on eurobonds see Fisher (1988), Chester (1991) Benzie (1991).

7   For variable rate notes, the spread over libor is reset every three months at an auction of investors and not fixed as is the case for FRNs. In the auction, investors not accepting the spread on offer can sell them back to the issuer. If there is no spread at which investors are ready to hold the VRNs, the spread reverts to a high 'default' level, which is defined at primary issuance and at which investors are obliged to retain the bonds.

8   The main differences between euro and foreign issuance are that the latter are more commonly straight fixed rate issues. Industrial companies, international institutions, French and Japanese borrowers are particularly active in foreign bonds.

9   Source for all data in this chapter except where otherwise indicated: Bank of England ICMS database.

10 See Benzie (1991) for a description of underlying factors.
11 See Davis (1991).
12 This has led to introduction of a hybrid traditional/fixed price procedure where bonds are sold at reoffer price to institutions on initial distribution and at issue price to retail investors subsequently.
13 In addition, it is somewhat slower than bought deals (reducing opportunities for swaps) so is unlikely to supplant them entirely.
14 Source: BIS.
15 Source: Euroclear. References to turnover count a purchase and sale once only.
16 Source: Euroclear.
17 Corporates with AAA ratings.
18 On the other hand, the small size of issues and the large proportion which remain 'locked' in accounts means that individual secondary market prices can often be manipulated by firms. The practice of 'ramping' where firms buy up all of an available stock in order to profit from short sales by other firms is a typical example.
19 Which in the case where the ratio of bonuses to salaries is low bears many of the features of fixed costs.
20 These changes may be traced by comparing the successive descriptions of the eurobond market in Geisst (1980), Levich (1985), *The Economist* (1987) and Chester (1991).
21 Sources: Bank of England ICMS database, *International Financing Review, Euromoney*.
22 Evidence for the first half of 1991 is somewhat contrary to this, in that a rise in concentration has coincided with buoyant issuance. This may partly related to introduction of fixed price reoffer syndication.
23 However, it is noted that these data are also consistent with an equal chance for each firm to drop out in each year. If the probability of dropping out is 0.9, then 16 firms would be consistently in the table. The suggestion here is rather that some firms ('incumbents') have low probabilities, all the others very high probabilities.
24 The advent of swaps may also have led to reduced commissions.
25 It also reported that a leading firm made only $15 million from eurobond issues in 1986 (although it made $25 million from swaps and $60 million from euro-equity and equity-linked bonds). Meanwhile, another made $86 million on international primary capital markets in 1986, of which equity business earned 40%, eurobonds and related swaps 30%, other swaps 30%. Secondary market trading made three times as much as primary trading of which 40% was from bonds.
26 Feldman and Stephenson (1988) offer an interesting analysis of the relationship between size and privileged information in financial markets. They suggest that while size does enable firms to gain a better 'feel' for market activity – and hence profit opportunities – there are discontinuities in information flows which create a virtually impenetrable barrier to firms trying to increase trading volumes. In the eurobond market this is often due to captive investor bases. More generally, firms which try to grow beyond minimal size in OTC securities markets are seen as 'potential competitors' by large established firms rather than 'privileged customers' and may actually *lose* access to market information (the information/market share tradeoff is 'U' shaped).

27 Excess capacity is difficult to identify in the case of financial services, but could include levels of dedicated capitalisation, dealing rooms, hired expertise and settlement staff.

28 The following quotations from *The Banker* (1988) illustrate these tendencies to predatory pricing. 'Dutch bankers complain that the Swiss firms are adopting the same policy that the Japanese did in the eurodollar market – expansion (in euroguilders) through purchase of market share. They reckon foreign-led deals are unrealistically tightly priced'. 'The (Coca Cola) deal (lead managed by the Swiss) wounded German pride and spurred Deutsche Bank to bid aggressively for deals wherever there was the slightest chance of a mandate slipping abroad'.

29 Courtadon (1985) suggested that the bought deal and r&d competition, together with placing power, were the main barriers to successful entry. The relative importance of these will of course fluctuate. Arguably, innovation was more important than placing prior to the crisis in the FRN market and the equity market crash, while placing power has now come to the fore.

30 It is not denied that a degree of innovation may be necessary for the efficiency of financial markets and there may be particular benefits to issuers.

31 The perpetual FRN is the best example – not only did it prove illiquid (a failed product) but it also helped to reduce liquidity (by externality) in the dated FRN market.

32 Examination of the innovations described in Mason (1986) illustrates the number of at most marginal products that have been put on the market, all at considerable resource cost in terms of research ('rocket scientists'), product development, legal advice, advertising and other marketing expenditure. These include reverse FRNs, minimax FRNs, step down FRNs, step up FRNs, floating then zero FRNs, double drop lock bonds, multiplier 'bunny' bonds, capped forex linked 'purgatory and hell' bonds, marginal reverse forex linked bonds, window warrants, wedding warrants, duet bonds and serial sinking fund bonds to name but a few. The collapse of the FRN market itself spawned a vast and fruitless r&d effort to find ways to revive it.

33 Evidence presented in Davis and Mayer (1991) shows a considerable degree of switching of lead management affiliations by corporate issuers in the eurobond market.

34 In an EC context, the Single Market Initiative will entail removal of some of these barriers, notably to international investment, but not the others. Even for investment, removal of restrictions is likely to be a slow process.

35 The key distinction between 'commodity' and specialised markets is that in the latter a firm may differentiate itself from its competitors in exploitation of factors such as its perceived reputation and expertise, its capacity to innovate, and asymmetries of information between intermediaries and customers. In these circumstances relationships are important. In 'commodity' markets the product tends to be homogenous, with strong competition limiting profitability; relationships tend to be less important. See, for example, Bleeke and Bryan (1988).

Bibliography

The Banker, (1988) Games without frontiers, May 1988, 16-21.

Benzie, R.S. (1991) *The development of the international bond market*, BIS Economic Paper No. 32.

Bleeke, J.A. and **Bryan L.L.** (1988) The globalisation of financial markets, *McKinsey Quarterly*, Winter 1988, 17–38.

Chester, A.C. (1991) The international bond market, *Bank of England Quarterly Bulletin*, **31**, 521–8.

Courtadon, C.L. (1985) *The competitive structure of the eurobond underwriting industry*, Salomon Brothers, Monograph Series 1985-1, Salomon Bros Center for the study of Financial Institutions, New York University.

Davis, E.P. (1988) Industrial structure and dynamics of financial markets; the primary eurobond market, *Journal of International Securities Markets*, February 1988, 253–68 and January 1989, 83–102.

Davis, E.P. (1989) Instability in the euromarkets and the economic theory of financial crisis, *Bank of England Discussion Paper*, **43**.

Davis, E.P. and **Latter A.R.** (1989) London as an international financial centre, *Bank of England Quarterly Bulletin*, **29**, 516–28.

Davis, E.P. (1990) International financial centres; an industrial analysis, *Bank of England Discussion Paper*, **51**.

Davis, E.P. (1991) International diversification of institutional investors, *Journal of International Securities Markets*, Summer 1991, 143–67.

Davis, E.P. and **Mayer, C.P.** (1991), Corporate finance in the euromarkets and the economics of intermediation, forthcoming, *Bank of England Discussion Papers (Technical Series)* **45** and forthcoming CEPR paper.

The Economist (1987) How and where to make money in the euromarkets, 3.1.1987, London.

Feldman, L. and **Stephenson, J.** (1988) Stay small or get huge – lessons from securities trading, *Harvard Business Review*, **663**, 116-23.

Fisher, F.G. (1988) *Eurobonds*, Euromoney Publications.

Geisst, C.R. (1980) *Raising International Capital*, Saxton House.

Hammond, G.M.S. (1987) Recent developments in the swap market, *Bank of England Quarterly Bulletin*, **27**, 66–79.

Hanna, J. and **Staley, S.** (1983) *The International Bond Manual – US Dollar*. Salomon Bros, New York.

Hendry, D.F., Pagan, A.R. and **Sargan, J.D.** (1983) Dynamic Specification, in Griliches, Z. and Intriligator, M.D., (eds) *Handbook of Econometrics*, **2**, North-Holland.

Jeanneau, S. (1989) Reform of the eurobond market, mimeo, Bank of England, London.

Levich, R.M. (1985) A view from the international capital markets, in **Walter, I.,** (ed.) *Deregulating Wall Street* John Wiley.

Mason, M. (1986) *Innovations in the structures of international securities*, Credit Suisse First Boston Ltd.

Mayer, C.P. (1985) The assessment; recent developments in industrial economics and their implications for policy, *Oxford Review of Economic Policy*, Vol. 1, **3**, 1–24.

Tirole, J. (1990) *The Theory of Industrial Organisation*, MIT Press.

6   The London money market

by Paul Temperton

The well developed, highly liquid and sophisticated money market in London today has, as its origins, the discounting of bills by the discount houses in the early nineteenth century. This remained the principal activity in the London money market for over a hundred years, until a wave of innovation hit the market in the late 1960s. First came the development of the eurodollar market in London, driven by the wish to avoid domestic banking regulations in the United States. This was given added impetus in 1971 with the removal of quantitative controls on the UK domestic banking system and the rapid development of the CD and interbank markets ensued. In the 1980s, commercial paper, euronote and eurocommercial paper markets were added to the range of money market instruments traded in London. The development of the futures market, especially the LIFFE short sterling contract, further enhanced market liquidity. Despite this wave of innovation, the principal operational relationship between the Bank of England and the money market has remained little changed: this is described in the next section. We then go on to discuss the size and structure of the money market and the individual characteristics of the most important constituent markets. We assess the factors behind the development of the markets, highlighting the importance of the regulatory environment and investor preferences. Finally, we look at some of the issues facing the money market in the rest of the 1990s.

6.2   The Bank of England and the traditional London money market[1]

6.2.1   The role of the Bank of England in the money market

The Bank of England has a pivotal role in the London money market in that it acts as the main banker to both the central government and the clearing banks. The government does not hold balances, other than working amounts, with other banks. As the rest of the banking system maintains the accounts of all other sectors of the economy, any net payment to central government will produce a net flow of cash from the banks to the Bank. The relationship is shown schematically in Fig. 6.1. The banks will typically seek to restore their liquidity by drawing down some of their funds which they keep in the form of call or short term deposits with the discount houses. The clearing banks keep operational balances at the Bank which are used for settling the final position at the end of the day between the Bank and the banking system, and their drawing down of money from the discount houses will be designed to keep these balances at a 'target' level considered appropriate given the uncertainty of the daily cash flows to the Bank. The cash shortage in the money market is, in this way, passed to the discount houses. Discount houses, in turn, balance their position, if short of funds, either by selling eligible bills to the Bank or by borrowing from the Bank.

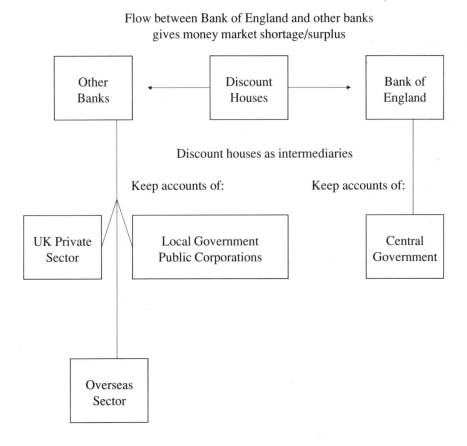

Figure 6.1 Money market structure and flows

The discount houses have their origins in the early nineteenth century. Their role at that time was to discount bills for holders requiring immediate cash for payments which were due in perhaps two or three months. From that time, they have continued to have an important role in the discounting of bills and as a result of this function have come to fill a pivotal role between the banks and the Bank of England in the determination of short term interest rates. There are nine discount houses in London, all members of the London Discount Market Association. The balance sheet of the discount houses is shown in Table 6.1.

Table 6.1 Balance sheet of discount houses (a)

£ Millions
Liabilities: borrowed funds

Sterling	Sept 1991
1 Bank of England	545
2 Other UK banks(b)	9,279
3 Other UK residents	2,802
4 Overseas	6
5 Total sterling liabilities (1 to 4)	12,632
6 of which, call and overnight	9,969
Other currency	
7 UK banks(b)	83
8 Other UK residents	160
9 Overseas	93
10 Other currency total (7 to 9)	336
11 Total borrowed funds (5+10)	12,969
Assets:	
Sterling	
12 Cash ratio deposits with bank of England	14
13 Bills: Treasury bills	571
14 Local authority bills	17
15 Other public sector bills	–
16 Other bills	4,908
17 Total bills (13 to 16)	5,496
18 Funds lent: UK banks(b)	100
19 UK bank CDs (b)	5,095
20 Building society CDs and time deps.	1,083
21 UK local authorities	6
22 Other UK residents	733
23 Currency assets	5
24 Total funds lent (18 to 23)	7,021
25 Investments: British government stocks	86
26 Local authorities	–
27 Building societies	202
28 Other	52
29 Total investments (25 to 28)	341
30 Other sterling assets	43
Other currency assets	
31 Certificate of deposit	145
32 Bills	8
33 Other	182
34 Total other currency assets (31 to 33)	335
35 Total assets (12+17+24+29+30+34)	13,250

Notes: a) Comprises all money-market dealing counterparties of the Bank of England which are authorised under the Banking Act 1987 regardless of ultimate ownership.
b) Comprises offices in Great Britain and Northern Ireland of institutions authorised under the Banking Act 1987, together with certain institutions in the Channel Islands and Isle of Man, and the Banking Department of the Bank of England.
Source: *Bank of England Quarterly Bulletin*, Nov. 1991, Table 4.

6.2.2 The Bank of England's day to day operations in the money market

The Bank of England's day to day operations in the money market are conducted primarily through the discount houses. Information on money market flows is provided by the Bank of England on various electronic screen based services (for example, on Reuters on pages RTCA through to RTCD, see Fig. 6.2).

```
1001                  MONEY MARKET OPERATIONS              RTCA
                    OFFICIAL BANK OF ENGLAND INPUT
   .            MORNING FORECAST, THURSDAY 16 JANUARY
   .       A SHORTAGE OF AROUND STG 1700 MN IS EXPECTED TODAY
   .        AN EARLY ROUND OF BILL OFFERS WILL BE INVITED
   .                  AMONG THE MAIN FACTORS ARE
   .           TREASURY BILLS & MATURING ASSISTANCE -832
   .     EXCHEQUER TRANSACTIONS -790   RISE IN NOTE CIRCULATION -55
   .              BANKERS BALANCES  BELOW TARGET -20
     IN EARLY OPERATIONS THE BANK HAS PURCHASED BILLS TOTALLING
   STG 158MN OF WHICH STG 30 MN OUTRIGHT -
   BAND 1 BANK BILLS STG 30 MN AT 10 3/8% AND STG 128 MN FOR

                         SEE PAGE RTCB
   ++++++++++++ REUTER ++++++++ Key Station 3 ++++++++ v. T2291 +++++++

   1212                  MONEY MARKET OPERATIONS              RTCB
                    OFFICIAL BANK OF ENGLAND INPUT
   RESALE TO THE MARKET ON 3 FEBRUARY AT AN INTEREST RATE OF
   10 7/16%
   THE FORECAST HAS BEEN REVISED TO A SHORTAGE OF AROUND
   STG 1750 MN, BEFORE TAKING ACCOUNT OF THE EARLY OPERATIONS.
   IN FURTHER OPERATIONS IN THE MARKET THIS MORNING THE BANK HAS
   PURCHASED BILLS TOTALLING STG 78 MN, OF WHICH STG 47 MN OUTRIGHT -
   BAND 1 TREASURY BILLS STG 18 MN AT 10 3/8%
   BAND 1     BANK BILLS STG 29 MN AT 10 3/8% AND STG 31 MN FOR
   RESALE TO THE MARKET ON 3 FEBRUARY AT AN INTEREST RATE OF
   10 7/16%
                         SEE PAGE RTCC
   ++++++++++++ REUTER ++++++++ Key Station 3 ++++++++ v. T2291 +++++++

   1453                  MONEY MARKET OPERATIONS              RTCC
                    OFFICIAL BANK OF ENGLAND INPUT
   THE FORECAST HAS BEEN FURTHER REVISED TO A SHORTAGE OF AROUND
   STG 1900 MN BEFORE TAKING ACCOUNT OF THE MORNING OPERATIONS.
   THE BANK HAS OPERATED IN THE MARKET THIS AFTERNOON PURCHASING
   BILLS TOTALLING STG 642 MN, OF WHICH STG 546 MN OUTRIGHT -
   BAND 1 TREASURY BILLS STG 175 MN AT 10 3/8%  **  PLEASE SEE NEXT
   BAND 1     BANK BILLS STG 357 MN AT 10 3/8%      PAGE FOR LATE
   BAND 2 TREASURY BILLS STG   4 MN AT 10 3/8%      ASSISTANCE  **
   BAND 2     BANK BILLS STG  10 MN AT 10 3/8% AND STG 96 MN FOR
   RESALE TO THE MARKET ON 3 FEBRUARY AT AN INTEREST RATE OF
   10 7/16%.
                         SEE PAGE RTCD
   ++++++++++++ REUTER ++++++++ Key Station 3 ++++++++ v. T2291 +++++++

   1452                  MONEY MARKET OPERATIONS              RTCD
                    OFFICIAL BANK OF ENGLAND INPUT
       THE BANK HAS PROVIDED LATE ASSISTANCE OF AROUND STG 560 MN.
```

Source: Reuters pages RTCA to RTCD Thursday 16 Jan. 1992.

Figure 6.2

The first piece of information to be released through this channel each day is the Bank's estimate of the overall cash shortage or surplus in the money market. The main factors contributing to this overall position are then listed. These fall into six main categories, information on the first five of which may be disclosed by the Bank. The six main categories are discussed below.

The Exchequer is broadly equivalent to central government and the category of 'exchequer transactions' comprises the main flows which are the result of the Bank of England acting as the banker to central government. The category comprises: a) payments to the Exchequer net of expenditure by it; b) the proceeds of net official sales of government debt (gilts, National savings, treasury bills etc.); and c) net receipts of sterling on the Exchange Equalisation Account (EEA). In all three cases net sterling payments to the government's accounts at the Bank reduce market liquidity. Thus, if the government receives tax payments from, or if it sells government debt to, the private sector the proceeds will act to reduce the money market's cash position. Conversely, government spending will increase the deposits of the banks and reduce those of the government at the Bank of England. If the EEA intervenes to support sterling (i.e. if it sells foreign currencies and buys sterling) then the receipt of sterling by the Bank will act to drain market liquidity.

Many elements of the Exchequer transactions total can be predicted with a reasonable degree of accuracy by the Bank of England on a day-to-day basis: the impact of foreign exchange transactions passing through the EEA is generally known since most such transactions are settled two days later; gilts transactions are generally settled on the next business day; and various government sources give information on both government expenditure and expected tax receipts. But the timing of some tax payments is not known with certainty and can lead to substantial changes in this component of the money market cash position during the course of the day. (These intra-day revisions to the cash position are very important to the discount houses and close observers of the Bank of England's operations and are discussed later in this chapter.)

If the demand for cash, in the form of notes issued by the Bank of England, rises, the clearing banks meet the rise in demand by obtaining notes from the Bank, at the same time running down their operational balances with it. Thus a rise in the note circulation leads to a money market shortage. Generally, the note circulation rises towards the end of the week (as the general public withdraws cash for the weekend and the banks anticipate the demand) and falls at the start of the week: thus on Mondays and Tuesdays the fluctuations in the note circulation generally raise money market liquidity and on Thursdays and Fridays generally reduce it. The note issue also follows a pronounced seasonal pattern throughout the year rising, in particular, at Easter and Christmas. The Bank has an estimate based on past experience of daily and seasonal patterns, and on the banks' declared requirements, of likely changes in the note circulation.

If the Bank holds bills which then mature, repayment will come from the rest of the banking system so market liquidity falls. Similarly, as the discount houses take up Treasury bills from the tender on the Friday of the previous week, net payment will be made to the Bank from the rest of the banking system. The Bank will know the extent of these influences on the market's cash position with certainty.

The Bank occasionally lends to the market or uses purchase and resale agreements (see below). The unwinding of such assistance (repayment of loans given by the Bank to the market or resale to the market of bills bought from it by the Bank) will drain market liquidity and will, of course, be known by the Bank in advance.

If the clearing banks' balances are above target – that is, if the final clearing on the previous day left the clearers with balances at the Bank above those which they desire to keep in order to meet day-to-day requirements – then there will be a corresponding easing of the market's cash position. The clearers tell the Bank of England of their target balances so this influence on the money market cash position will be known with reasonable certainty.

As well as acting as the government's banker, the Bank also acts as banker for other customers, for example, overseas central banks and international organisations. Flows due to the transactions of these customers influence the cash position of the money market but are not disclosed by the Bank. Such customers generally provide information to the Bank on flows on their accounts and hence help in the process of predicting the cash position in the money market.

6.2.3   The objective of the Bank of England's money market operations

The objective of the Bank when operating in the money market is broadly to offset the cash flows between the Bank and the money markets and to leave the clearing banks within reach of their desired operational balances. The Bank thus provides whatever assistance is necessary to offset the daily cash position in the money market: the terms (that is, the interest rates at particular maturities) at which the cash position is offset are, of course, determined by the Bank. The Bank's forecast of the daily position of the money markets is designed to help this process. The Bank's initial forecast and the factors behind it are made available at 9.45 a.m. each day, but revisions to the overall shortage may be made during the course of the day, typically being announced at noon and 2 p.m. Revisions to the individual components of the shortage are not made, but generally it is the estimate for exchequer transactions which is subject to the greatest uncertainty. When deciding on the amount of intervention needed, however, the Bank also takes account of the reports of their positions from the discount houses and the major banks, and the behaviour of short term interest rates. Different techniques are used depending on whether there is a shortage in the money market or a surplus.

The preceding section has emphasised the day-to-day actions in the money market, but it is also useful at this stage to look at the aggregate position in recent years which is shown in Table 6.2. There are several ways of expressing the factors affecting the cash position in the money market, but this is the method used most often in the Bank's *Quarterly Bulletin*.

The Bank of England uses three principal techniques to relieve money market shortages: outright purchases of bills from the discount houses; purchases of bills with associated resale agreements; and lending to the market. Information on the technique(s) used by the Bank in alleviating the cash position are made available via the electronic screen based services. The techniques are discussed below.

Under the arrangements first introduced in late 1980, emphasis is placed on bill dealings as a method of relieving money market shortages and the outright purchase of bills from the discount houses is the most common form of assistance provided. If the Bank informs the market that it is prepared to buy bills, the discount houses will generally offer bills to it, specifying a discount rate, for each combination of instrument and band – or, if they wish, different rates for separate amounts within each combination. Bills are classified as falling into one of four remaining (rather than original) maturity bands:

Table 6.2 Influences on the cash position of the money market and official offsetting operations

£billion, increases in market's cash (+)	81/82	82/83	83/84	84/85	85/86	86/87	87/88	88/89	89/90	90/91
Factors affecting the market's cash position										
CGBR(+)	+7.6	+12.7	+12.2	+10.2	+11.0	+10.5	+0.9	−6.9	−5.6	−2.5
of which, on lending to local authorities and public corporations	+1.0	+5.0	+4.1	+3.7	+6.7	+6.0	+4.2	+6.0	−0.3	+0.4
Net sales (−) of central government debt [1]	−10.8	−9.2	−14.7	−14.1	−8.2	−8.7	−9.3	+13.3	+17.2	+1.4
of which: Gilt edged	−6.0	−5.1	−11.7	−10.2	−5.7	−6.1	−7.0	+13.3	+15.8	+2.9
National Savings	−4.3	−3.0	−3.3	−3.1	−2.1	−3.3	−2.3	−0.6	+1.7	−1.4
CTDs	−0.6	−1.0	+0.2	−0.8	−0.4	+0.7	0.0	+0.6	−0.3	−0.1
Currency circulation (increase−)	−0.2	−1.2	−0.3	−0.9	−0.7	+0.3	−1.9	−0.8	−0.8	−1.0
Reserves etc	−1.3	−1.6	+0.1	−0.5	+0.9	+1.5	+11.4	+1.5	−5.8	+0.6
Other	−0.4	+0.1	−0.3	−0.3	+0.7	+0.9	−0.6	−0.8	−0.4	+0.3
Total factors affecting cash position	−5.1	+0.8	−3.0	−5.7	+3.7	+4.4	+0.6	+6.2	+4.5	−1.2
Official Offsetting Operations										
Net increase (+) in Bank's commercial bills [2]	+4.7	−0.3	+3.8	+1.5	−2.0	−3.3	+2.5	−5.7	+1.1	+2.2
Net increase (−) in Treasury bills in market	+0.1	−0.2	−0.1	+0.2	−0.1	−0.7	−0.8	−0.5	−5.7	−1.3
Securities acquired (+) under sale and repurchase [3]	0.0	+0.6	−0.6	+3.4	−1.1	−1.2	−1.1	0.0	0.0	0.0
Other	+0.3	−0.6	−0.1	+0.7	−0.4	+0.9	−1.5	+0.1	−0.2	+0.5
Total Official Offsetting Operations	+5.1	−0.5	+3.0	+5.8	−3.7	−4.2	−0.9	−6.1	−4.8	+1.4
Change in bankers' operational balances at the Bank	0.0	+0.3	0.0	+0.1	0.0	+0.1	−0.3	+0.2	−0.3	+0.2

Notes: 1) Other than Treasury bills 2) By the Issue and Banking Departments of the Bank of England. 3) Gilt edged stocks and promissory notes related to guaranteed export credit and shipbuilding paper.
Source: Bank of England Quarterly Bulletins; various issues and Temperton (1991)

band 1:   1–14 days
band 2:   15–33 days
band 3:   34–63 days
band 4:   64–91 days.

Since May 1989, the Bank normally purchases bills only in bands 1 and 2. Normally the Bank operates in the markets at midday and 2.00 p.m., but on days of very large shortages, it may offer to buy bills earlier in the day (9.45 a.m.) as well.

When the discount houses offer bills to the Bank, the Bank decides which offers to accept. During the course of the day the Bank's objective will be to provide enough assistance to the money market (through outright bill operations and the other techniques discussed below) to relieve the overall expected shortage, but purchases of bills by the Bank at the early rounds of assistance during the course of the day might only account for a small proportion of the overall assistance provided, for four main reasons.

First, the Bank may, in each of the 9.45 a.m., midday and 2.00 p.m. rounds of assistance decline to buy the amount of bills offered by the discount houses in order to keep the market short and sustain short term interest rates at a relatively high level.

Second, when the discount houses want to 'test the water' for an interest rate cut, they might offer paper 1/2% lower than on the previous day at the first opportunity (that is, at 9.45 a.m. or midday). If the Bank refuses to accept these offers then the amount of assistance provided in the first round could be a long way short of the overall amount of assistance needed during the day. The houses will then almost certainly return to the rates established on the previous day at the next round of assistance.

Third, a relatively small amount of assistance at the earlier rounds could also occur if the Bank estimates of the shortage were unusually uncertain: for example, it might not be known whether a particular tax payment were to be passed through the money market on that day.

Fourth, the discount houses collectively may offer a smaller quantity of bills for sale than apparently needed by the market as a whole, either because they take a different (to the Bank) view of the overall shortage in the market or because of the relationship in the market between the short term interest rates at which they fund themselves and the relevant bill yields.

The amount of bills bought in each band, the type of bill and the interest rate at which the deal was made are published after both the morning and afternoon sessions.

Purchase and resale agreements are occasionally used as an alternative to outright purchases. In this case, the Bank buys bills but agrees to sell them back to the market at an agreed price some time in the future. The technique is used for three main reasons. First, to smooth out a known future market position (for example, arranging for the unwinding of the repo on a date of large central government spending). Second, to prevent a particular interest rate structure from becoming too entrenched. Third, when the market is reluctant to sell bills outright because of interest rate expectations. Thus, if interest rates are expected to fall, market participants will be unwilling to sell bills outright to the Bank. In particular, they will not wish to sell longer dated bills, the prices of which rise by a larger amount for a given change in interest rates. Another form of repo which has been used at times of particularly heavy tax receipts by the government is one undertaken directly with the banks. The repo is generally in gilts, although other instruments have also been acceptable.

Lending to the discount houses takes three principal forms. First, the Bank can lend to the discount houses as a method of providing further assistance if it has not provided adequate assistance earlier in the day. Discount houses have borrowing facilities at the Bank, with limits related to the capital base of each discount house. If a discount house finds itself short of funds after the Bank's main bill business has been concluded, it can request to borrow on a secured basis from the Bank. The Bank publishes the total amount of this so called late assistance, although not the terms on which it has been granted.

Second, the Bank can, by refusing to relieve market shortages through bill operations, force the discount houses to borrow from it. This technique may be used when the Bank is keen to produce a change in interest rates faster than that which could be obtained by waiting for bill offers to respond to an initial rejection of bids by the Bank: it was used more frequently in 1988 and 1989, especially as a method of signalling the Bank's desire to see higher short term interest rates. Typically, the Bank will announce that discount houses wishing to use their borrowing facilities are invited to do so at 2.30 p.m.; on such occasions the interest rate at which loans are made is usually published. The limits on the size of borrowing facilities are suspended for 2.30 p.m. lending. A variation on this technique is for the Bank to announce a Minimum Lending Rate which, for a short period ahead, it will apply in any lending to the discount houses. This technique was last used on 5 October 1990 at the time of ERM entry in order to bring a 1% reduction in interest rates to 14%.

Third, the Bank may lend to relieve 'technical shortages' due to, say, oversubscription to a privatisation issue (for example, on 30 October 1981, the Bank lent £121 million over the weekend through the discount window because of the heavy oversubscription for shares in Cable and Wireless). In such circumstances, lending will be at rates close to market rates and will be designed to avoid any distortion to bill rates.

If there is a surplus, the Bank normally acts only in the afternoon to absorb it. Such operations are carried out in Treasury bills, of one or more specified (usually short) maturities. The clearing banks as well as the discount houses have the opportunity to buy Treasury bills on such occasions, as otherwise they would be at a substantial disadvantage compared with the discount houses in finding an outlet for surplus funds.

Looking ahead, there is one other technique which could be used to offset a money market surplus: a call for special deposits. All monetary sector institutions with eligible liabilities of £10 million or more may be called upon to place special deposits with the Bank. Such deposits would normally earn a rate of interest close to the equivalent of the average rate of discount at the most recent Treasury bill tender and would be called in amounts set as a percentage of eligible liabilities. Although the scheme has not been activated since December 1979, it remains available as a method of withdrawing cash from the banking system. Since a call for, or a repayment of, special deposits requires a period of notice, the scheme is best suited to occasions when there is the prospect of a protracted period of surplus cash which the Bank wishes to offset. Once special deposits have been called, their release can be timed to match an expected money market shortage.

6.2.4 Money market flows and the government's funding policy

During the early and mid-1980s, there were persistent shortages in the money market and the Bank of England found itself regularly providing assistance to the market in the form of purchases of commercial bills. The Bank accumulated a substantial portfolio of commercial bills which came to be termed the 'bill mountain'. As these bills were of short maturity (up to three months) they 'rolled over' rather quickly. This factor, described as 'bills maturing in official hands' above, came to be an important influence on the daily cash position of the money market. Overall shortages often amounted to more than £1 billion per day in the mid-1980s.

The growth of the bill mountain in the first half of the 1980s was due largely to the policy of overfunding the PSBR – that is, selling more public sector debt to the non-bank private sector than was needed to match the size of the PSBR.

The combination of the abandonment of overfunding and continued heavy borrowing by central government for on-lending to the local authorities and public corporations led to a move to overall money market surpluses in the later 1980s and a fall in the amount of money market assistance outstanding. From a peak level of £17 billion in July 1985, the amount of assistance outstanding fell to £4.1 billion by the end of March 1989. The Bank's holdings of commercial bills – the 'bill mountain' – fell from a peak level of £14.3 billion in February 1985 to £2.4 billion at the end of June 1989.

6.2.5 Relationship between Bank of England interest rates and market interest rates: administered versus market related interest rates

Up until the early 1970s, the Bank of England's Bank Rate was the pivotal interest rate in the money market. Bank Rate was the rate at which discount houses could borrow from the Bank in order to meet any shortage of liquidity. The Bank could, and did, make Bank Rate effective by open market operations. In particular, as the discount houses were obliged to take up the whole of the weekly offering of Treasury bills by the Bank, the Bank could, by deliberately overissuing Treasury bills, leave the discount houses short of cash balances and force them to borrow from the Bank.

Bank Rate was the rate charged for such 'last resort' lending. Any rise in Bank Rate would induce the discount houses to raise their lending rates and this in turn would be reflected in the clearing banks' interest rates.

The importance of Bank Rate was recognised to the extent that this process became short circuited. From the 1930s, the clearing banks directly linked their interest rates to Bank Rate. The rate became the central rate in a system of 'administered' rates.

In September 1971 a new system of competition and credit control was introduced. Under the new system, the role of quantitative controls on bank lending was reduced and greater reliance was placed on the role of market determined interest rates in the allocation of credit. The role of Bank Rate as the pivotal interest rate was reduced. In particular, the clearing banks ceased to tie their deposit and lending rates to it. However, Bank Rate remained as the 'last resort' rate for lending to the discount houses and, furthermore, continued to have a high political profile.

In order to make the rate more flexible, but still leave it as a penalty rate, a new system of determining the Bank's lending rate to the market was introduced. From 13 October 1972, Bank Rate was replaced by Minimum Lending Rate (MLR). MLR was set at ½% above the average rate of discount for Treasury bills at the most recent tender, rounded to the nearest ¼% above. The rate was automatically determined by this formula and announced each Friday afternoon with the results of the Treasury bill tender. The right to suspend the formula was, however, reserved. If the Bank decided, with the approval of the Chancellor, to make a special change of this kind, the announcement would normally be made on Thursday at midday.

Although the formula related MLR was considered a more satisfactory system at the outset, the new system itself was found to be lacking when interest rates became much more volatile in the mid-1970s: high and variable inflation was accompanied by sharp changes in interest rate expectations and in the term structure of short term rates. Lending to the discount houses at MLR was never for periods longer than seven days but that rate was tied to the three month Treasury bill rate. Such a firm link between interest rates for different periods proved inappropriate in such volatile conditions. Indeed, it was only a year after the formula was introduced that the first suspension took place (on 13 November 1973, when MLR was raised from 11¼% to 13%). On 7 October 1976 and on 3 February 1977 the formula was again suspended. On the fourth occasion of suspension, 11 April 1978, when MLR was raised from 6½% to 7½%, it was stated that the formula would remain suspended until it was capable of being applied without a change in the rate: that is, until market rates had risen to a level consistent with the administered rate. After two further administered rises in rates, it was announced on 25 May 1978 that from then onwards MLR would be a purely administered rate.

Disenchantment with this regime soon set in. Changes in the official interest rate once again took on a high political profile and this led to problems with the conduct of monetary policy. Specifically, as soon as market interest rates started to rise, expectations of an increase in MLR were generated and the government's funding programme became difficult. Because official sanctioning of a rise in interest rates could be slow, a 'funding pause' could result: this led to problems with controlling broad money, which in turn could reinforce expectations of a rise in interest rates.

These problems, coupled with the Conservative government's free market philosophy, led to a move back towards more market related official rates in the early 1980s. On 20 August 1981, it was stated that MLR would no longer be announced continuously. Greater reliance was to be placed on market forces in the determination of interest rates, although the Bank would still aim to keep 'very short term' interest rates within an unpublished 'band'. This is generally interpreted as a band for overnight money rates. As discussed above, the range of signals at the Bank's disposal is quite wide. At the least subtle end of the range the Bank can announce in advance the rate which will apply in its 2.30 p.m. lending to the market. This technique has been used increasingly often in the recent past as a way of signalling the Bank's wishes on the appropriate level of interest rates. Its use can be regarded as a move back to a more 'managed' approach to the determination of interest rates. More subtle techniques include not doing an early round of assistance when there is a large shortage.

6.3   Size and structure of the London money market

Before going on to discuss the characteristics of each market we set out in Table 6.3 the size of each of the markets that constitute the London money market.

Table 6.3 The London money market: size and structure

£billion, 1991 Q2

CD Market	£	50.9	(1)
	other currency	73.6	(1)
Interbank Market	£	90.3	(1)
	other currency	79.2	(1)
Treasury bills	£	13.6	(2)
Eligible Bank bills	£	} 21.2	(3)
Ineligible Bank bills			
Commercial Paper	£	6.2	(4)

Sources: (1) *Bank of England Quarterly Bulletin* Aug 1991 Tables 3.1 to 3.7
       (2) *Bank of England Quarterly Bulletin* Aug 1991 Page 350 Table F
       (3) *Bank of England Quarterly Bulletin* Aug 1991
       (4) Sterling Commercial Paper: May 1991 Bank of England Press Release.

6.3.1   Treasury bills

Treasury bills are normally of three months to maturity. They are sold at a discount, the rise in price bringing a return to the holder as no coupon is paid. They are allotted by tender each Friday and issued on each working day by the Bank of England. The discount houses have a traditional undertaking to underwrite the whole of the Treasury bill tender. Historically, this arrangement provided a residual form of financing for the government – meeting any financing requirement not satisfied by sales of other forms of debt. When the Bank of England receives the proceeds of the Treasury bill tender a shortage in the money market is created. Indeed, in the 1960s and 1970s, deliberate over issuance of Treasury bills was the way in which the Bank of England enforced Bank Rate. The discount houses, in the face of the shortage which was created in the money market, were forced to borrow from the Bank of England's discount window at Bank Rate.

From the mid-1970s onwards greater reliance was placed on control of broad money and sales of gilts replaced the need for the government to finance its borrowing requirement through the issue of Treasury bills. Indeed, the money market shortages created by greater reliance on sales of gilts were initially relieved by buying back Treasury bills from the market. In the early 1980s the process went one stage further with the Bank buying commercial bills as a means of providing assistance in the money market; the need for this was exacerbated by the policy of overfunding the PSBR to reduce broad money growth. Issuance of Treasury bills therefore amounted to only £100 million per week, with the largest part of this taken up by the banking sector. In the early and mid-1980s purchases of Treasury bills by the UK private sector contributed only a modest amount to funding the PSBR.

The end of the 1980s, however, saw a return to surpluses in the money market, a reduction in the Bank of England's outstanding holdings of commercial bills and, in 1989, an enlargement of the Treasury bill issue. In May 1989 the size of the weekly three month Treasury bill tender was increased from the customary £100 million to £500 million, and for the first time a weekly six month tender of £100 million was introduced. In September 1989, nine week bills were also offered. Although the banking sector continued to be the largest purchaser of these Treasury bills, some were purchased by the M4 private sector (i.e. the UK private sector excluding banks and building societies) (see Table 6.4). In the first half of the 1989/90 financial year purchases by that sector amounted to £1.5 billion at an annual rate.

Table 6.4 Treasury bills
£ millions, net purchases by the public +/sales −

	Total Treasury bills	Overseas sector: CMIs (1)	Other overseas	Banks	Discount houses	Building societies (2)	Other public sector	Private sector (3)
1975/76	2,166	−517	1	1,404	471		0	807
1976/77	−1,192	−399	4	−697	179		70	−349
1977/78	−572	−387	−3	−547	35		0	330
1978/79	−840	93	2	100	−300		−59	−676
1979/80	56	285	18	237	−500		9	7
1980/81	−1,025	−318	−14	−531	−163		−73	74
1981/82	−111	−113	12	−19	−68		−25	102
1982/83	195	101	42	−120	−22		2	192
1983/84	126	−31	37	−38	57		74	27
1984/85	−185	58	46	−84	−23		−7	−175
1985/86	124	−61	5	128	14		51	−13
1986/87	670	262	−17	72	205		−51	198
1987/88	789	683	96	−58	−232		133	167
1988/89	460	163	38	−182	−87	103	442	−17
1989/90	5,733	778	−87	3,358	343	1,010	−560	891
1990/91	1,029	−111	0	−742	79	1,123	52	628

Notes: 1) Central Monetary Institutions and international organisations (for example, the IMF). 1990/91 figure relates to total overseas sector.
2) Up to and including 1987/88, building society purchases are included in purchases by the private sector.
3) The UK private sector excludes banks and discount houses and, from 1988/89, building societies as well.
Source: Bank of England Quarterly Bulletins, various issues, and Temperton (1991).

Given that the government was buying in gilts with the purpose of unfunding the Public Sector Deficit Requirement (PSDR), such purchases meant that an even larger amount of gilts had to be repurchased from the M4 private sector, but these purchases themselves further increased the surplus in the money market and hence the requirement for issuance of Treasury bills. The Chancellor of the Exchequer thus announced in October 1989 that 'it has become increasingly anomalous to chase our own tails in this way. Accordingly, we have decided to treat Treasury bill sales as outside the definition of funding irrespective of who buys them.'

As the public sector debt repayment is now contracting in size (to only £0.4 billion in 1990/91 compared with £14.7 billion in 1988/89 and £7.9 billion in 1989/90) and as a public sector borrowing requirement is expected for the 1991/92 and 1992/93 financial years, it seems likely that regular issuance of Treasury bills will be maintained.

In the recent past the Bank of England has been issuing between £300 and £500 million per week of 91 day bills and £200 million per week of 182 day bills. Both are regularly three times oversubscribed.[2]

6.3.2 Sterling bank bills[3]

The bill of exchange has been used as a method of raising short term finance since the seventeenth century. It is an unconditional order in writing, addressed by one person or company to another, signed by the person or the company to whom it is addressed, to pay on demand or at a fixed or determinable future date a certain sum of money to, or to the order of, a specified person or company, or to bearer.

Bills of exchange may be drawn in any currency. Those drawn in sterling are the most easily negotiated in the London market although there is a ready market for foreign currency bills providing they are accepted payable in London. Bills can be drawn for almost any amount but the maximum usually negotiated is £500,000. The period for which a bill is drawn is not normally longer than six months or less than fourteen days.

The method of creating a bill is for the customer to arrange an acceptance credit facility with his bankers. This procedure involves the bank in accepting full liability to pay the bill on maturity and this is granted subject to the terms on which bills are drawn by the company. Very often this is combined with an option to take money instead should bill rates be unfavourable. This is commonly termed an 'either or' facility. Bank bills are classified as either eligible or ineligible. Eligible bank bills are accepted payable by one of the banks on the Bank of England list whose paper is rediscountable at the Bank of England (that is, such bills can be bought by the Bank in its money market operations). Ineligible bank bills are accepted payable by banks whose paper at present is not rediscountable at the Bank of England but whose names trade in the money markets. The discount market helps to make a secondary market in this type of paper. Trade bills are bills drawn by one trade customer and accepted by another rather than a bank. Their rate of discount depends on the financial status of the two companies.

6.3.3 The interbank market

In the interbank market, banks offer surplus deposits which they might have to other banks. Banks who wish to acquire additional deposits in order to match their loan commitments bid for such deposits. These deposits are for a range of maturities from overnight to one year. Generally, the shorter maturities are the most actively traded. The interbank market is the largest of the London money markets, with close to £100 billion of sterling interbank deposits outstanding (see Table 6.5). It is thus more than twice the size of the sterling CD market. Rates in this market have taken on particular importance in the recent past for three main reasons. First, the UK clearing banks have come to rely heavily on raising funds in the interbank market. Second, many companies have loan facilities at rates linked to interbank rates. The London Interbank Offered Rate (LIBOR) has come to be widely used as a

Table 6.5 The interbank market: size and structure

£billion, 1991 Q2 Held by:	Denominated in: Sterling (a)	Other currencies (a)
UK Retail banks	26.3	7.1
British Merchant banks	11.0	5.4
Other British banks	16.6	0.8
American banks	3.9	8.5
Japanese banks	10.4	28.8
Other overseas banks	22.2	28.8
Total	90.3	79.2

Source: Bank of England Quarterly Bulletin, Aug. 1991
(a) Totals may not add due to rounding

benchmark rate, deposit and loan rates being set on margins related to LIBOR. Many corporate customers now have access to both traditional base rate related loan facilities as well as LIBOR related facilities. Third, the launch of the LIFFE short sterling contract in 1982, and its subsequent successful development into one of the most active of the LIFFE contracts, has enhanced trading opportunities in the interbank market.

In the light of these two developments, the clearing banks have moved to a system whereby their base rates are now largely determined by the prevailing inter-bank rate. Barclays Bank plc took the step in March 1984 of announcing that it would aim to keep its base rate within ¼ – ⅜% of the prevailing three month interbank rate, but there no longer seems to be a very precise linkage between the two rates.

Rather, the term structure of interbank rates, which gives an important indication of expected interest rates, will also be considered. If interbank rates are determined solely by expected future interest rates, then the current structure of rates can be 'unwound' in order to obtain expected future rates. As an example of how this can be done, refer to Table 6.6.

In this table we show interbank interest rates at maturities from one to twelve months. From one month and four month rates we can derive the three month interest rate which, if prevailing in one month's time, would lead to the same return being achieved from investing either in a combination of a one month deposit followed by a three month deposit, or in a four month deposit from the outset. Similarly, the two month and five month rates can be used to derive the expected three month rate in two months' time. In this way, we can build up a profile for expected three month interest rates, shown in the right hand column of Table 6.6. Given the close relationship between three month interbank rates and base rates, this provides a good guide to the money market's expectation of the path of base rates over the next twelve months.

6.3.4   LIFFE short sterling contract

Alternative information on expected interest rates is available more directly from the prices of the short sterling contract traded on the London International Financial Futures Exchange (LIFFE) and in practice developments in this market often lead developments in the cash market. This contract is deliverable on the first business

Table 6.6 UK money market term structure

Interbank rates (%pa):		Expected 3 month rates:	
One month	10.94		
Two months	10.84		
Three months	10.81		
Four months	10.75	in 1 mnth –Sep 91	10.59
Five months	10.69	in 2 mnths –Oct 91	10.40
Six months	10.66	in 3 mnths –Nov 91	10.23
Nine months	10.63	in 6 mnths –Feb 92	10.04
One year	10.63	in 9 mnths –May 92	9.85
Short sterling contract	price:	implied 3m rate:	
Sep 91	89.28	10.72	
Dec 91	89.78	10.22	
Mar 92	89.98	10.02	
Jun 92	89.86	10.14	
Sep 92	89.78	10.22	
Dec 92	89.67	10.33	
Mar 93	89.53	10.47	
Jun 93	89.46	10.54	

Source: Data for 23 August 1991 from Reuters pages FULB (interbank rates)/LIIA (futures)

day after the third Wednesday in the relevant month (that is, usually about the 19th). The contract is expressed as 100 minus the three month interest rate to be delivered. Thus an 8.5% expected rate gives a contract price of 91.50.

The corresponding data on interest rate expectations from the LIFFE market are shown in the lower section of Table 6.6.

6.3.5   The CD and euro-CD (ECD) market[4]

The CD market in London started in 1967 with the issue of the first US dollar CD (that is, it was strictly the euro-CD, ECD, market). It is currently the second largest section of the London money market, after the interbank market. The current size and structure of the market are set out in Table 6.7 and the development of the non-sterling CD market in Table 6.8. Any bank with a UK banking licence can issue a CD in London, which can be denominated in sterling, US dollars, yen, Canadian dollars, Australian dollars, SDR and ECU (although the Bank of England is prepared to accept issues in other currencies, subject to approval from the relevant central bank) with no minimum maturity and a maximum maturity of five years. Authorised building societies can also issue London CDs.

The US dollar sector of the market is still the largest and most active, and of the £74 billion (US$119 billion) outstanding in 'other currencies' in mid-1991, around £65 billion (US$105 billion) was probably dollar denominated.

In the early 1980s the eurodollar CD market received its growth momentum from two forces: the high level of dollar interest rates and reserve requirements on dollar domestic (i.e. issued in the US) CDs. Both of these favoured issuance of CDs

Table 6.7 The CD market: size and structure

£billion, 1991 Q2 Issued by:	Denominated in: Sterling	Other currencies
UK Retail banks	22.4	7.7
British Merchant banks	3.9	0.7
Other British banks	0.7	0.2
American banks	1.1	7.1
Japanese banks	7.0	25.1
Other overseas banks	15.8	33.0
Total	50.9	73.6

Source: Bank of England Quarterly Bulletin Aug. 1991, Tables 3.1 to 3.7

Table 6.8 London non-sterling CDs outstanding (US$ bn)

Yr end	Total	US banks	% of total	Japanese banks	% of total	British banks	% of total	Other banks	% of total
1980	48.7	26.8	55.0	8.8	18.1	4.6	9.4	8.5	17.5
1981	76.1	43.8	57.6	11.9	15.6	6.6	8.7	13.8	18.1
1982	92.6	50.3	54.3	19.0	20.5	9.3	10.0	14.0	15.1
1983	99.8	46.0	46.1	29.2	29.3	8.6	8.6	16.1	16.1
1984	94.7	34.0	35.9	33.5	35.4	7.6	8.0	19.7	20.8
1985	92.1	32.1	34.9	28.9	31.4	8.9	9.7	22.2	24.1
1986	114.8	27.8	24.2	45.4	39.5	12.5	10.9	29.0	25.3
1987	134.9	26.5	19.6	59.2	43.9	12.8	9.5	36.4	27.0
1988	140.7	23.2	16.5	67.5	48.0	9.8	7.0	40.3	28.6
1989	135.3	18.9	14.0	67.2	49.7	11.9	8.8	37.1	27.4
1990	137.0	13.3	9.7	58.3	42.6	14.5	10.6	50.9	37.2
1991	119.2	11.5	9.6	40.5	34.0	13.9	11.7	53.4	44.8

Sources: Jeanneau (1989); *Bank of England Quarterly Bulletin*, Tables 3.1 to 3.7, various issues.

in the euro rather than the domestic market. Reserve requirements on domestic CDs increase the cost of funds to banks.[5] Suppose the reserve requirement is 3%. Then for every dollar obtained through a CD, only 97% is available to lend. If a bank's CD offers a 10% yield then the additional costs imposed by reserve requirements is 31 basis points (10%/0.97=10.31%).

In 1980, with interest rates as high as 20% and an 8% required reserve, the implicit cost of issuing a domestic CD would have been 174 basis points (20%/0.92=21.74%). In 1991, with interest rates around 6% and a 3% reserve requirement, the implicit cost was down to 19 basis points (6%/0.97=6.19%). The relatively less marked advantage for American banks of issuing in the euro markets explains the fall in issuance by American banks in the late 1980s and into the 1990s.

The principal issuers of US dollar CDs are now the Japanese and European banks (see Table 6.8), a sharp turnaround from the situation of the early 1980s.

Domestic US investors form the largest part of the holders of the US$ CDs issued in London, probably accounting for around three quarters of all holdings.

Of the relatively small amount of CDs issued in other currencies, yen and ECU make up the bulk. ECU CDs are typically held by EC nationals, although some are also held by central banks. Yen CDs are mainly held in the Far East.

In the sterling CD market, the UK clearing banks and the Japanese banks are the largest issuers, although the UK building societies are also playing an increasing role. UK corporates, building societies, local authorities and banks themselves are the main investors.

US dollar CDs are broadly traded by a large number of institutions. The market is overseen by the International Certificates of Deposit Market Association (ICDMA). Up until very recently, a trader was obliged to make a two way market in any CD from one month to one year to maturity, in which he held an inventory (traders not being allowed to go short). Issues are divided into individual months, and within each month into early (the first half of the month) and late (the second half). Up until recently there was also a generic list for issues by Japanese, Americans and Europeans. Thus a trader might be asked for his price in 'American early threes', meaning CDs issued by American banks with a maturity in the first half of the three month maturity period. The trader would be obliged to make at least a bid in one of the generic runs and in a size of at least $5 million. The generic list system has declined in use, however, given growing concern about the credit worthiness of individual members of the list. The issuers in the generic American list, for example, no longer all trade on the same basis. Trading is now more 'name' orientated.

In the sterling CD market, trading is split into clearing bank, building society and other issuers. Clearing bank CDs form the most actively traded component of the market. No overall body, such as the ICDMA, has set up rules for trading and trading is generally more fragmented than in the dollar CD market. There are no clearly defined maturity bands or formal minimum or maximum dealing sizes as in the dollar market.

6.3.6   The role of brokers in the CD market[6]

In the secondary market, around three quarters of trading is principal to principal, with one quarter conducted through brokers. In the primary CD market, brokers have a larger role, with the proportion broadly reversed. This reflects the importance of structured deals in the primary market which in turn often hinge on taking advantage of arbitrage opportunities. For example, a broker might know that one market maker has a strong demand for CDs of six month maturity, but can only find an issuer willing to issue at three months. By bringing the two parties together and structuring a transaction involving the use of Floating Rate Agreements (FRAs), an overall package can be brought to the market. The FRA, an agreement as to the level of LIBOR at a certain date in the future, often plays a crucial role in such structured deals. For example, the broker could identify a potential issuer of CDs of six months maturity at LIBOR minus $\frac{1}{8}$, and then lend the funds for three months at LIBOR. By entering into an FRA, which sets the reinvestment terms when the three month CD matures, an overall return to the issuer higher than LIBOR minus $\frac{1}{8}$ can be achieved. Although CDs are still to a large extent an instrument of liability management, such arbitrage has become increasingly important in driving new issuance recently.

155

In the dollar CD market, dealing spreads are typically 5 basis points for CDs between one month and one year to maturity, for a minimum size of $5 million, with the spread normally being the same up to $100 million. In the sterling market, spreads for one month to one year maturity are $\frac{1}{16}$ for clearing bank CDs, $\frac{1}{8}$ for others.

For CDs over one year maturity spreads are generally wider, 10 basis points in the dollar market and in the sterling market $\frac{1}{8}$ for the clearers and variable for others. The CD market at this maturity is generally driven by the interest rate swap market with, in particular, banks issuing fixed rate in order to obtain LIBOR-related funding.

6.3.7 The ECP market[7]

The euro-commercial paper (ECP) market made its first appearance in the early 1970s. At that time it developed as a means of circumventing US restrictions on foreign direct investment, but when those restrictions were lifted in 1974 the market contracted sharply. It was not until the early 1980s that a sustained development of the ECP market took place.

The renewed development of the market in the 1980s can be traced to three principal factors. First, convergence between euro and domestic interest rates. In particular, with lower short term interest rates and reserve requirements in the US, domestic CD and euro CD rates converged from the mid 1980s onwards, as described above. Second, there was a changed source of the supply of capital in the world financial markets away from the Middle East and towards Europe and Japan. These investors had a preference for securities rather than bank deposits. Third, a number of factors combined to make CP finance relatively cheap in relation to bank finance. The reduced credit ratings of the banks meant that good quality corporates could issue directly in the capital markets on relatively more favourable terms. Moreover, corporates issuing directly in the CP market did not have to bear the costs associated with reserve requirements, requirements which encouraged the banks themselves to favour off balance sheet instruments. The banks thus switched, to some extent, from an intermediary role (taking deposits and making loans) to an agency role (the placing of securities in the market).

The ECP market itself developed from the euronote market. The euronote market developed in the early 1980s with the success of such underwritten facilities as RUFs (Revolving Underwriting Facilities), NIFs (Note Issuance Facilities) and SNIFs (Secured Note Issuance Facilities). These were arrangements through which a stream of notes and CDs were issued. The principal difference between ECP and euronotes is that euronotes are issued with the backing of a syndicate of underwriters whereas ECP is issued on a non-underwritten tap basis.

The growth rate of the ECP market has been impressive, growing from around $10 billion outstanding at the end of 1985 to $70 billion at the end of 1990.

6.3.8 Commercial paper[8]

On 29 April, 1986 H.M. Treasury and the Bank of England announced changes in existing regulations to allow the issue of Sterling-denominated Commercial Paper and the first issue was launched on 20 May 1986. The market received added impetus on 11 January 1990 when the Bank made two further moves: the maximum maturity of paper was extended to five years (it was previously one year), with paper of a maturity between one and five years designated 'medium-term notes' (MTNs); and issues could be in any currency, not just sterling.

Since the opening of the Sterling Commercial Paper (SCP) market in 1986, there have been regular issues but the market has not developed as quickly as national (as opposed to euro) commercial paper markets in many other European countries.

SCP takes the form of negotiable short term unsecured promissory notes denominated in sterling and payable to bearer. It is similar in kind to US dollar commercial paper which has been issued in the United States for many years. It may be issued by UK or overseas companies which satisfy certain conditions. The main restrictions on issuance are that the issuer must have shares listed on the Stock Exchange and have net assets of at least £25 million. The minimum face value of paper is £500,000 and maturities can range from 7 days to one year.

The issue and distribution of SCP in the primary market can be effected in various ways. The most common method is by means of a continuous programme, for which one or more banks or securities houses are appointed by the issuer to act as dealers. In a dealer programme, an appointed dealer normally acts as a principal, purchasing SCP from the issuer for onward distribution to investors. Alternatively, a dealer may act as agent on behalf of the issuer, placing paper with investors on a best endeavours basis. As alternatives to a dealer programme, a company may issue SCP direct to investors or through a tender panel of banks which are invited to bid competitively for the paper.

Normal market practice is for SCP to be issued on a non-interest bearing basis at a discount to its face value, although provision has also been made for it to bear a stated rate of interest. In either case, it is issued and dealt in the primary and secondary markets on the basis of a yield to maturity, which is usually expressed in basis points.

An issuer will need to appoint an issue and paying agent, to be responsible for the safekeeping of bearer notes, completing and authenticating the notes prior to issue and handling the payment flows between the issuer and holder at issue and at maturity. As a domestic sterling instrument, the delivery, settlement and clearing arrangements for SCP are similar to those for other domestic instruments such as sterling certificates of deposit. In the first five years of the market's existence, between May 1986 and May 1991, 222 companies issued sterling commercial paper. Of these 197 still had commercial paper outstanding in May 1991 with a total value of £6.25 billion (see Table 6.9).

Table 6.9 Sterling commercial paper

£ billion, May 1991	
Total outstanding: of which:	6.25
UK company issues	5.34
Overseas company issues (guaranteed by UK parent)	0.09
Overseas company issues (other)	0.82

Source: Bank of England 'Sterling Commercial Paper', Press Release; May 1991.

The development of the market has not been as rapid or as extensive as in many other European countries. In France, for example, the domestic CP market was launched at around the same time, but by the end of 1990 it had grown in size to FF165 billion, around four times the size of the UK market (see Table 6.10 for a comparison of commercial paper markets in Europe, the ECP market and the US CP market).

There are several interrelated explanations for the relatively limited development of the SCP market. Perhaps most important is the well developed nature of the domestic bank bill markets. As the Bank of England conducts its money market operations predominantly in such instruments, there has been a continued demand for such paper. There is a question as to the importance of the bank guarantee on such bills. SCP does not have a guarantee and, traditionally, 'name recognition' has been the principal way of ascertaining the credit risk associated with SCP. The spate of defaults in the ECP market, and the default of Polly Peck in the SCP market in 1990, however, brought into question whether such a system provided adequate information as to credit standards for the investor. In response to the spate of defaults, the use of credit ratings has become more widespread in commercial paper markets recently, with up to 90% of new programmes now rated.[9] Moodys estimate that around 40% of outstanding SCP programmes have a credit rating.

The domestic banking system has (since the early 1980s) been completely free of formal restrictions on the supply of credit and has not been subject to reserve requirements. The imposition of credit restrictions in other markets (for example, in Spain in 1989) stimulated the development of the domestic commercial paper market in that country.

These problems can be seen as having prevented the SCP market developing sufficient 'critical mass' and this, in itself, has brought its own problems. For example, documentation standards in the market have been criticised, and are generally regarded as falling well behind standards in the US CP and ECP markets. The structure of a commercial paper programme is generally determined by the type of credit support, if any, on the programme. A CP programme can be issued with or without: i) support from the issuer's parent; ii) credit support from a bank or surety support from an insurance company, and iii) collateral support. The type of support is not always perfectly clear in SCP programmes: for example, the extent to which the parent company is responsible for SCP formally issued by a subsidiary company may not always be clear. In a better developed market such documentation problems would be less likely to occur. The relatively underdeveloped nature of the market has also meant that consistent historical data for SCP interest rates are not readily available, so potential issuers in the market find it difficult to ascertain the interest rate they need to offer in the market. Some of the larger issuers have simultaneous ECP and SCP programmes, being easily able to switch between the two markets in order to take advantage of perceived arbitrage opportunities and with the ECP programme providing a 'benchmark' interest rate for the SCP programme.

Access to the ECP market, in itself, may also explain the underdeveloped nature of the domestic CP market. Many ECP programmes include options to issue in more than one currency, although the majority still only allow for issuing in US dollars. UK corporates might find it attractive at times to borrow in a currency other than sterling (most commonly US dollars) through such a programme and fully hedge the proceeds into sterling, hence creating a synthetic SCP. The flexibility of ECP programmes, with issuance often taking place within a day of the decision to

Table 6.10 Overview of commercial paper markets

Criterion	UK	France	Domestic markets				ECP Market	USCP Market
			Sweden	Finland	Spain**	Netherlands		
SIZE OF MARKET								
Outstandings (approx)	£4.7bn ECU 6.7 bn December 1990	FF 165.1 bn (BdT) ECU 23.7 bn December 1990	SEK 160 bn* ECU 20.9 bn September 1990	FIM 30.2 bn ECU 6.1 bn December 1990	Ptas 500 bn ECU 3.9 bn Autumn 1990	HFL 2.8 bn ECU 1.2 bn Jan 1991	US-$ 70.2 bn ECU 51.1 bn December 1990	US-$ 557 bn ECU 404 bn December 1990
Total program volume (approx)	£19.465 bn	N/A	SEK 345 bn	FIM 50bn	Ptas 1162bn	HFL 13.9bn	US$ 187bn	N/A
Number of programs (approx)	156	117	270	270	40	65	780	2144 issuers
DEALERS								
Number of active dealers	5 to 7	20	5 to 7	3 to 5	20 to 30	3 to 4	10 to 25	45
Average number of dealers per program	3 to 4	1 to 3	2 to 3	1 to 3	20 to 30	1 to 3	4 to 5	2 to 3
DEFAULTS								
Name of defaulting issuers and year of default***	Polly Peck (1990)	SFEC (1987) CODEC (1990)	Nyckeln Gamlestaden Independent Finansor Beijer Capital (all in 1990)****	Mancon (1989) Bensow (1989)	FECSA (1988) Corporacion Intra (1991) (unreg mkt)	None	See: Moody's Special Report on CP defaults 1972–1990	See: Moody's Special Report on CP defaults 1972–1990
TRANSACTION FEATURES								
Maturity range	7 days to 1 year	10 days to 7 years	1 day to 2 years	1 day to 5 years	1 to 18 months	14 days to 2 years	1 day to 1 year	Max of 270 days
Average Maturity (days)	30	60–90	60–90	80–100	N/A	80–120	60	30
REGULATION								
Supervisory institution	Bank of England	COB/Banque de France	Sveriges Riksbank	Bank of Finland	CNMV	DNB	None	SEC
Restrictions on issuers	Min asset size of 25mn	Corporate: B/S for last 2 yrs	None	No banks	No banks	No banks	None	None
DISCLOSURE								
a) Initial	Info Memo/ Prospectus	Prospectus	No	No	Prospectus (registered)	Info Memo	Info Memo in practice	Info Memo
b) Ongoing	Annual update	Annual update	No	No	Annual update	No	None	Annual update

Notes: * Foretagacertificat – SEK 130bn, Marknadebevis – SEK 30 bn
**Registered market only (if not indicated otherwise)
***Losses may have been (partly) absorbed by dealers
****All defaults occurred in the Marknadebevis segment
Source: Moodys Special Comment on Commercial Paper Markets in Europe, 1991.

issue being taken, means that it is relatively easy to take advantage of such short term opportunities. The UK building societies, with well recognised 'names', have been active in this respect. The fact that the foreign issuer premium (i.e. the amount by which the interest rates on issues by foreign names exceed those on US domestic issues) in the US market is now close to zero has facilitated such fully hedged issues.[10]

6.4   Issues for the future

The ECP market is a convenient point at which to end the discussion of the current structure of the London market as many of the issues facing the London money market generally are exemplified in that particular market.

A key issue is the extent to which the money market continues to be dominated by the markets in which the banks play a role either as intermediary or guarantor. The interbank, CD and eligible bill markets remain by far the largest elements of the London money market. The commercial paper market might still challenge these established markets, although for the reasons discussed above it has not yet developed critical mass. More widespread concern about bank credit risk or the imposition of credit controls on the banking system could stimulate the development of the market, but they are presumably not the routes through which the Bank of England would prefer development to take place. The Bank of England could help the market develop further by purchasing SCP as part of its daily money market activities, rather than just eligible bills. With the size of overall shortages in the money market having been reduced, however, the technical position in the money market is unlikely to warrant such a move. The Bank, however, does regularly review its list of banks who are eligible to have their bills rediscounted at the Bank of England and it is arguable that the credit risk of many UK corporates is lower than some of the banks on that list.

There is a more general issue here about the interface between the Bank of England and other sectors of the economy. In the early 1980s when the policy of overfunding led to persistent money market shortages, the Bank's bill mountain was criticised from the standpoint that it entailed the Bank acting essentially as a clearing bank, lending to the corporate sector (albeit indirectly) via its bill purchases. Moreover, the bill purchases were due to a large extent to overfunding of the PSBR through sales of gilts so the Bank was effectively carrying out a maturity transformation in the market and one which, at times, entailed a 'cost' (as bill yields were lower than gilt yields).

Although the abandonment of overfunding has meant that this problem has (although maybe only temporarily) been resolved there still remains an issue as to the relationship between central government and the local authorities. As a way of alleviating shortages in the money market in the mid 1980s the central government borrowed heavily to on-lend to the local authorities. This raises the CGBR (within an unchanged PSBR) and eases the cash position of the money market. Favourable financing from the Public Works Loan Board is still made available to the local authorities, although the money market rationale has largely disappeared and local authorities borrow only limited amounts directly in the capital markets. But with questions raised about the credit worthiness of some local authorities, is the provision of cheap finance from central government the best way of financing such institutions? Ought they to be forced to borrow more directly in the capital market, so that their credit worthiness can be assessed in the market and an appropriate interest rate be charged?

The absence of new gilt issues for a period from 1988 to 1991 and the steeply inverted yield curve for much of that time meant that the eurosterling bond market developed strongly. To some extent this market was tapped by UK corporate borrowers who then swapped the funds to achieve LIBOR related funding. Such long term fixed rate financing opportunities may not be so readily available in the future, with the chance of the corporate sector being crowded, or priced, out of the long end of the market. First, the Bank of England has already returned to the gilt market as an issuer and the prospect over the next few years is one of a larger PSBR and gilt issuance. At the same time, the yield curve has taken on a flatter shape and could, especially given Exchange Rate Mechanism membership, take on a more typically continental European upward sloping nature. Both developments could push the non-central government borrowers towards the shorter maturities.

The move towards more unified European financial markets and a single European currency during the 1990s are potentially the most important, but at this stage the most unfathomable, forces acting on the London money market in the 1990s. For example, will London become the operational centre for a new European central bank and if so how will its responsibilities be defined? To what extent can restrictions or controls on the domestic (that is, the UK) market be maintained in the face of integration of financial markets? Can the Bank of England's restricted list of counterparties with which it deals in the money market be maintained in the face of EC Directives on capital liberalisation? Will the UK be left behind as the majority of other countries in the ERM use a common currency?

Finally, there is the problem of regulation and supervision. The development of banks' off-balance business was a source of concern for regulators in the 1980s and early 1990s, but the problem may well become larger if the credit risk of the banks is further undermined and the banks no longer act as intermediaries in a growing number of capital market transactions.

Notes

1   This section draws heavily on descriptions of the Bank of England's operations in the money market in various editions of the *Bank of England Quarterly Bulletin*. The most recent description was contained in Bank of England (1988). This, in turn was an updated version of Bank of England (1982). See also Bank of England (1983).

The suspension of minimum lending rate was described in the *Bank of England Quarterly Bulletin*, Sept. 1981, p. 333. For the most recent developments in money market assistance see Bank of England (1989a, 1989b, 1989c).

The 'Operation of monetary policy' section of each *Bank of England Quarterly Bulletin* provides a regular update of developments in market assistance.

2   See Table 9.2 in the *Bank of England Quarterly Bulletin* for the latest details. Details of each Friday's Treasury bill tender are also available on Reuters page RTCE.

3   See Gerrard and National (1981).

4   This section draws on the British Bankers' Association (1990).

5   This example comes from Jeanneau (1989).
6   See Bank of England (May 1990).
7   This section draws on Jeanneau (1989) and Heller (1988).
8   This sections draws on British Bankers' Association (1986).
9   Bank of England (1991).
10 Estimates produced by Warren Sparr of Lehman Brothers.

Bibliography

Bank of England (1982) The role of the Bank of England in the money market, *Bank of England Quarterly Bulletin*, **22**, 86–94

Bank of England (1983) The Bank's operational procedures for meeting monetary objectives, *Bank of England Quarterly Bulletin*, **23**, 209–15.

Bank of England (1988) Bank of England dealings in the sterling money market: operational arrangements, *Bank of England Quarterly Bulletin*, **28**, 403–9.

Bank of England (1989a) Recent developments in money market assistance, *Bank of England Quarterly Bulletin*, **29**, 212–13.

Bank of England (1989b) Recent developments in the commercial bill market, *Bank of England Quarterly Bulletin,* **29**, 342.

Bank of England (1989c) Recent developments in the Treasury bill market, *Bank of England Bulletin*, **29**, 505–6.

Bank of England (1990), The role of brokers in the London money markets, *Bank of England Quarterly Bulletin*, **30**, 221–7.

Bank of England (1991), Developments in international banking and capital markets in 1990, *Bank of England Quarterly Bulletin*, **31**, 234–45.

British Bankers' Association, *Sterling Commercial Paper*, December 1986.

British Bankers' Association, *Certificates of Deposits on the London Markets*, November 1990.

Gerrard and National, *The London Discount Market*, 3rd edn, 1981.

Heller, L. (1988) *Eurocommercial Paper*, Euromoney Publications.

Jeanneau, J.G.S. (1989) Structural changes in world capital markets and eurocommercial paper, *Bank of England Discussion Paper*, **37**.

Temperton, P. (1991) *UK Monetary Policy: The Challenge for the 1990s*. Macmillan.

7 The regulation of securities business in the UK

by David Miles

The activities of institutions which operate in London's financial markets are subject to forms of regulation which are complex and varied; many of these regulations are unique to the financial sector. Under the system of regulation established following the Financial Services Act (FSA) in 1986 institutions which deal in equities, bonds, futures and options and other investments; offer portfolio management services; provide financial advice; operate and market collective investment schemes; and sell long term insurance contracts, have to satisfy various conditions including:

- demonstration that the institution is run and controlled by persons 'fit and proper' to undertake investment business;
- separation of the institutions' own funds from those of clients;
- provision of 'sufficient' own capital – that is funds which act as a cushion to absorb losses, thereby preventing investors from sustaining losses and/or the stability of the markets in which the firm operates from being threatened, as a result of adverse conditions;
- compliance with rules regarding the way in which business is conducted, designed to prevent institutions taking advantage of information which clients do not have and which might allow financial firms to benefit at their expense.

Furthermore, many institutions are required to pay for compensation paid to investors in the event of insolvencies. The cost of operating this system of regulation is covered by levies made upon the firms regulated.

Several fundamental economic questions are raised by the system of regulation outlined above. First, what is the rationale for the existence of a complex system of rules which govern the operation of financial institutions many of which – limits on the balance sheet structure of firms, rules on the establishment of a compensation scheme, restrictions on the range of products which may be offered – do not apply to non-financial firms? Put another way, what are the problems which the unfettered operation of financial institutions might produce and which regulation is designed to counter? Second, does the system really succeed in correcting types of market failure which would otherwise reduce economic welfare? Third, how did the current system of regulation come into being? Fourth, will the process of greater integration of European financial markets necessitate major changes to the system of regulation?

In this chapter I aim to address each of these questions. Section 7.1 considers the economic case for special forms of regulation for financial institutions and markets. In the light of this section 7.2 describes the current system of regulation and analyses the effectiveness of existing rules given the market failures to which regulation should be addressed. Section 7.3 describes in more detail the evolution of the current rules regarding both the conduct of investment business and the operation of organised financial markets and compares the sytem of regulation in the UK with that in the US. The final section looks at the implications of liberalisation in the provision of financial services within Europe.

7.1 Regulation – the economic issues

Most financial intermediaries in the UK are subject to forms of regulation; these are over and above the requirement to comply with company law and many of them are unique to the financial sector. This prompts a fundamental question. Is there something special about the financial sector? The existence in many countries of forms of regulation of financial intermediaries which are specific to the financial sector suggests that supervisors – often central banks – believe that there is. Both banks and non-deposit taking financial intermediaries in the UK, for example, operate in an environment where supervisors monitor the structure of their balance sheets; the suitability of their key personnel; their exposures to particular types of risk and the internal control mechanisms for assessing those risks. There are no comparable forms of regulation of, say, a car company or a hotel chain.

Two questions arise from this. First, what, if any, might be the special features of financial markets which warrant particular forms of supervision? Second, what are the effects upon financial intermediaries of regulation?

7.1.1 Why regulate?

Economists have suggested several reasons as to why special regulations should be applied to financial institutions:

1. Macroeconomic, and in particular monetary policy, considerations
2. Protection of the payments system
3. Prevention of financial collapse, sometimes described as the avoidance of systemic failure
4. Protection of the interests of the clients of particular institutions from fraud, negligence or excessive risk-taking
5. Promotion of competition.

The first and second factors are clearly more relevant to banks than to financial firms undertaking investment business whilst the final issue is not specific to financial firms. Consequently it is the prevention of systemic risks (3) and the protection of individual consumers (4) that have been seen as the *raison d'être* of non-bank financial supervision. But whilst it is not hard to agree that risks to the stability of the whole financial system, or large parts of it, and losses sustained by individual consumers are in themselves undesirable, it is far from clear that a regulatory response is required.

The fundamental question is *not* whether unregulated, or free market, outcomes create *some* risk of major disturbances and result in *some* consumers losing money but whether unregulated outcomes would be *excessively* risky. If all agents could accurately assess the overall risks entailed by entering into transactions and were prepared to accept them at the terms offered, it is not clear that free market outcomes, which certainly might create risks of default and bankruptcy, are sub-optimal. But if firms and their clients are unable to assess all the risks of deals, one of the conditions for the efficient operation of markets – knowledge of the characteristics of commodities – fails to hold. It is therefore not surprising that underlying nearly all arguments that unregulated outcomes would be excessively risky is the premise that there are information problems – in particular information asymmetries – in financial markets which are different in degree, and perhaps in kind, from other markets. The effects of asymmetric information in financial markets and the likely scale of such information problems in different markets is therefore a key issue.

7.1.2 Information problems

Chant (1987) provides an excellent review of several arguments for and against special regulation of financial firms and concludes that it is the existence of asymmetries of information between intermediaries and their clients which both explains the existence of particular, common forms of contract offered in financial markets (e.g. deposit contracts and standard loan contracts offered by banks) *and* justifies a role for supervision. More generally, it is clear that the large theoretical and (smaller) empirical literature on bank runs and other financial panics relies heavily on information problems to explain these phenomena. (See the seminal paper by Diamond and Dybvig (1983) and papers by Merrick and Saunders (1985), Tobin (1985 and 1987), Miles (1990) and Goodhart (1987a and 1987b).)

Although the case for regulation is often couched in terms of externalities – e.g. the failure of one institution might reduce confidence in others and cause a chain reaction of failures – such externalities as are quoted generally stem from information problems. To make the point another way, one could ask whether a plausible case could be made for special forms of regulation of financial intermediaries if there were not information problems specific to such firms. The fact that financial intermediaries might be heavily interconnected through inter-bank loans in a world with perfect information, and that the failure of one firm would have knock on effects upon other firms and those that own their liabilities, would not be enough to justify regulation if all the parties to financial contracts understood the nature of the interconnections and saw clearly the risks. In other words, if all agents know the risks involved in entering into contracts there is no clear case for *special* regulation of the balance sheets of financial intermediaries any more than for similar types of regulation of the balance sheets of car manufacturers. In short, with full information there is no obvious market failure one can identify which regulation is to correct.

But if asymmetries of information between a financial intermediary and its clients exist it has been argued that these seriously impede the operation of markets. This argument has generally been used to justify banking regulation which has several specific features most notably:

- that the majority of clients (at least by number if not by weight of money) are relatively unsophisticated;
- that banks operate the payments system thereby making failures in banking markets necessarily spill over into the wider economy in ways in which problems in equity or bond markets (or in the firms which operate in them) might not.

Before considering the relevance of the information problems to non-banks we should note that for banks it is not hard to see the problems which might arise with unregulated outcomes. If potential depositors find it hard to evaluate a bank's assets which will back their money they may, rationally, assume that with limited liability a bank's managers, acting in the interests of shareholders, may go for high risk portfolios. The economy may then be driven to a low level of intermediation as depositors are scared off from using banks, an outcome which the argument first formalised by Akerlof would suggest likely (see Akerlof 1970 on the market for lemons). But there are two alternative scenarios one can imagine. First, while managers of banks with limited liability have an incentive to acquire an excessively risky portfolio of assets, depositors may be unaware of this incentive. In this case the scale of intermediation through the banking sector may not be reduced as a result of asymmetric information, though the riskiness of bank asset portfolios would be excessive relative to the efficient outcome. But a very different set of outcomes will become plausible once a time element is added to the story. The further ahead banks look, the more important will be the benefits to them of establishing a reputation as a sound institution and the less the inefficiency stemming from asymmetric information (in the presence of limited liability) is likely to be.

So, even if asymmetries of information are serious it is not clear, at least in theory, what effect this may have even upon intermediation in banking markets. Nor is it clear whether a regulatory, as opposed to a free market, response is optimal. If financial intermediaries do have incentives to take excessive risks then supervision of balance sheets may be welfare-improving and could, because of lemons arguments, increase intermediation. If reputation is crucial then free market outcomes could be optimal.

On top of this, of course, it remains hard to gauge just how serious asymmetries of information are in financial markets. What this means is that the argument between those who believe that special forms of supervision of financial markets are welfare-improving (e.g. Chant, 1987) and those who argue that they are unnecessary and indeed welfare-reducing (for a particularly strong version of this case see Dowd, 1989) is hard to judge. There has been virtually no empirical work to try to settle this issue, yet we noted above that theoretical arguments cannot answer the practical question of whether a system of regulation of financial intermediaries is desirable. Empirical investigation of the seriousness of information asymmetries in financial markets is therefore a matter of some policy relevance.

7.1.3 The case for regulating non-deposit taking financial firms

Many economists have argued that the economic case for externally imposed capital adequacy restrictions, for 'fitness and properness' criteria and for the construction of compensation schemes is not compelling, even for banks. (See, for example, Dowd, 1989.) There is even greater doubt as to that case as applied to non-bank financial firms. (See the excellent discussion in Franks and Mayer, 1989.) First, the systemic problems which may arise from the collapse of a major bank are harder to imagine as resulting from the failure of many types of non-banks. Certainly the failure of an investment manager – who invests funds in marketable instruments on behalf of others – hardly seems likely to threaten the stability of the bond or equity markets. The collapse of Barlow Clowes in 1990, whilst meriting media coverage on the grounds of regulatory failure and human interest, hardly did so because of a plausible threat to global financial stability. (The collapse arose because funds raised from the public on the expectation that they would be invested in low risk securities were used for other purposes.) The same argument – that fears of systemic risk cannot plausibly be seen as a good justification for a complex system of regulation – is surely relevant for a whole range of institutions offering financial advice.

166

But systemic risks, which have long been seen as the *raison d'être* of banking regulation, are relevant to certain types of investment business. Firms acting as dealers in bonds and equities and firms trading financial futures stand more nearly at the centre of the operation of the organised markets in assets. Here interlinkages between firms, who trade great quantities with each other and often hold claims on each other which are large relative to capital, are important. Mayer (1989) reports that respondents to a survey of over 30 UK investment managers found that the average loss that a firm could have suffered on the day of the survey (31 March 1988) had *one* of their counterparties defaulted was £3.9 million. If *all* counterparties had defaulted, admittedly a somewhat apocalyptic scenario, average losses for each institution would have been £55 million. In short, the failure of a bond or equity market maker is far more likely to create problems in the securities market than is the failure of a firm which offers financial services to the public. Furthermore, the link between banking firms and securities dealers, many of whom fund a substantial proportion of their stocks of assets with short term bank loans, is direct and quantitatively important. One of the major concerns of the monetary authorities and bank regulators during the October 1987 stock market crash was that insolvencies amongst securities firms caused by the decline in asset values might generate substantial losses for, and a reduction of confidence in, banks.

7.1.4   Implications of the heterogeneity of investment business for regulation

The great variability in the level of systemic risk posed by the failure of market makers and other securities dealers, on the one hand, and firms offering retail financial services, on the other, suggests that the system of regulation applied to different types of non-bank financial institutions should vary greatly. This is not to suggest that the phenomenon which has been taken ultimately to justify regulation – the existence of asymmetric information between parties to deals – does not exist across all markets, albeit to differing degrees. Rather, the wider economic implications of such asymmetries will vary greatly across institutions and consequently the form of regulations applied to different types of non-bank financial intermediaries should also vary.

To be specific, asymmetries of information between investment managers and their clients would seem to be a good reason to compel managers to separate own funds from client funds. (Part of the notoriety of the Barlow Clowes affair arose because this principle had apparently been breached.) But the likely absence of any systemic risks makes the relevance of capital adequacy requirements far from clear. Rules to prevent convicted fraudsters – fitness and properness criteria – are far more likely to be useful in such markets where fraudulent uses of investors' money creates greater risks than the insolvency, *per se*, of a particular investment trust or unit trust. Risks stemming from the activities of institutions which operate primarily with other professionals – most obviously market makers, equity dealers and traders in bonds whose counterparties are generally other dealers or large financial institutions such as investment houses or institutional investors – are of a very different nature. First, the players in these markets tend to know their counterparties well and have long established relations; risks of being ripped off by fraudulent firms are relatively low. This suggests that fitness and properness criteria are less relevant than are capital adequacy rules which reduce risks that adverse price movements will bankrupt counterparties. When asset prices are moving rapidly (October 1987 being only the most memorable of the recent examples), firms with low capital may find it hard even to know themselves whether they are solvent. The uncertainty about the credit worthiness of counterparties can create major system wide problems if trade dries up at precisely the time that many players most want to deal to reduce existing exposures. Minimum capital adequacy requirements are at least the right sort of tool to handle this problem.

There is a third class of institutions – or rather range of activities – which does not fall into either category, involving neither the direct sale of investment services to the public nor trading in securities. Merchant banks and the banking arms of large securities houses which offer advice to corporate clients are not directly involved in trading securities and are removed from the mechanics of making securities markets work. In that sense they are more like investment managers for whom we argued capital adequacy requirements were of limited value. But their clients are generally not small private investors but rather large non-financial corporations taking advice on financial structure and buying corporate banking services. The relative sophistication of these clients in itself suggests that regulation need be less than for either retail financial services firms (investment managers) or for securities dealers. But a particularly acute form of information asymmetry which can exist for large financial institutions offering corporate banking services may require a special form of regulation. Specifically, there exists the potential for large institutions who both trade securities and take positions in particular stocks to use privileged information available as a result of their also providing financial services to corporate clients. The scope for conflicts of interest of this sort to arise has become far greater in the 1980s as distinctions between financial institutions have become blurred and there have been created financial supermarkets providing clients with a full range of products and services 'under one roof'. In the UK this process was made possible by the abolition of the distinction between jobbers and brokers – the so called 'Big Bang' of October 1986.

The economies of scale and scope advantages enjoyed by the 'under one roof' financial conglomerate create the potential for conflicts of interest. The corporate banking arm of such institutions may be party to information which allows the trading arm to make a killing. The possibility of insider trading of this sort creates several problems for regulators. The economic issues are subtle. First, who loses as a result of insider trading? Is it a crime without a victim? One plausible answer is that everyone loses in the long run – corporate clients no longer trust the motives of financial advisers and fear that prices of securities might move adversely or prematurely as a result of putting cards on tables; clients of securities houses may come to distrust the advice offered by financial supermarkets if the supermarket has its own incentives to see clients buy or sell a particular stock. For these reasons the much publicised financial scandals of recent years which have involved insider trading are serious. In both the Blue Arrow affair and the Guinness scandal in the UK share dealing by insiders was claimed to have distorted the value of traded securities and misled outsiders (see below). In the US, Ivan Boesky and Michael Milken took advantage of information on takeover bids to buy underpriced securities.

The problems for regulators in designing appropriate rules to try to control abuses stemming from these types of asymmetric information are severe. First, how is inside information to be defined? If any information used by a financial supermarket which makes earning a profit more likely is deemed inside information then houses which both provide financial advice to corporate clients and trade their securities may simply stop trading. Second, even if a useful definition of inside information is available, how are uses of such information to be spotted? Third, what is the best way to deal with insider trading – assuming we know what it is and how to spot it? Is the best policy to dole out big penalties to those found guilty or to limit the range of permitted activities of companies such that conflicts of interest are minimised? We return to these points below when we consider the current system of regulation in the UK.

7.1.5   Implications of the economic issues

What this overview of the economic issues in the regulation of investment business suggests is that the types of market failure which might arise in different markets, whilst all ultimately stemming from information problems, vary enormously. This is because the *scale* of information asymmetries varies (professionals dealing with each other are likely to know more about what they are getting than are members of the public) and because the *implications* of a given level of information asymmetry differ greatly across institutions. Consequently, the aims of regulation should vary depending on what type of activity, and between what types of player, is being undertaken. One simple distinction of which much is made in the literature is that between regulation aimed at protecting investors and regulations aimed at reducing systemic risk. (See Goodhart, 1988a; Goodhart *et al.*, 1988; and Mayer, 1989.) In analysing the system of regulation of securities business in the UK it is useful to keep asking what types of problem specific rules are designed to reduce.

7.2   The design of the regulatory system

In the previous section I argued that consideration of the fundamental economic problems which regulations should be designed to counter suggests that a uniform system of regulation for all non-bank institutions which, either directly or indirectly, operate on the organised financial markets is almost certain to be sub-optimal. In this section I describe the current system for the regulation of investment business established under the FSA and consider whether it allows enough flexibility. More specific issues – in the design of capital adequacy schemes and in the operation of rules on insider trading – are also considered.

7.2.1   The Financial Services Act

The legal framework for the regulation of all investment business in the UK was established with the passage of the Financial Services Act, which followed the publication of the Gower Report. Gower, a lawyer, had been commissioned to report on investor protection. He completed his study in 1984. The scope of the Act is enormous, covering the activities of all securities dealers, brokers, pension funds, investment and unit trusts, futures and options traders, investment managers and financial advisers as well as some activities carried on by banks and life assurance companies. The Act also establishes criteria for the recognition of investment exchanges – the organised markets where bonds, equities, financial and commodity futures and options are traded.

Under the terms of the Act, regulatory powers are delegated to the Securities and

Investment Board (SIB). The SIB is a private body financed by charges levied on the investment industry. The main purpose of the SIB is not to regulate directly individual firms but rather to monitor Self Regulating Organisations (SROs). The role of regulating financial institutions is thus delegated to SROs which are required to meet the criteria established by the Act; the SIB's main role being that of certifying that the SROs' rule books are, at a minimum, consistent with the aims of the Act and that arrangements for monitoring compliance with those rule books are adequate. The SIB has established ten principles and a set of core rules on the conduct of business which 'together form the essential spine of the UK regulatory system for the conduct of investment business' (Securities and Investment Board, 1991). The rule books of individual SROs must be consistent with these essential principles.

7.2.2 The principles of the SIB

The ten principles of the SIB are:

1. Firms should observe high standards of integrity and fair dealing.
2. Firms should act with due care, skill and attention.
3. Firms should observe high standards of market conduct.
4. Firms should seek information from clients which could be expected to be relevant to their fulfilling their obligations to them.
5. Firms should provide information to clients which will allow them to make balanced and informed decisions.
6. Firms should aim to avoid conflicts of interest. Should conflicts arise fairness in treatment of all customers is to be preserved by disclosure, by internal rules of confidentiality or else by declining to act.
7. Firms should protect assets of customers for which they have control and are responsible.
8. Firms must ensure that they have adequate financial resources to meet their business commitments and to withstand the risks which they face.
9. Firms must keep proper records and should ensure that staff are properly trained and supervised for the tasks they undertake.
10. Firms should deal in an open way with their regulators and keep them informed of anything which they might reasonably be expected to disclose.

Clearly the principles are very general and are probably too vague to be helpful; they prompt numerous questions but offer no answers. What is 'adequate' in the context of financial resources? How much information is it 'reasonable' for customers to be given about financial products? What is 'proper protection' of clients' assets? Just how high are 'high standards of market conduct'? What is 'due care, skill, and attention'? Many economists' first reaction is to see these principles as unquantified (and perhaps unquantifiable) and therefore useless. Worse, they might be interpreted as meaning that each firm has to observe standards of conduct no lower than those of firms with the highest standards – an interpretation which many commentators placed upon the original Gower Report (see Goodhart *et al.*, 1988) and one which would be very hard to justify on economic grounds.

But to criticise the SIB's principles in this way is to miss much of the subtlety of the system. First, these are broad principles which the, far more specific, rule books of the SROs must be consistent with rather than a set of workable regulations to guide day to day business practice. Second, the core rules established by the SIB are far more specific than these general principles. In particular they distinguish between rules which apply whoever the customer is and those which are designed to protect the private customer. Third, there is recognition that firms that undertake business solely in the wholesale markets (for sterling, foreign currency and bullion) are best regulated separately by the Wholesale Markets Supervision Division of the Bank of England (see below).

7.2.3   The SROs and wholesale markets supervision

Under the terms of the Act all institutions undertaking investment business are to be monitored by one of the SROs, or by the Wholesale Markets Supervision Division at the Bank of England or else directly by the SIB. In practice most firms have opted to be regulated by one of the SROs, each of which specialise in regulating institutions in particular lines of business.

The system is a subtle blend of self regulation and statute. The SROs are private bodies funded by, and generally run by, practioners; the SIB, to which statutory powers have been delegated under the terms of the Act by the Secretary of State for Trade and Industry, has the sanction of refusing to recognise SROs. Individual firms have to be regulated by an SRO which has been designated by the SIB.

There are currently four SROs:

The Securities and Futures Authority (SFA) whose members include financial institutions dealing in securities and derivatives – bonds, equities, gilts, eurobonds, commodity options and futures – and firms undertaking corporate finance business.

The Life Assurance and Unit Trust Regulatory Organisation (LAUTRO) whose members are life assurance companies and unit trust managers.

The Investment Managers Regulatory Organisation (IMRO) whose members include investment managers and pension fund managers.

The Financial Intermediaries, Managers and Brokers Regulatory Association (FIMBRA) whose members are firms advising on retail investment products (unit trusts, life insurance, pension products).

The SIB has recognised five Recognised Investment Exchanges; the London Stock Exchange, the London Metal Exchange, the London International Financial Futures Exchange (LIFFE), the London Commodity Exchange (London FOX), and the Options Market (OM London Ltd). Again the role of the SIB is to ensure that exchanges continue to meet the criteria for recognition laid down in the Act. This implies that exchanges should ensure that agents trading (and perhaps more importantly, clients on whose behalf deals are undertaken) are provided with sufficient information and that business can be carried out in an orderly way. Although somewhat vague, in practice this means that agents should know details of the timing of transactions, the prices at which trades are made and sufficient information to establish whether deals are made at fair prices – for example, prices at least as good as those quoted by other traders.

Section 43 of the Act provides for the exemption of certain transactions undertaken by firms in the wholesale markets in sterling (the money market), the foreign currency market and the market for bullion. The participants in these markets are professionals usually dealing in large amounts. Many of the players on these markets are banks who were already supervised by the Bank of England and it seemed natural that a division of the Bank should regulate the securities business undertaken by all firms who chose to be exempted from the terms of the Act under Section 43. Exemption is dependent upon the type of instruments traded by the firm (money market instruments, futures and options, foreign exchange and bullion), the size of transactions (minimum size of £100,000 for most cash instruments – see Bank of England, 1987) and by the nature of the institution (generally specialist brokers or institutions 'acting on their own account in a general market making sense').

7.2.4 An appraisal of the FSA

This brief description of the current regulatory organisations shows the enormous diversity in the activities which are regulated. One might be sceptical as to whether a single piece of regulation – the FSA – could successfully establish useful principles simultaneously to guide the regulation of, say, the London Stock Exchange and an independent investment adviser working from a small office and dealing with twenty clients. Despite the enormous length and complexity of the Act it is therefore not surprising that the charge has been made that it has insufficient flexibility to address adequately the specific forms of market failure that arise in very different markets. Franks and Mayer (1989), for example, question whether capital adequacy requirements, which we noted above may be appropriate for market makers whose failure could trigger systemic problems, are suitable for investment managers. Provided client funds are kept separate from the firm's money there would not seem to be significant costs associated with the insolvency of an investment manager. Since capital requirements are designed to reduce, or at least set a minimum level to, the probability of bankruptcy their usefulness for investment managers is questionable. Goodhart (1988b,) has questioned the policy of establishing so called best practice rules which if taken literally require firms offering financial services to provide a product no worse than the best on offer. Again the degree of inflexibility implied by the rule could create real economic costs as lower quality, and presumably lower cost, products for which rational and informed investors might have a preference are regulated out of existence.

The principle of polarisation, whereby institutions marketing retail financial services face the choice of either selling only in house products or selling only the products of independent firms, has been criticised as being unduly inflexible.

But the dangers and costs of the imposition of excessively uniform regulations can be exaggerated by focusing on the terms of the Act. In practice there is great flexibility in the system – both because the rules established by different SROs vary greatly and because those rules have evolved since the system was established. For example, although capital requirements are made of firms operating in very different lines of business, the way in which minimum levels of capital are calculated differs across firms. Equity and bond traders face minimum capital requirements which depend upon the net stocks of securities held and upon the historical variability of the values of those stocks as well as upon assessment of the risk of counterparty default and of currency movements. Investment managers' minimum levels of required capital depend upon their average level of expenditures, not the value of funds managed. This distinction reflects the different aim of regulators – to reduce systemic risk from the failure of a trader (or market maker) on the one hand and to prevent insolvency of an investment manager leading to clients losing money on the other.

Furthermore, the system of self regulation by practioners has the advantage that SROs are quickly made aware of (at least some of) the costs that compliance with rules creates. Few have failed to notice that the there have been attempts by the SIB under Sir David Walker to simplify the rule book so as to reduce compliance costs following complaints by member firms of the SROs that reached a peak in the final months of Sir Kenneth Berrill's term of office as the first Chairman. (See articles in the *Financial Times* of 31 October, 1990 and *The Observer*, 28 April 1991.)

Despite the flexibility that the current system allows SROs in establishing rules which are consistent with the FSA it remains the case that that Act simply ignored the question of the relative costs and benefits of regulation. It is here that the real economic issues arise. Ideally, and obviously, one requires of a system of regulation that the sum of social benefits stemming from the amelioration of various forms of market failure, net of *all* the economic costs of regulation, be maximised. In practice the difficulties in measuring costs and benefits are enormous. The least difficult to measure are the direct compliance costs of regulation and it is therefore not surprising that these have been the focus of so much of the criticism of the system of regulation administered by the SIB. (Lomax, 1987, for example, estimates that the direct cost of running the regulatory bodies is over £20 million a year and the cost of compliance by firms is around £100 million a year.) But there are other potentially far greater, though harder to quantify, costs and benefits. I will focus on two sets of regulations in order to bring out some of the issues in measuring these wider costs: a) capital adequacy guidelines for securities dealers and b) rules on insider information.

7.2.5   Establishing optimal capital adequacy weights

Optimal capital adequacy weights for a financial institution reflect three things: an accurate assessment of the way in which greater capital affects the probability of insolvency; measurement of the economic benefits from reducing the frequency of insolvencies; and measurement of the economic cost of compliance with capital requirements. It should come as no surprise that measuring each of these three things is difficult.

In principle, the reduction in the probability of insolvency for any institution from a given increase in capital can be calculated given the probability distribution of the value of the assets and the value of the (non-equity, or non-capital) liabilities of the institution. Let the net value of those assets and liabilities of an institution – i.e. the net worth – be:

$$\sum_{j=1}^{J} P_j S_j \tag{1}$$

where P_j is the market price of the j'th asset or liability and S_j is the quantity of the asset (+ve) or liability (–ve). Insolvency occurs when net worth is negative, i.e. the value of the assets falls beneath that of the liabilities. If individual asset prices are joint normally distributed, the probability of bankruptcy can be measured by evaluating how many standard deviations away from zero the net worth of the institution is; i.e. by calculating

$$\sigma_I / \sum_{j=1}^{J} P_j S_j \qquad (2)$$

where σ_I is the standard deviation of the value of the institution. Knowing the value of this statistic would enable a regulator to calculate the probability of bankruptcy. The statistic expresses the variability in the value of the net worth of the institution, (σ_I), relative to the current net worth of the firm, $\left(\sum_{j=1}^{J} P_j S_j \right)$.

The variability in the total value of the institution, o_I, is simply the square root of the variance of the net worth. Net worth is given by equation (1) and the variance of net worth is given by the expression:

$$\sigma_I^2 = \sum_{j=1}^{J} \sigma_j^2 S_j^2 + \sum_{j=1}^{J} \sum_{k=1}^{K} \sigma_{jk} S_j S_k \qquad (3)$$

where σ_{jk} is the covariance in the prices of the j'th and k'th securities; σ_j^2 is the variance in the price of the j'th security. What equations (2) and (3) reveal is that the appropriate level of capital required of an institution to reduce its probability of insolvency below a certain level depends on the structure of its balance sheet and the variances and covariances of the values of all its assets and liabilities. Equation (3) suggests that the optimal extra amount of capital needed to sustain a given probability of bankruptcy following a change in balance sheet structure depends upon the covariances of the assets which have been acquired with the returns on *all* other securities. The amount of information required to devise such an appropriate set of capital weights is enormous – there are $\frac{1}{2} (J.(J+1))$ variances and covariances in equation (3). With as few as 100 types of security over 5,000 independent estimates of asset price moments are needed.

In practice regulators have relied upon aggregating classes of assets into a few broadly defined categories and assuming that the covariability of prices with those of the value of a diversified portfolio is a sufficient measure of risk; this greatly reduces the number of covariances to estimate but probably at the cost of underestimating the degree of portfolio diversification inherent in balance sheets. (The procedure used by the SFA for calculating the risk of portfolios is based on major simplifying assumptions but is of far greater sophistication than methods which may be adopted as a result of international harmonisation in the regulation of securities firms (see *Financial Times*, 26 September 1991)).

Even if one could accurately assess the probability of insolvency for a given capital structure, the question of the optimal (minimum) level of risk to accept remains. The benefits of reduced insolvency risk to securities dealers are easy to list – less disruption in the market; fewer legal costs; and greater confidence in counterparties which is likely to enhance liquidity – though extraordinarily difficult to quantify.

Perhaps even more difficult to assess are the costs to financial institutions of complying with minimum capital requirements. If regulations bite they force institutions to have a greater level of capital than they would otherwise choose. ('Capital' can come in various shapes; core capital can be thought of as equity capital and it is core capital which we shall focus on here.) The financial costs of forcing firms to have more equity, or lower debt gearing, are not well understood. If the Modigliani-Miller theorem holds the costs of having lower gearing are zero (see, for example, Copeland and Weston, 1988, Chapter 13). If there were any costs of insolvency in such a world it would therefore make sense in cost-benefit terms to force firms to have infinite capital. Firms themselves, perhaps not surprisingly, react to capital adequacy requirements in a way which suggests that they pay penalties for increasing equity; i.e. they complain. To assess the efficiency of a capital adequacy scheme requires measurement of these costs.

One strategy is to see if the stock market valuations of financial corporations who make (unexpected) announcements of equity issues fall. If the Modigliani-Miller theorem holds there should be no change in the value of outstanding equity claims; but if equity really is costly we might expect market values to fall on announcements. Miles (1991) investigated the impact of rights issue announcements by UK banks on their stock market valuations. He analysed in detail the capital issue announcements made over the last ten years by the large UK retail banks, paying close attention to other news revealed at the time and attempting to gauge the extent to which the announcement was a surprise. His results, although not directly related to securities firms, throw some light on the costs to financial institutions in general of complying with capital adequacy guidelines.

Table 7.1 shows the background to thirteen announcements of major new share issues by large UK retail banks in the 1980s. The announcements are split into two groups – those which were reported as 'news' and those which commentators described as already having being largely discounted.

Table 7.1

a)   Surprise announcements

Bank	Date of announcement	Amount		Press comment	Other news	Price change	
		Absolute	Relative to market value			Absolute %	Relative to standard deviation
Barclays	7 April 1988	£921m	26%	'Both the size and the timing were a surprise '(*FT*)	-	−12	−7.0
Nat West	14 May 1986	£714m	23%	'...it is none too easy to see what made Nat West move just now' (*FT*)	-	−11	−6.9
Bank of Scotland	18 April 1984	£42m	20%	announcement not reported as expected	record profits announced	−1.6	−1.6
Bank of Scotland	22 April 1985	£81m	21%	'news caught stock market by surprise' (*FT*)	profits grow 36% on year	−5.6	−5.5
Nat West	19 July 1984	£236m	31%	'the move caught the market by surprise' (*FT*)	profit figures announced	−4.5	−2.9

175

Table 7.1 *Cont.*

Bank	Date of Announcement	Amount		Press Comment	Other News	Price Change	
		Absolute	Relative to market value			Absolute %	Relative to standard deviation
Midland	13 Nov 1987	£400m	24%	whole package reported as surprise	Hong Kong and shanghai to take stake; LDC provisions announced	+7.8	+2.6
Royal Bank of Scotland	11 Jan 1985	£121m	26%	neither share issue nor acquisition expected	purchase of Charterhouse Japhet; base rate rise	−8.8	−7.2
Midland	26 Jan 1978	£96m	18%	'Midland jolts the banking sector' (*FT*)	good profits figures	−5.6	−3.3

b) Expected (in part) announcements

Bank	Date of Announcement	Amount		Press Comment	Other News	Price Change	
Midland	7 July 1987	£700m	46%	'The measures, which were long anticipated.'(*FT*)	profits figures higher provisions	+1.0	+0.6
Barclays	7 March 1985	£507m	25%	'...the stock market had been anticipating it for some time..'(*FT*)	poorish profits figures	−1.2	+0.9
Nat West	17 Sep 1986	£121m	3%	issue to secure listing on US exchange rather than to raise funds	-	−0.2	+0.1
Midland	27 July 1983	£155m	21%	*Economist* reports issue as widely discounted	good profits	+3.5	+1.7
Barclays	16 April 1987	£210m	6%	issue seen as means to secure overseas listing	-	+1.0	+0.8

Source: Miles, 1991.

The table shows the size of the announced issue, both absolutely and relative to the market value of the institution, and the reaction of the share price on the day of the announcement. To allow one to gauge whether a change in the share price is unusually large, these price changes are computed relative to the standard deviation of the daily change in the price of each firm's share in the one hundred days prior to the announcement day.

The table appears to reveal that those share issue announcements which were described as having been surprises usually caused significant falls in share prices, whilst those which were reported as having been expected, or those not primarily designed to raise funds (i.e. the overseas issues), did not generally cause a fall in price. Unfortunately, it is possible that financial journalists might decide whether or not a capital issue announcement was expected or not in the light of what happens to the share price in which case the table gives a biased picture of the effect of share issue news. But even ignoring any attempt to classify issues into expected or unexpected it is still true that on announcement days most share price movements, and all of the larger ones, were downwards.

The results suggest that unexpected announcements of large rights issues by major UK financial institutions are associated with significant falls in market values. It would appear that the Modigliani-Miller theorem does not hold, at least for this sample of financial firms. This implies that there is likely to be a real trade off between the costs of complying with capital adequacy requirements and any benefits stemming from greater stability in the financial system.

The structure of the SIB and SRO rules on minimum capital implicitly recognise the subtle nature of the trade offs involved – for example, portfolio theory is used to calculate adequate capital for equity dealers thereby reducing the capital required by firms with diversified balance sheets in a way which suggests the SIB is not unaware of the potential costs of holding more capital. It may be unrealistic to expect greater subtlety in the construction of capital adequacy rules; calls for the application of cost-benefit analysis which do not recognise the sort of difficulties in measurement outlined above are of little value.

7.2.6   Insider trading

Insider trading is the opposite of apple pie. Everyone knows what apple pie is and agrees that it is a good thing. Few people really know what insider trading is and there is widespread disagreement about its moral status. (For a useful discussion of the problems in defining insider trading see Herzel and Katz, 1987.) The 1985 Company Securities Act, subsequently amended and extended by the Financial Services Act which amongst other things conferred new investigative powers on the Secretary of State for Trade and Industry, defined the crime of insider dealing in the UK. Insider dealing occurs when an individual in possession of unpublished price sensitive information trades on that information on a recognised exchange. What makes someone an insider is not entirely clear but a necessary condition is some 'connection' with the company – either direct (e.g. someone employed as a financial adviser to a company, perhaps on a takeover deal) or indirect (acquiring information from someone who is in direct contact with the firm). There are exemptions; market makers are not precluded from trading on information if the information was obtained in their usual business of market making.

To an economist the issue with regulations about insider dealing is to assess exactly what harm they are designed to prevent and to estimate what might be the costs of legislation whose side effects may be to reduce the degree to which prices come to reflect underlying value. The issues are related. For stock markets to work effectively it is desirable that prices of securities are close to fundamental value – that is, accurately reflect the underlying profitability of associated real assets. If prices are to play this role there must be a mechanism whereby relevant information which is acquired, possibly at cost, by individuals should come to be reflected in price. The obvious way for this to happen, ignoring public anouncements by the altruistic of the findings of their costly research, is that trades by the informed move market prices. One cost of outlawing individuals who hold information from trading is that this mechanism is short circuited. (See Grossman, 1986).

It has been argued that there is no compensating benefit to offset this cost and that outlawing insider deals is an economic bad (see Demsetz, 1969). But it is clear that the legality of trading on any information, however obtained, might also undermine the role of prices as providing information on fundamental value. There are several ways this might occur.

First, corporations might simply stop seeking advice from financial firms for fear that their secret plans be revealed. Supposing that the services of financial advisers make prices more nearly reflect underlying value, for example by encouraging takeover bids for undervalued firms, the informativeness of stock market valuations would then be reduced.

Second, traders – market makers – might be wary of trading with other professionals for fear of being stung by insiders (i.e. selling something for much less than it is worth or buying something for much more than it is worth). In protecting themselves against these risks they may increase bid-ask spreads resulting in greater trading costs for all agents.

Third, outsiders may simply stop wishing to hold stock if they believe that insiders who want to trade with them have far superior knowledge.

Liquidity would be diminished by each of these.

The Blue Arrow affair shows some of the potential costs of insider trading. In September 1987 merchant banks, including County NatWest, advising Blue Arrow on a major rights issue secretly bought unsold shares to increase the take up level from 38% to 49%. Subsequently several investors who did take up shares argued that they would not have done so if the take up rate had been lower. Senior executives at County NatWest were tried on the charge of conspiring to create a false market in the shares. It is not hard to see the damage that might be done if such practices were widespread; rights issues might be harder for all companies if shareholders felt they could not deduce much about the attractiveness of the issue from the aggregate take up rate.

The economic costs of the kind of insider trading which are claimed to have occurred in the Guinness scandal are equally clear, at least in principle if not in magnitude. In the course of the 1986 takeover bid for Distillers, secret buying of Guinness shares was undertaken on a large scale so as to increase the share price. This improved the chances of the Guinness bid, which was favoured by the Distillers' management, succeeding. The manipulation of the Guinness share price by the company, with the aid of its financial advisers and the cooperation of several other companies, reduced the informativeness of the stock price to those who were considering the merits of the Guinness offer. If shareholders came to believe that manipulation of this sort was common, takeover bids involving offers of the raiders' equity would become harder.

The real issue with insider trading is how to outlaw those types of trading where costs of reduced activity due to diminished trust are greater than costs of diminished price informativeness due to the discouragement of informed traders. Again it is not difficult to think up nice principles like this but where do they lead us?

One thing the principle suggests is that some rules on insider trading are wrong headed. For example, the Securities and Futures Authority has a rule to prevent what are seen as abuses stemming from the revelation of price sensitive information to analysts prior to public announcements. Specifically, trading on such information in a way which moves market prices is forbidden. What is strange about this rule is that the economic benefit of 'early trading' is that other market participants may be able to infer something about the information from changes in price. To allow early trading only when prices do not move seems to leave the costs – unfair access to information, reduction in trading by outsiders – while removing the potential for wider benefits from prices moving early into line with fundamentals.

7.3   How did we get where we are today?

The current system of regulation – a subtle blend of self regulation within a massively detailed legislative framework – is relatively recent. To gauge its success it is instructive to make two comparisons. First, to describe the position in the UK prior to the Financial Services Act. Second, to briefly consider the very different regulatory system in the US.

7.3.1   UK regulation before 1986

It would be quite wrong to think that regulation of investment business did not exist before 1986. The Prevention of Fraud Act of 1958 required dealers in securities to be licensed and to abide by rules regarding the conduct of business (see Mayer, 1989). Whilst trading in eurobonds and eurodollar securities has always been undertaken in relatively unregulated markets, there were severe restrictions on the way in which domestic securities – equities and bonds – could be traded on the London Stock Exchange. Before 'Big Bang' the distinction between brokers and jobbers was rigidly preserved. A system of self imposed rules on takeovers and mergers was administered by the Takeover Panel – a body with no statutory powers. Provision of financial services was subject to ordinary commercial law. The organised insurance market of Lloyds had, and continues to have, its own form of self regulation.

In short, a system of self regulation operated in many markets within the overall framework of ordinary commercial law. What changed with the passage of the Financial Services Act was not that self regulation was abandoned but that the rules established by self regulatory organisations had to comply with criteria set out in statute. This prompts the question as to why self regulation cannot be left to itself. Membership of private clubs has a long tradition in many professional services, not least in the financial sector (see Goodhart, 1988b). It is generally in the collective interest of firms providing services where there is a high degree of asymmetric information that clients have confidence in the integrity of practitioners. (See Akerlof, 1970, for a classic analysis of the implications of lack of trust.) Professionals are in a good position to judge the integrity of other professionals and have the self interest to pass on their information to outsiders. One way in which this happens is by allowing agents who satisfy certain conditions to become members of professional bodies. Membership of the body comes to be seen as a signal of quality and integrity.

There are two problems with relying upon such a system of self regulation in the financial industry. First, while the opinions of other professionals might be accurate on questions of integrity – and thereby useful as a means of screening out crooks – preventing fraud is not the only desideratum of certification. As noted above, systemic problems are likely to arise in securities markets if a major player were to fail, not through ill intent but because of the structure of the balance sheet and a bit of bad luck. Since precise detail of balance sheet structure – as opposed to personal details on integrity or competence – is not something most financial institutions would want to pass on to other players it is hard to see how self regulation can effectively monitor system wide risks. It may therefore be in everyone's interest to play by the rules of an honest outsider backed by the force of law.

Second, there are obvious dangers of restrictive practices being followed, either consciously or not, by existing members of a club to exclude outside competition. This claim is often heard from free marketeers in regard to the medical profession and was common prior to 'Big Bang' which, in the face of entry by major new overseas players, opened up membership of the Stock Exchange.

Finally, there are clear benefits to having the rules which self regulatory clubs impose on their members being open to public scrutiny. One of the advantages of the Financial Services Act is that the rule books of the SROs have become public information.

Whilst these arguments suggest that some statutory backing to the regulation of financial services is likely to be desirable, the optimal blend of legal and self regulation is not clear. The US system of regulation of securities business, based on statute to a far greater extent than the UK system, provides a point of comparison.

7.3.2 Regulation of investment business in the USA

Regulation of securities business in the US is a legal matter. (For a brief but excellent description of the US system of securities regulation see Foley, 1991.) In the wake of the stock market crash of 1929 several pieces of legislation were passed which made the US securities markets the most heavily regulated in the world. The Glass Steagall Act 1933 separated banking from securities dealing, making it illegal for US banks to deal in, or issue, securities. The Securities Act 1933 and the Securities and Exchange Act 1934 established a system of rules designed to ensure disclosure of information and established principles on which margin requirements (which limit the ability of institutions to take speculative positions) were based. The Acts led to the creation of the Securities and Exchange Commission (SEC). The SEC is a federal agency which registers securities exchanges – i.e. certifies exchanges subject to compliance with rules about membership and disciplinary procedures – and requires that extensive information be made available to potential investors in securities. The operations of futures traders and the rules of the exchanges in which they trade are regulated by a different agency – the Commodity Futures Trading Commission (CFTC). Differences in rules between the two Commissions, for example on margin requirements, have created a lobby in the US to place regulation of the futures exchanges under the SEC. The US system has been the subject of much criticism. The effectiveness of margin requirements has been questioned by Miller and Hsieh (1990) and Miller and Upton (1989). The usefulness of disclosure requirements has been analysed by Benston (1969) and Stigler (1964). But the greatest attention has been paid to the enforced separation of securities and banking business. Originally designed to prevent systemic problems in securities markets spreading to the banking system, or vice versa, the legislation has been seen as increasingly damaging for US firms competing in a world where giant overseas financial conglomerates have been able to operate across the spectrum of financial markets.

The repeal of the Glass Steagall Act now seems inevitable but is only one part of wider dissatisfaction with a system which, despite more legislation than any other country, has avoided neither financial scandal (Boesky, Milken) nor systemic risk (the crash of 1987). If the US experience suggests anything for the optimal design of regulation of investment business in the UK, it is that a system based almost entirely on statute and with a minimum of self regulation is unlikely to be desirable.

Although the current UK system avoids excessive reliance on statute and most certainly has a strong element of self regulation, it is unclear whether the system will continue to preserve this balance. The implications of the creation of a single market in financial services within Europe will be the major factor here, a subject to which we now turn.

7.4   The future of securities market regulation in Europe

The 1992 programme in Europe, whose aim is to establish a single market in the provision of goods and services, will force changes in the system of securities market regulation in the UK. The most significant factor will be the acceptance in the Community of a Directive for Investment Services which is likely to establish the same principles for securities business regulation as those explicit in the Second Banking Coordination Directive. (For a discussion of the economic issues see Mayer and Neven in Giovannini and Mayer, 1991.) The key feature of the plans for financial regulation of securities business is that of (eventual) home country supervision. (See the preliminary EC Directive on Investment Services published in December 1989.) Under the principle of home country regulation a firm that is authorised to undertake investment business in one member state will be allowed to undertake business in any other state without further authorisation. It has been widely suggested that this principle necessitates uniformity in the system of regulation of investment business across member states – the Directive certainly suggests that uniformity is desirable. The much abused term 'level playing fields' has also been used to justify the principle that regulations should be EC wide.

There are three important economic issues which arise here. First, is it inevitable that the freedom to provide investment services throughout the Community should lead to uniformity in regulation? Second, is uniformity desirable? Third, how would the UK system need to change if Community wide principles of regulation are to be adopted? On the first point it has been argued that unless regulations were the same throughout the community, institutions would establish their base in countries with the minimum of regulation and use the single Community investment services licence to set up branches and supply services in other member countries. Competition between financial centres in Europe would drive regulations down to a (sub-optimal) minimum. Hence coordination and, more specifically, uniformity is desirable. The argument is flawed. It assumes that investors would always prefer to deal with firms offering the cheapest service, regardless of the system of authorisation that the firm complies with in its home country. If that argument were true, people would never buy used cars from dealers authorised by car manufacturers and would always buy what appear to be bargains from unauthorised dealers.

Second, Mayer (1989) has argued forcefully that uniformity in regulation across Europe is undesirable. Whilst regulations designed to prevent systemic problems may necessitate harmony across countries, he argues that a diverse range of levels of protection for customers buying financial services can, and should, coexist. There is no reason why regulations designed to protect investors, rather than preserve financial stability, should be the same everywhere. Some people simply don't want to buy their second hand car from (relatively expensive) authorised dealers; should they be forced to?

Whether desirable or not, what might be the consequences of a single system of regulation for all investment business within the Community? The experience of banking regulation within Europe, where there has been far greater 'progress' towards what is, somewhat euphemistically, called harmonisation, suggests that a common system would need to rely upon explicit minimum standards which are set out in detail. One must fear that in the lengthy meetings between national regulators, central bankers and government officials where such details are worked out the principle which should guide the design of regulation – that of ameliorating the undesirable consequences of market failures – will be forgotten.

Bibliography

Akerlof, G. (1970) The market for lemons: qualitative uncertainty and the market mechanism, *Quarterly Journal of Economics*, **84**, 488–500.

Bank of England (1987) Change in the Stock Exchange and Regulation in the City, *Bank of England Quarterly Bulletin*, **27**, 54-65.

Benston, G. (1969) The value of the SEC's accounting disclosure requirements, *The Accounting Review*, **44**, 515-32.

Chant, J. (1987) Regulation of financial institutions – a functional analysis, *Bank of Canada Technical Report*, **45**.

Copeland, T. and **Weston, J.** (1988) *Financial Theory and Corporate Policy*, third edn. Addison Wesley.

Demsetz, H. (1969) Perfect competition, regulation and the stock market', in H.G. Mann (ed.) *Economic Policy and the Regulation of Corporate Securities*. American Enterprise Institute.

Diamond, D. and **Dybvig, P.** (1983) Bank runs, deposit insurance and liquidity, *Journal of Political Economy*, **91**, 401–19.

Dowd, K. (1989) *Free Banking*. Macmillan.

Foley, B. (1991) *Capital Markets*. Macmillan.

Franks, J. and **Mayer, C.** (1989) *Risk Regulation and Investor Protection*. Oxford University Press.

Goodhart, C. (1987a) Why do we need a central bank?, *Oxford Economic Papers*, **39**, 75–89.

Goodhart,. C. (1987b) Financial regulation and supervision: a review of three books, *National Westminster Bank Quarterly Review*, August, 55–64.

Goodhart, C. (1988a) The regulatory debate in London, *Financial Markets Group Special Paper*, **7**, London School of Economics.

Goodhart, C. (1988b) *The Evolution of Central Banks*. The MIT Press.

Goodhart, C., Kay, J. and **Seldon, A.** (1988) *Financial Regulation or Over Regulation?*, Institute for Economic Affairs, London.

Grossman, S. (1986) An analysis of the role of 'insider trading' on futures markets, *Journal of Business*, **59**, Part 2.

Herzel, L. and **Katz, L.** (1987) Insider trading: who loses?, *Lloyds Bank Review*, **165**, July, 15–26.

Lomax, D. (1987) *London Markets After the Financial Services Act*. Butterworths.

Mayer, C. (1989) The regulation of financial services: lessons from the UK for 1992, mimeo, City University Business School.

Mager, C. and **Neven, D.** (1991) European financial regulation: a framework for analysis, in A. Giovannini and C. Mayer (eds) *European Financial Integration*, Cambridge University Press.

Merrick, J. and **Saunders, A.** (1985) Bank regulation and monetary policy, *Journal of Money, Credit and Banking*, **17**, 691–717.

Miles, D. (1990) Some economic issues in the regulation of financial markets, *Managerial Finance*, **16**, 15–25.

Miles, D. (1991) What is different about financial firms?', *Manchester School*, **LIX**, 64–79.

Miller, M. and **Hsieh, D.** (1990) Margin regulations and market volatility, *Journal of Finance*, **45**, 298–316.

Miller, M. and **Upton, C.** (1989) Strategies for capital market structure and regulation, *A Report Prepared for the Center for Business and Policy Studies*, Stockholm.

Securities and Investment Board (1991) *Principles and Core Rules for the Conduct of Investment Business*, January.

Stigler, G. (1964) Public regulation of the securities market, *Journal of Business*, **37**, 117–42.

Tobin, J. (1985) Financial innovation and deregulation in perspective, in J. Tobin, *Politics for Prosperity* (ed.) P.M. Jackson (1988), Wheatsheaf.

Tobin, J. (1987) A case for preserving regulatory distinctions, *Challenge*, Vol **30**, No **5**, November–December, 10–27.

Author Index

In this index the suffix n indicates reference in note, and suffix b indicates entry in bibliography

Subject Index

alpha stocks, 33, 40, 41, 42, 44, 47, 48, 49
American Depository Receipts (ADRs), 29, 57n
Amsterdam, 6, 88, 90, 106
  see also European Options Exchange
ask-price, 3, 4, 32, 48, 49, 73, 92
auctions, 69, 70–1, 72, 134

bank bills, 149, 151, 158, 160
Bank for International Settlements, 22, 62, 79, 81, 134
Bank of England, 6, 7, 23, 29, 30, 43, 44, 66, 67, 68, 69, 70–2, 73, 74, 75, 98, 156, 158, 160–1, 171, 172
  and traditional money market, 138–48, 149–51
Bank Rate, 147–8, 149
banks, 6, 7, 8, 9, 43, 66, 73, 75, 76, 90, 93, 105, 107, 111, 113, 114, 117, 118, 127, 132, 138–48, 149, 150, 151–2, 153–5, 156, 157, 158, 160, 161, 164, 165–6, 167, 169
  American, 7, 9, 111, 154, 155
  clearing, 138, 142, 143, 147, 151, 152, 155, 175–6
  commercial, 17, 116, 123, 133
  investment, 17, 116, 123, 128–9, 131, 133
  Japanese, 9, 128, 154, 155
barriers to entry, 30, 123, 129, 130, 135
bearer securities, 76, 112, 115, 118, 156
beta stocks, 33, 41, 44, 47
bid-price, 3, 4, 32, 48, 49, 73, 92
Big Bang, 8, 31–4, 37, 39, 41, 43, 44, 45–53, 68, 119, 168, 178, 180
bill of exchange, 6, 151
bonds, 6, 163, 165, 167, 169, 171, 172, 179
  see also eurobonds, gilt-edged, government bonds, sterling bonds
bought deals, 36–7, 113, 116, 124, 125, 129, 135, 136
broker/dealers, 32–3
brokers, 7, 27–30, 43, 68, 73, 155–6, 169, 172, 178

building societies, 22, 74, 150, 153, 155, 160
Bund (German government bond), 9, 82, 92, 94, 95, 96, 100, 118

capital adequacy requirements, 113, 163, 167, 168, 172, 173–7
cash settlement, 86, 97, 101
Central Gilts Office, 23, 68, 70, 75
certificates of deposit (CDs), 138, 149, 151, 153–6, 160
Chicago financial markets, 85, 88, 90, 91, 92, 95, 97, 99–102, 103, 108–9
clearing house, 87–8, 93, 97, 98, 106
clearing systems, 117, 118
clustering of financial activity, 18–20
commercial bills, 147, 149, 150
commercial paper, 134, 138, 156–60
commissions, 21, 23, 45, 49–50, 55, 73, 97, 122, 127, 128, 131
Commodity Futures Trading Commission, 99, 100, 180
commodity markets, 9, 86, 88
compliance costs, 173
computer technology, 26, 30, 32, 43, 75
  see also electronic trading systems
contestable markets, 5, 48, 129–30, 131
convertibles, 76, 113
corporate finance, 10, 134, 168, 169, 171
coupon, 64, 65, 76, 122
crash (October 1987), 32, 36, 41, 49, 52, 53, 95, 97, 124, 167, 168
credit controls, 138, 147, 158, 160
credit ratings, 8, 135, 156, 158
cross subsidisation, 123, 128, 131, 133
crowd trading, 26, 31

dealer markets, 25–6, 54
debentures, 76, 77
debt crisis, 8
default risk, 87, 128, 167, 172
depth, 47–9
deregulation, 8, 20, 23, 30, 93, 104, 125, 132